MARY BYWATER CROSS

Quilts of the Oregon Trail

Schiffer Publishing Ltd

4880 Lower Valley Road, Atglen, PA 19310 USA
Printed in China

Other Schiffer Books on Related Subjects
Quilts of Virginia 1607-1899, by the Virginia Consortium of Quilters' Documentation Project
Quilting Traditions: Pieces From the Past, by Patricia T. Herr
Amish Quilts of Lancaster County, by Patricia T. Herr
Quilts and Quiltmakers Covering Connecticut, by the Connecticut Quilt Search Project
Quilts: The Fabric of Friendship, by the York County Quilt Documentation Project and the York County Heritage Trust

Dedication

To the memory of my grandmother
Harriet Louisa Smith McNeill
1887-1976

Front cover image: *Blue Mountain*, painting by William Henry Jackson. National Park Service/Scotts Bluff National Monument, Gering, Nebraska, SCBL44

Copyright © 2007 by Mary Bywater Cross
Library of Congress Control Number: 2006933127

Designed by John P. Cheek
Cover design by Bruce Waters

Type set in Zapf Humanist Demi BT/Aldine 721 BT

ISBN: 0-7643-2316-4
Printed in China

Published by Schiffer Publishing Ltd.
4880 Lower Valley Road
Atglen, PA 19310
Phone: (610) 593-1777; Fax: (610) 593-2002
E-mail: Info@schifferbooks.com

For the largest selection of fine reference books on this and related subjects, please visit our web site at
www.schifferbooks.com
We are always looking for people to write books on new and related subjects. If you have an idea for a book please contact us at the above address.

This book may be purchased from the publisher.
Include $3.95 for shipping.
Please try your bookstore first.
You may write for a free catalog.

In Europe, Schiffer books are distributed by
Bushwood Books
6 Marksbury Ave.
Kew Gardens
Surrey TW9 4JF England
Phone: 44 (0) 20 8392-8585;
Fax: 44 (0) 20 8392-9876
E-mail: info@bushwoodbooks.co.uk
Website: www.bushwoodbooks.co.uk
Free postage in the U.K., Europe; air mail at cost.

Contents

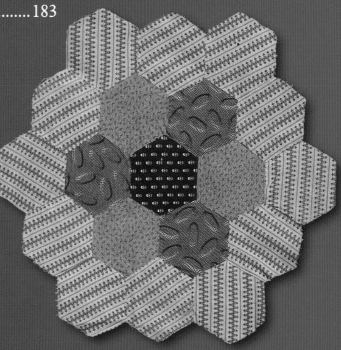

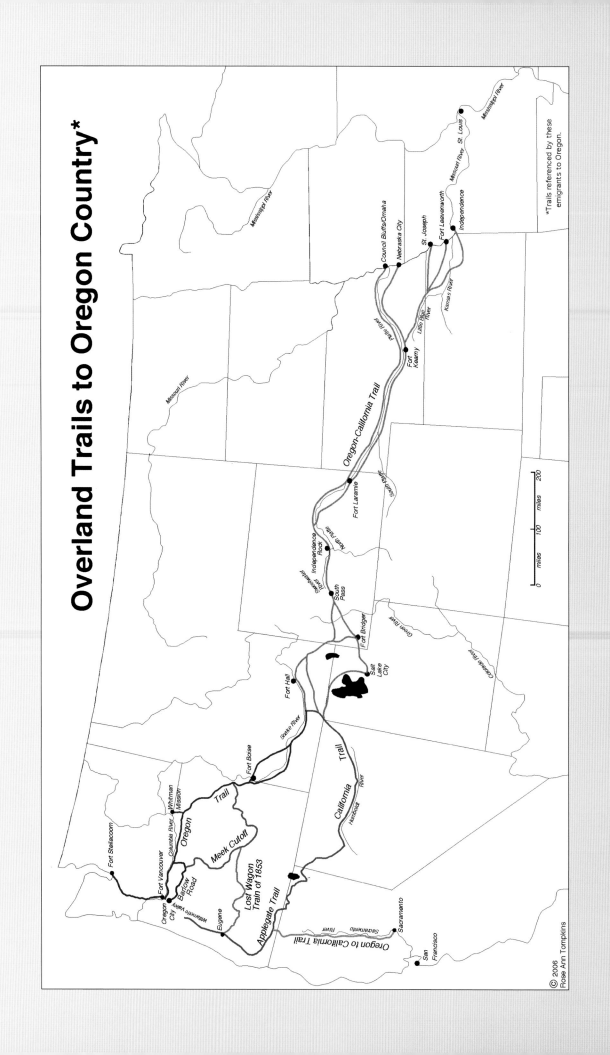

Overland Trails to Oregon Country*

*Trails referenced by these emigrants to Oregon.

© 2006
Rose Ann Tompkins

Introduction

Between 1840 and 1870, a quarter of a million Americans crossed the continent to Oregon and California in what was considered one of the great migrations of modern times. These men, women, and children sought to make a major transformation in their lives. The year 1993 marked the 150th anniversary of the first wagon train into Oregon. The first edition of this book, and a traveling quilt exhibition celebrated this sesquicentennial. The first edition drew national attention to women's western migration and their stitched records of human experience. It brought new awareness and appreciation to owners of similar family migration-themed quilts that had been stored away for years. The book's reissue by a new publisher provides the opportunity to incorporate additional quilts and new scholarship on migration and community development in the Pacific Northwest.

The settling of the West has long been portrayed through the visual arts in paintings, films, photographs, and drawings; and innumerable books, journals, diaries, and letters have been written about the experience. Many of these were contributed by men and therefore represent a male perspective. At the time they were written, these contributions were an important resource to describe the physical characteristics of the landscape and the encounters with Indians, traders, and animals. In general, they gave recommendations to others planning to explore the West.

Popular literature about the period featured the adventures of such heroes as Davy Crockett and Daniel Boone foraging and fighting to lead the settlement effort. Focusing on the Oregon experience were men like Francis Parkman, author of *The Oregon Trail*; artist William Henry Jackson, who accompanied a freight-wagon train and returned to his Boston studio to paint his watercolors; and Ezra Meeker, the only pioneer to cover the route by wagon, train, automobile, and airplane. Their works did much to promote knowledge of the trip to Oregon and to educate the public about this experience.

At the same time (1840-1975), the female perspective was ignored or avoided. With an increased focus on women's history, contemporary contributions have been made to understand the Westward Movement from their point of view. Works by Julie Roy Jeffrey, Sandra Myres, Lillian Schlissel, Glenda Riley, Dean L. May, and Shannon Applegate, through their studies of literate American women's recorded documents—diaries, letters, journals, and books—have been major resources for this long-overdue emphasis.

Jeffrey, in her book *Frontier Women, The Trans-Mississippi West 1840-1880*, examines how nineteenth-century American society's definition of women as agents of civilization and keepers of morals was challenged by the experience of living on the frontier. Working from the long-established and challenged thesis of Frederick Jackson Turner that as Americans moved west the new environment gradually weakened inherited culture and forced them to create new institutions and values, Jeffrey concluded that women held to society's definition of their role and were proud of their contributions of creating social and educational institutions for their families and communities.

The focus of Sandra Myres's *Westering Women and the Frontier Experience 1800-1915* was to identify women's place within the context of the American frontier by reviewing preconceptions about the experience held by both men and women, and to see how they were changed by their participation in it.

Lillian Schlissel, in *Women's Diaries of the Westward Journey*, used her study of 103 different white women's writings to reconstruct the daily lives of these women in an effort to define their role in the Westward Movement. A goal of her work was to understand the design of the emigrant family and to see its dimensions of emotional balances and work roles.

According to Schlissel, women went West because there was no way for them *not* to go once the decision was made by their husbands and fathers, whom they were committed to support. She concluded:

> The period of the overland trail migration (1840-1860) produces over-whelming evidence that women did not greet the idea of going West with enthusiasm, but rather that they worked out a painful negotiation with historical imperatives and personal necessity.[1]

Within cycles of childbearing and childrearing, women managed a kind of equity for their lives. They were neither brave adventurers nor sunbon-neted weepers. They were vigorous and given to realism and stoicism. To them, the West meant the challenge of rearing a family and maintaining domestic order within the disordered life on the frontier. Once embarked on the journey, they were determined and energetic in their efforts to make the move a success.[2]

It is the scholarship in the last fifteen years focusing on settlement patterns, community development, and economic and environmental features of the Pacific Northwest that has given depth and further awareness of women's lives to this edition. Beginning with Glenda Riley's *A Place to Grow: Women in the American West*, it was recognized that women seized the opportunity to make a difference in their personal and family lives as well as in their community. In *Three Frontiers: Family, Land, and Society in the American West 1850-1900*, Dean L. May demonstrates the importance of land ownership and kin/neighbor relationships in women's adjustment to life in the Pacific Northwest. Shannon Applegate's *Skookum: An Oregon Pioneer Family's History and Lore* and *Life Among Headstones* added an honest personal dimension to the women's stories.

Because the focus of this book is on quilts as products of needlework skills, I studied the role of needlework within the framework of the nineteenth-century woman's life. Quilt historians have been gathering data about quilts made in America over the last two hundred years. Most of this work has been done within the framework of state quilt projects that have recorded the history of quilts made within politically and geographically defined borders. More often than not, the quilts reflect the static aspect of American society; they were made by women who stayed home and were later kept at home by the children who chose to remain there. These projects have analyzed regional trends, individual styles, ethnic group quilts, and industrial influences. State project publications as complete as *Quilts in Community: Ohio's Traditions*, by Ricky Clark, George Knepper, and Ellice Ronsheim, have been an important resource to this study because many of the cross-country emigrants originally came from that midwestern region.

In the last fifteen years, the continuing contributions by quilt historians and enthusiasts to the field of quilt study has expanded the amount and quality of scholarship available for use. Barbara Brackman's works have been extremely helpful in dating the quilts, placing styles and techniques within the spectrum of American textile history, and identifying pattern names and sources.

These studies have shown that women used their needles to make quilts that reflected the passages of their lives. Studies ranging from state documentation projects to museum exhibitions have yielded information showing that quilts were produced for such major events as birth, childhood, coming of age, marriage, death, and involvement in church and community activities. The coming of age passage has shown a general group of quilts related to becoming an adult, to serving in the military, and to taking leave of home.

This book differs from many others in that it is the first to look at quilts made in an extended span of time and sweep of distance. It looks at the quilts and at the women who made them, and considers quilts in three categories: those made before the journey, those made during the journey, and those made afterward, covering the period from 1825 to 1925. The quilts are presented within four parts. The first three fall within definite periods when the women or family connected to the quilt made the journey; 1840-1850, 1851-1855, and 1856-1870. These periods are defined by the conditions that influenced and affected the migration. The fourth part, expanded in this edition, features quilts made by those women who waited—either for a loved one to return, or to join a loved one in the West after they were established.

Quilts of the Oregon Trail presents quilts as documents of history, similar to diaries, in order to learn about the lives of the women who made the migration. To be considered valid documents of history, according to textile historian Rachel Maines, quilts must meet several necessary requirements: they must have a continuous and traceable history; they must reflect the experience of the mainstream of society at the time they were made; and they must be honest in representing the free expression of the maker.[3]

I have sought to validate all of the possible quilts and their connection to the family, the maker, and the Oregon Trail experience in terms of when they were made, by whom, and the years the family crossed the Plains. Documentation on the makers includes the dates of their lives, their birth and settlement locations, locations where they began their migrations, their immigrant ancestors (including when and where they came to America, if available), and information about their husbands and families. In this edition, I have also included material about the role each played in the settlement of the Northwest. Current Internet resources for genealogy and historical information have been most useful, helping to enrich the stories of these women's lives.

Using the original study's quilts and adding eight more that have surfaced over the last fifteen years, I have been able to add further depth to the original edition of this book. In addition, new works by history scholars have enabled me to add interpretation and broader awareness to the role these women played in establishing their homes, farms, and communities in the Pacific Northwest during the nineteenth and early twentieth centuries. I continue to infer how the quilts celebrated the lives of these quilt makers.

In this new edition, I have changed the order of the quilts' presentation from the date they were made to the migration date of the maker/owner. References to a specific maker or family are identified by their assigned number. I have revised the chart of all quilts in Appendix A so it lists the quilts alphabetically by maker/owner's last name. I have learned that important benchmarks are the family's name and the year of their migration.

My major research directives have been: what are the quilts; who were the makers; how do the quilts reflect the lives of these westering women; where are the quilts located; how were the quilts used on the Trail and in the homes; and what was the woman's role in her family and community.

My conclusions are drawn from study of the quilts as a body of work done within each maker's lifetime. Looking for common patterns, fabrics, quilting motifs and styles, I sought to identify themes of nature, movement, friendship, and celebration, all related to the common overall theme of migration.

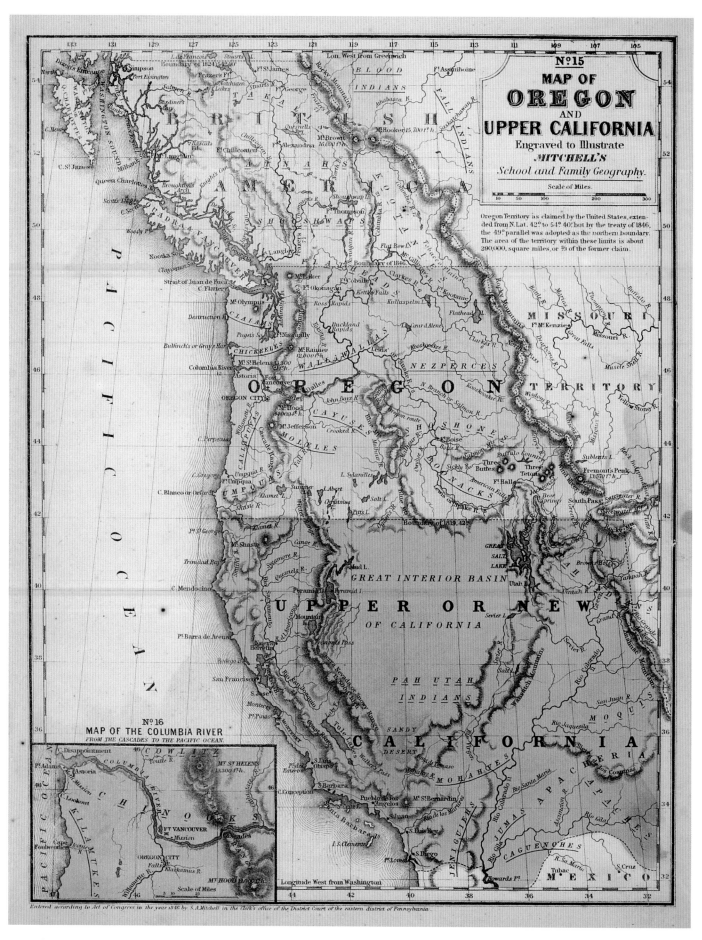

Map of Oregon and Upper California before Anglo-American settlers arrived. *Collection of Robert Hamm, West Linn.*

Preface

The gay colored quilts which came across in a big chest, and which had been used as wrapping for a few cherished dishes and other treasures, were unpacked. ... Other bits from the old home three thousand miles away were placed on the crude shelves; a picture of grandmother's parents; a few books, the family Bible, the little treasures which had been slipped between the bedding in a an old chest and a queer looking trunk lined with bright flowered paper. They were now at home.[1]

And so it was, as thousands of women arrived in the Northwest by way of the Oregon Trail. This migration, or "leave-taking," would consume the longest time and widest distance undertaken by these nineteenth-century women to establish new homes for themselves and their loved ones. Many would have experienced shorter moves previously from one location to another.

The Migration

The 1804-1806 Lewis and Clark Expedition sparked interest in the Pacific Northwest when the two men successfully returned from mapping and recording the land of the Louisiana Purchase. Jesse Applegate (Quilt A-2) credited his reading of the 1814 edition of the Lewis and Clark journals with making him aware of the possibilities in the Pacific Northwest. He also met William Clark in 1825 and Wilson Price Hunt in 1828, who both spoke favorably of Oregon.[2] Hunt was one of the earliest fur traders and Mountain Men who sought beaver skins to meet the fashion demands of the world's society. Interest in the fur trade was quickly followed by religious-affiliated missionaries from the New England-based American College Society of Commissioners for Foreign Missions. They came seeking to convert the Native Americans, but soon realized the value to and interest of Anglo-Americans in migrating to the Pacific Northwest for land and opportunity. In the first years of Trail activity, prior to 1850, the Trail population was a mix of missionaries and Mountain Men, as represented in this study by Adeline Brown Crawford (Quilt A-1) and James Washington Chambers (Quilt A-5). They were soon joined by young adults, both male and female, who came for the opportunity and were without strong ties to the Midwest. These included Medorem Crawford (Quilt A-1) and the orphaned young Foster adults (Quilt A-9-11).

The desire for available land was encouraged by the 1848 Provisional Government of Oregon, which allowed each married couple six hundred and forty acres for the cost of living on the land and improving it for agriculture. The migrating population began to explode, as this land appealed greatly to families experienced in migrations who desired to own land as a symbol of property and independence. Extended families making the journey at this time included the Applegates (Quilt A-2), Chambers (Quilt A-5), Glovers (Quilts A-14-15), Weavers (Quilt B-9), and Riddles (Quilts B-1-2). Families were also drawn to this area by the opportunity to join a family member who had already migrated. Such was the case in the early years for the Perkins (Quilt A-4) and Simpsons (Quilt B-20); these families had sons in the Northwest who encouraged

Westward Migration★

Year	Estimate
1841	100
1842	200
1843	1,000
1844	2,000
1845	5,000
1846	1,000
1847	2,000
1848	4,000
1849	30,000
1850	55,000
1851	10,000
1852	50,000
1853	20,000
1854	10,000
1855	5,000
1856	5,000
1857	5,000
1858	10,000
1859	30,000
1860	15,000
1861	05,000
1862	5,000
1863	10,000
1864	20,000
1865	25,000
1866	25,000
Total	350,000

★From *The Great Platte River Road* by Merrill Mattes

them to make the migration. In the early years, most people came from the Mississippi and Missouri River Valleys. By virtue of being close to the Trail's jumping off points, they got an early start on claiming land in the Willamette Valley.

In addition to the "pull" to Oregon country, there was the "push" from the Midwest. The harsh climate, crowded population, fear of illness, and economic recession of the 1830s all contributed to the conditions that encouraged people to "take leave" and head out over the Oregon Trail.

The California Gold Rush of 1849 had a major effect on migration over the Oregon Trail in several ways. Many of the families' men who were already in Oregon took the opportunity to go south to seek their luck in the gold fields. The Oregon men were the closest to the fields when word spread of the strike in the American River in January 1848. News of this strike was communicated to Oregon pioneers by friends from their Trail migration days who had gone to California instead of Oregon.[3] Among the men who went were Lindsey Applegate (Quilt A-2), Harrison Wright (Quilt A-3), Elaim Morris (Quilt B-5), and Elisha Buell (Quilt A-13). Other families took advantage of the financial opportunity to offer services for those headed to the gold fields. The Applegate family (Quilt A-2) provided food and lodging while William Riddle (Quilt B-2) worked his trade as a blacksmith. Other men from the Midwest went to California, liked what they saw in terms of settlement opportunity, and returned home to bring their families to Oregon. Many were said to have "Oregon Fever," the desire to live in the Pacific Northwest. Among these were Zadoc Riggs (Quilt B-1), James Greer (Quilt B-6), Charles Drain (Quilt B-10), John Whiteaker (Quilt B-7), Royal Hazelton (Quilt A-19), Abel Helman Quilt (D-2), Alexander Berry (Quilt D-3), and Francis Simpson (Quilt B-20).

All of these factors affected the number of people migrating to Oregon between 1849-1853, when the totals jumped from several thousand a year to over ten thousand a year (see table, "Westward Migration").

Communication back to families, friends, newspapers, and other publications about living conditions and opportunities in the Pacific Northwest also had an effect on increasing migration (see Appendix B, Triumphs and Tragedies, #2-5). Such communication encouraged loved ones to sell their farms, pack their wagons, and take leave from the Midwest and East. Among the families lured West by this communication were the Robbins (Quilt B-11), the Riddles (Quilts B-2-3), and the Propsts (Quilt B-12).

Others, as they learned about Oregon and the offerings there, saw the migration as an opportunity for a new beginning in a far-away location. These included the Stones (Quilt B-18), and the Aurora Colony (Quilts B-19, C-3-4). For the Aurora Colony and its leader, William Keil, migration provided the opportunity to practice their communal society beliefs in an environment away from public criticism and to retain control over their membership.

The desire to practice their faith also encouraged a number of religions to encourage their pastors to migrate west. These included the Circuit Riding Methodist preachers, who came to serve the population and grow their congregations. Among the Methodists represented in this book are the Crawfords (Quilt A-1), Greers (Quilt B-6), Royals (Quilt B-13), and the Wingville Methodist Episcopal South Church (Quilt C-2).

By the 1860s, during the Civil War years, strife over the slavery issue and the physical confrontation in Missouri especially became the reasons why many families moved to Oregon. At least eleven of the quilts (shown in Part III), connect to multiple families who chose to leave Missouri for a calmer, quieter living environment. In 1864, John Wesley Lieuallen, the only one of the seven Lieuallen brothers who did not migrate to Oregon during this time, wrote of the despair he and their father felt continuing to live in Mercer County, Missouri:

> Times are very troublesome here, and so they were, but nothing to compare with what they are now. And they get worse every day, my language fails me to tell how low and degraded the people have got, mind cannot think of anything too mean for them to do. They kill and rob the blind, the dead and the dumb, the widow and orphan…there has been murder and stealing all around us.[4]

By the end of the Trail era, with the completion of the transcontinental railroad across western America in 1870 and the link to the Pacific Northwest by 1883, most of the population in Oregon was quite homogenous, consisting primarily of white married families from the rural sections. The quilts validate this conclusion.

The Women

All would begin the journey with individual life experiences that would depend on their age, their stage in personal relationships and society, their background, and their expectations. Slowly covering the distance at a rate of five to twenty miles a day for four to nine months, each woman would experience a personal transition, whether physically, emotionally, mentally, socially, or culturally.

All challenges—pregnancy, illness, death, exhaustion, isolation, cultural identity, and moral beliefs—were to be confronted in a sphere of an emerging, unknown world, far from that original home. This experience would have a major impact on their lives, changing their views, their expectations, and their outcomes.

A major part of how the women reacted and interpreted their Trail experience would be directly related to their educational background. For the nineteenth-century daughter lucky enough to have formal education, it would be defined as in the following sampler verse stitched by my great-great-grandmother, Lydia Louisa Whittemore in 1824 in Massachusetts:

> How blest the maid whom circling years improve
> Her God is the object of her warmest love
> Whose youthful hours successive as they glide
> The book, the Needle, and the Pen divide[5]

This verse reflects the attitude and environment of the "proper" nineteenth-century young woman. While she focused privately on her world as expressed through her pen and needle, her public image was being defined by the sermons, etiquette books, and literature written and published on the East Coast.

Nineteenth-century women compiled a private history, recorded in Bibles, diaries, letters, and needlework, rather than in public documents of military, court, legislative, and town records. Part of this project is a review of the diaries and letters left by the women who made the quilts, as well as those left by their family and friends.

The extent and role of education in women's lives was as varied as their life experiences. While some learned to read and write, all learned needlework skills because of the need to make the clothes they wore and the household linens they used.

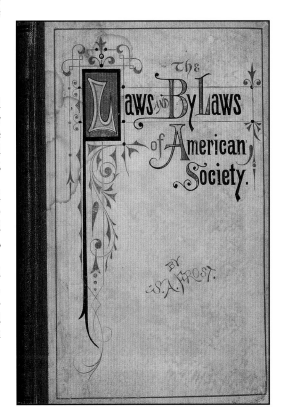

Nineteenth-century etiquette book

Sampler by Lydia Lousia Whittemore, circa 1824

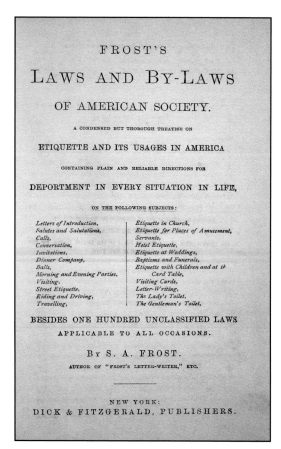

Title page of etiquette book

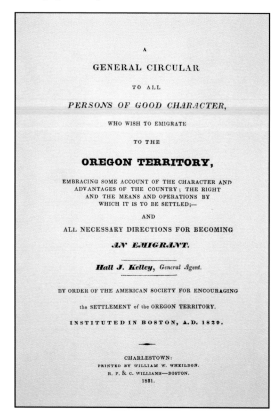

Hall J. Kelley's general circular, 1831. *Oregon Historical Society, OrHi83930.*

The Quilts

Bed quilts were a major part of the household linen production in nineteenth-century America. Answering the demand for such large numbers of items, women became extremely proficient in their needlework capabilities, and their work received encouragement and recognition. Many women began to spend leisure time planning and creating quilts to honor and commemorate important events in their lives. Citing an 1883 issue of *Arthur's Magazine*, which estimated that as many as three-quarters of the bed coverings were quilts, Elaine Hedges stated that sufficient numbers were made to allow women to create special ones meant to be kept as records of life's passages.[6] As early as 1855, women in Oregon were able to stay current in fashion and trends by subscribing to magazines featuring needlework projects, including *Harper's Monthly, Godey's Lady's Book, Leslie's Weekly,* and *Putnam's Monthly Magazine.*[7]

Based on the vast extent of work in quilt history over the last twenty years, it is generally accepted that quilts were the most universal form of needlework produced by all women. They were made by all socioeconomic levels of society, all ethnic groups, all cultural groups, in all parts of the country. They are valid artifacts for studying the broadest range of women and their experiences throughout American history.

The Frontier Experience

In general, women's actual frontier experiences were defined by several factors. Most important was the "shaping power" of the West, as described by historian Anne Hyde. The territory's landscapes presented new perceptual challenges, forcing people to create new expressions. Studying the history of perception involves considerations of what women expected to see, what they saw, how they interpreted it, and what they learned from it. Citing not only a woman's background of experience in age and role, Hyde also noted the importance of the mode of transportation and the medium through which the perceptions were interpreted.[8]

Another factor on the frontier that shaped women's response in quilts was the sharing of resources and creative skills before, during, and after the Trail journey. Discussing particularly experiences on the Trail, Julie Roy Jeffrey quotes the following:

> There was "commendable reciprocity in the exhibition and distribution of new patchwork quilt designs. The display was made with quite as much pride as is the showing of artistic fancy-work today. All plans, patterns, ideas, or innovations were pleasantly passed along ... This was true, likewise, of clothing cutting. Exclusiveness in the cut or trim of apparel was unthought of."[9]

For women experienced in needlework, interpretation of the Oregon Trail through their quilts was a natural creative enterprise. Themes reflecting their perceptions of the leave-taking from family and friends, the six months of living outdoors, and the reliance on equipment and divine guidance appeared in quilts connected to migration. Women translated the geometric shapes of colored fabrics into what they saw in flora and fauna, what they experienced in weather and exposure on the Trail. They pieced, appliquéd, and quilted their response to people and places in their new home in the West.

PART I
1840-1850

Westport Landing, painting by William Henry Jackson. *National Park Service/Scotts Bluff National Monument, Gering, Nebraska, SCBL280*

Estimate of an Outfit

The following estimate of an outfit for one year, for three persons, with ox teams, is copied from *The Emigrants' Guide to California* by Joseph E. Ware:

Four yoke of Oxen*, $50 each		$200.00
One wagon, cover, etc.		100.00
Three rifles, $20		60.00
Three pair pistols, $15		45.00
Five barrels flour,	1,030 lbs.	20.00
Bacon	600 "	30.00
Coffee,	100 "	8.00
Tea	5 "	2.75
Sugar	150 "	7.00
Rice	75 "	3.75
Fruit, dried	50 "	3.00
Salt, pepper, & c.,	50 "	3.00
Saleratus,	10 "	1.00
Lead,	30 "	1.20
Powder,	25 "	5.50
Tools, & c.,	25 "	7.30
Mining tools,	30 "	12.00
Tent,	30 "	5.00
Bedding,	45 "	22.50
Cooking Utensils,	30 "	4.00
Lard,	50 "	2.50
Private baggage,	150 "	
Matches,		1.00
One mule,		50.00
Candles and soap,		5.50
Total:	2,585 lbs.	$600.00

*The teams for the journey should be oxen or mules, either of which can be purchased at the frontier towns. Cows are often taken along for their milk, being sometimes the only dependable source for drink.

The Trail Preparation

The weeks, months, or years before planned departures were active and busy with preparations. While men dealt with the disposal of land at home and gathered the necessary supplies and livestock, women prepared the food and sewed clothes, tents, wagon covers, and bedding. Making quilts as bedding to use or to keep as heirlooms was an activity often noted in writings of the period.

The cost estimated by the guidebooks for a family of four to move West was about six hundred dollars for overland, while coming by ship around the Horn was six hundred dollars per person. With the exception of the very early years of migration, there were guidebooks, letters, and journals that described the preparations to make, the supplies to bring, and the routes to take including the best locations for food and water.

An interesting footnote to the list of recommended items says "Do not leave home, or St. Louis without possessing the above Guide, also the *best map* of California etc that can be procured." The recommendation sounds not unlike one of today's credit card commercials: "Don't leave home without it".

The recommendation for bedding was forty-five pounds for a party of three persons, children or adults for one year when traveling with oxen. This cost approximately $22.50.[1] Other guidebooks were more specific and suggested two or three blankets and comforters for each traveler.[2] The idea was to have sufficient bedding to last the trip plus several years after arrival in Oregon.

Quiltmaking became an important part of the preparation for moving West or leaving the States, as women focused on the need for bedding or retaining emotional connection with family and friends. As they made the quilts to be used on the Trail, they referred to them in diaries, letters, and logs. They made quilts to honor their families and friends who stayed behind and they made quilts to record items from their past. For example, Elizabeth Currier Foster made the Poke Stalk (Quilt A-9) before migrating with her older brother and sister to Oregon in 1846. The Poke Stalk is a plant that does not exist in the Northwest.

Another part of preparing for the trip meant talking to other family members to encourage them to join the migration. Persuasive letters were written and visits were made among relatives. Since the family was the social unit on the Trail, often the woman's goal was to maintain that unit at all costs. Even single men and women attached themselves to family units and hired on to do specific tasks in order to travel in safer numbers. Whenever possible, families traveled with a group of kin and neighbors. They would gather extended families from various places and then travel West together, as did the Chambers family (Quilt A-5), Eli Perkins family (Quilt A-4), Philip Glover family (Quilts A-14-15), Jacob Robbins family (Quilt B-11), William Riddle family (Quilt B-2), and the Royal family (Quilt B-13). For 1843, the first year of migration, the majority of the nine hundred emigrants came from Missouri, Illinois, and southern Ohio. These were the starting places with the shortest and easiest distances to cover by riverboat and wagon train.[3] As the charts in Appendix D indicate, for many of the migrating families this was at least a second migration if not more when they chose to make the long westward trek.

Of special interest were the three widowed women who either came with or later joined their sons and daughters. The commitment to make the long journey as an older woman shows the strength of their bond to families—the journey was easier than facing the loneliness without them. Mary Whitely Gilmour (Quilt D-4) understood that when she decided to travel with her grandchildren in 1870 at the age of eighty-two. Nancy Calloway Nye (Quilt D-3), a pioneer of 1865, realized it after seeing most of her children leave home for the west between 1847 and 1862. And for Sarah Moody Fuson (Quilt D-5), going to Oregon meant not going to the poorhouse in Missouri.

Who the quilters in this study came with:

	1840-50	1851-55	1856-70	Those who wait
Parents	4	4	1	1
Husband	1	12	4	1
Extended family	8	5	3	0
Brother/Sister	1	0	0	0
Widows/adult children	0	0	2	3
Unknown	0	0	2	0

The Trail

During the first days on the Trail, as the settlers crossed the Missouri River and headed over the Plains along the Great Platte River Road, women's feelings tended to be a mixture of concern and confidence.

Popular imagery of the period referred to this section as "the Elephant." Embarking in slow-moving wagon trains, the people traveled at great personal risk into a world of unknown experiences and challenges. One diarist wrote of it on the first day out: "All hands early up anxious to see the path that leads to the Elephant."[4]

Yet, as long as they were healthy, eager, and confident, the women were ready to share the journey with family and friends, old and new. Life along the Trail at first tended to be relaxed and enjoyable. Although they were busy with the tasks of providing child care, and preparing meals, women still found time to appreciate each other and the surroundings. Often, they would walk or ride and chat together. Catherine Haun wrote in 1849:

> During the day, we womenfolk visited from wagon to wagon or congenial friends spent an hour walking, ever westward, and talking over our home life back in "the states"; telling of the loved ones left behind; voicing our hopes for the future ... and even whispering a little friendly gossip of emigrant life.[5]

Seeing the elephant. *Oregon Historical Society, Portland, OrHi55094*

Women continued their normal tasks of baking, washing, mending, sewing, and taking care of others. These routines were simply an extension of their roles back home, where much of this work was done outdoors. Carrying out these domestic roles provided some assurance of control over the adverse physical environment, and repetition of the routine provided a sense of importance. As Charlotte Stearns Pengra noted in her 1853 diary on May 18th:

> ... washed a very large washing, unpacked dried and packed clothing—made a pair of calico cases for pillows and cooked two meals—done brave, I think. Those who come this journey should have their pillows covered with dark calico and sheets colored, white is not suitable.[6]

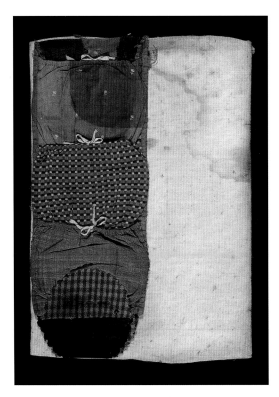

Housewife brought by Watson family

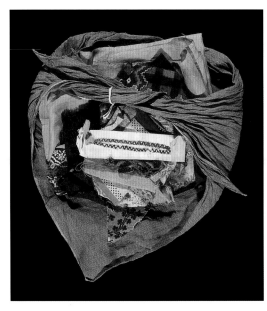

Bundle of fabrics brought by Rachel Bond

Women went prepared to do their needlework, as several important artifacts given to public collections indicate. These include a gourd used to hold the knitting yarn as a woman walked, which is in the Douglas County Museum of History and Natural History in Roseburg, Oregon. A pair of scissors kicked up from the dust at a burial site is another treasure, housed in the Lane County Museum of History in Eugene, Oregon. Several needlework items remain from the family of Sanford and Maria Watson, pioneers of 1849. A "housewife," the holder of personal items and needlework tools once sewn to the lining of a wagon, is now at the DAR Pioneer Mothers Cabin at Champeog State Park. A needlebook, made by Selina Venable of Springfield, Illinois, as a gift for pioneer Virginia Watson, was given to the Oregon Historical Society by her great-granddaughter Virginia Ann Woodworth in 1935.

For some women, this was the first time they had been confronted with being on their own and totally responsible for the homelike setting. These were the newlyweds and the women who had previously had slaves to assist in their work.

> Teenage Rachel Bond, pioneer of 1853, works long and hard at the cooking and clean up. Her young husband Allen toils into the night tending the herd and keeping the wagons tarred and greased. The two young people got married and joined Uncle Vincent's (McClure) train without money or rigs and supplies of their own—so they've agreed to work their way to Oregon.
>
> Rachel has found an old discarded copper kettle along the roadside, not too bruised she thinks. And as she walks westward she runs a needle and thread through squares of old fabric, storing each stitched piece inside the kettle hanging from her arm like a handbag. She tells Allen she'll have enough of these pieces sewn by the end of the trip to make a quilt. He agrees. That's about all they will have—a kettle and a quilt—but it's worth it.[7]

Sharing of Trail Tasks

As wagon trains moved westward, with parties splitting up and situations changing, women on the Trail showed their commitment to the trip by being willing to perform the additional chores usually regarded as a male's. These included such tasks as pitching tents, gathering wood and buffalo chips for fires, loading and unloading wagons, yoking oxen, and driving teams. On the other hand, men also did women's work, especially if they were single or if their wives were ill. "A man assuming female responsibilities was doing a favor. A woman doing a male job was doing what was necessary.[8]

Women were also interested in the economies of the trip—the mileage covered, the quality of water and grasses, the cost of supplies. They carefully noted these figures in their diaries along with notes about gravesites, Indian encounters, births, and deaths.

Layover Days

Most trains had a "laid over" day at regular intervals to wash and do other chores not possible to be accomplished during the regular "nooning" or in the evening at camp. Washdays occurred about every two weeks, when the whole train would participate in doing their laundry. Layover days were also used to clean and air the wagons, dry the bedding and clothing after one of the frequent heavy rains, and to repack the load.

Wagon Trains

Westward wagon trains were assembled at jumping off places along the Missouri River near Independence, St. Joseph, or Council Bluffs and Omaha, where various parties were gathered before heading west along the Platte River. Most trains would have about twelve wagons, with each driver having his turn at the head of the line. They rotated places each day so that everyone would have a turn at being at the end in the dust.

The 1846 train that brought fourteen-year-old Elizabeth Currier Foster (Quilt A-8) and her brother and sister to Oregon was called the Applegate Southern Cutoff Train. They were the first to follow Lindsay and Jesse Applegate's route, avoiding the Columbia River. There were fifty wagons at the start, but after they got past the worst danger from Indian attack, they divided because there were too many cattle to manage. By comparison, the 1863 wagon train from Bethel, Missouri, to Aurora, Oregon was made up of forty-two wagons and 252 people making up fourteen companies.

Wagons were customized to the family's needs. A feature of the wagons used by William and Margaret Fuson Lieuallen (Quilts C-8,9) was they were built with a double floor providing storage space on the lower level for imperishable foods such as wheat, corn, and garden seeds. If there was a death in a caravan, each wagon would contribute a board from the false floor to build the coffin.[9]

The Burt family, traveling with the Royal family (Quilt B-13), outfitted one of their wagons with seats projecting out over the wheels where their ten children sat and worked on lessons and sang songs as they rode west. Thomas Fletcher Royal called it "the Band Wagon," a veritable country school on wheels.[10]

Interior of covered wagon. *Oregon Historical Society, Portland, OrHi55997*

A-1

Quilt: Seth Thomas variation
Category: Pieced and appliqué
Size: 94" x 72"
Date: circa 1870
Maker: Adeline Brown Crawford (1821-1879)
Year Over Trail: 1842
County Where Settled: Clackamas, then Yamhill County, Oregon

This appliqué or laidwork pattern shows the maker's interpretation or variation to the original Seth Thomas pattern. Although many women of the late nineteenth century got their quilt patterns through exchanges with friends or from attending county and state fairs, it is not known what source this maker used.

It is masterpiece quality stitched by a woman with skilled ability. The quilt shows late nineteenth-century regional characteristics and trends that happened earlier on the East Coast by 1850, but not on the West Coast until after 1870. In the East, the popularity of red and green appliqué quilts had begun to wane after the Civil War because of the poor quality of aniline dyes, the growing availability of machine printed textiles, and the growing popularity of home sewing machines.

This quilt's fifteen-inch block arrangement is equally balanced so it can be read from all sides of the bed. The vine border is continuous around the quilt. There are triple rows of quilting stitches in the appliqué blocks. In the solid white blocks, there is a floral stem with leaves in two of the large blocks and in the small triangular blocks. In the other white squares are quilted wreaths. The quilt is finished with a red binding.

The quilt block is a traditional nineteenth-century pattern, first published in the *Kansas City Star* in 1929 and labeled "Seth Thomas Rose." It was a common practice during the Colonial Revival era for companies and newspapers to publish quilt patterns from earlier times as part of the effort to "recapture" the country's disappearing heritage.

Adeline Brown was born in Missouri on November 22, 1821. She and her mother, Mary DeWitt Brown, continued their plans to journey west in 1842, even after the sudden death of her father, the Reverend William Brown. This early wagon train was organized by Dr. Elijah White and included many Methodists headed for the Mission on the Willamette River. There were one hundred and five people, fifty-one men over eighteen in sixteen wagons with horses, mules, and cattle.[11] Also in the company was young Medorem Crawford, the man Adeline married in April 1843. The couple lived in Oregon City from 1845 until 1853

Adeline Brown Crawford with daughter Mary Elizabeth and son John Morrison, circa 1858

Medorem Crawford, circa 1860

when they purchased 640 acres in Yamhill County. Between 1844-1858, Adeline gave birth to ten children; only six survived infancy. In 1862, Medorem's sister, Elizabeth Stevens, came from New York and joined the family. Soon, she became ill and required much care. Adeline became her caregiver. In 1866, Adeline was taken ill and could only leave her room for meals. In 1869, she moved from her Portland home to the new brick house on the family farm in Dayton. By this time, her surviving children had grown to adulthood. The quilt was probably made during this period of her life.

Adeline died on May 20, 1879 from cancer, at the age of fifty-eight. She had been ill for several years. At the time of her death, Medorem's diary entry was only "wife died at 10:30."[12]

As was common with many women, little was recorded about her personal history including educational background, contributions to the community, and personal experiences. In a photo album of family and friends at the Clackamas County Historical Society, there is not a photo of Adeline, although there is one professional photo of her husband Medorem. Even in oral interviews conducted with her two daughters, Mary Stevens and Henrietta Crawford, no mention was made of their mother while history with great detail and emphasis was recorded about their father. This unfortunately was common when the husband was as active as Medorem.

While Adeline lived a private life managing the family and home, Medorem lived an active public life. He was typical of the young men who went west to seek adventure and opportunity. Starting out in Oregon, he was the first person to haul freight around the falls of the Willamette River at Oregon City. He was a member of the territorial legislature of 1847-1849. He sought political federal appointments. He served as a Captain in the Quartermaster Corps as leader of the Emigrant Escort Service, leading wagon trains over the Oregon Trail from Omaha west between 1860 and 1864. In 1864, he was appointed U.S. Government Internal Revenue Collector, a post he held until 1869. In 1871, he was appointed as Appraiser of Merchandise for the Port of Portland, a position he held for three years. Medorem participated in the Oregon Pioneer Association, serving as president from 1878-1881.[13]

Seth Thomas Rose Quilt Variation. *Museum of the Oregon Territory, Oregon City #C-72-10*

A-2

Quilt: "Wedding Dress" Quilt
Category: Pieced
Size: 82" x 68.5"
Date: circa 1880
Maker: Melinda Miller Applegate (1813-1888)
Year Over Trail: 1843
Came: As a wife with husband Charles Applegate
and nine children; his two brothers, their
wives, and their combined thirteen children
County Where Settled: Yamhill, then Umpqua, area
later named Douglas County, Oregon

Melinda Miller Applegate (1818-1888)   Sewing box with heirloom fabrics

This treasured family heirloom is kept in the
"Grand Mammy room" located in the west side, or
Women's Side, of Charles and Melinda Applegate's
home in Yoncalla in southern Oregon. Here the
eight daughters were taught to sew and quilt to
provide clothing and bedding for the family of
eighteen. In this historic house, one can still see
the hooks and pulleys on the rafters used to raise
and lower the quilting frame.

The quilt serves as a visual record of the extended family of Charles and Melinda Applegate,
his two brothers Jesse and Lindsay and their
wives, and the combined total of forty children.
As noted earlier, Jesse Applegate had met William Clark in 1825 and Wilson Price Hunt in
1828; both spoke favorably of Oregon.[14] Lindsay
was married to Elizabeth (Betsy) Miller, (1816-
1882), Melinda's younger sister. The quilt also
marks the separation for the first time of the two
Kentucky sisters who had traveled west together
in one of the earliest and largest wagon trains of
nine hundred people. Theirs was one of the most
difficult journeys because of the triple drowning
of family members and friends as they rafted along
the Columbia River's treacherous waters below
The Dalles. Settling first in Yamhill County, the
families moved south in 1852 to the Yoncalla area.
In 1859, Lindsay Applegate moved Betsy and their
family further south to an isolated toll road stop,
"ten days hard riding" from Yoncalla.

The pattern is the traditional nine-patch
made up of one size template (finished two and
a quarter inch). The fabrics are those from the
handmade dresses worn by family members in the
1850s through 1880s. Each fabric serves to trigger a
visual memory, a reminder of the person who wore
it, the period of time worn, and the occasion for
which the dress was made. There are five different
mourning prints of black and white, indicating the
need for such fabric within the family. There are
also five different blue and white prints and four
burgundy and white prints, showing the family's
interest in current fashion fabrics of the period.
There are at least two fabrics of an earlier era, both

dark brown with a green motif. What they represent is a mystery. The quilt is
backed and tied but the binding created by folding the backing to the front is
only basted in place. This would indicate an unfinished project, perhaps caused
by the death of Melinda Applegate in 1888.

For the current owners, the heirloom quilt has another significance. It
marks a change in Melinda's maternal experience. In 1856, at the age of forty-
three, she gave birth to her sixteenth child, Milton. Yet, she remained involved
with many birthings as she was the area's midwife. She was also recognized by
family and friends for her skill in handling illness and disease. Taking a sick
child "over to the Applegates" meant visiting Melinda for her guidance and
wisdom.

In 1852, when her daughter Ellen married George Burt, Melinda became
a mother-in-law, extending her family circle beyond blood relatives.   T h e
quilt's main fabric, a blue-green with black and white woven lightweight
woolen, was very likely the actual wedding dress. A string-tied roll of the fabric
with the inked label "Ellen Applegate Burt Wedding Dress Dec. 26 – 1852"
remains in a family sewing basket. The note was written by Flora Applegate
McKee, who recorded the information from interviews and house tours with
two of Melinda's daughters, Irene and Lucy. Ellen died in 1868 at the age of
thirty-six, leaving six young children in the care of her family.

This quilt's fabrics mark for Melinda the closure of her pioneering days
and the beginning of permanent residency in a gender-divided household.
This was the time the family completed their move from the Willamette Valley to southern Oregon with the building of this unique historic landmark
home. The two-story house, constructed between 1852-1856, was divided by
a common interior wall, with the west half known as the women's side and
the east half as the men's side, with separate entrances, separate fireplaces,
and separate stairways to the two separated rooms above. It was reminiscent
of a Tennessee-style house with a second story balcony across the front.[15] It is
now the oldest pioneer home still owned by a direct descendant of its original
builders. This home and its family cemetery represent what Dean May refers
to as the "iconography" of a successful migration and settlement, where the
Applegate clan "played out the transcendent spiritual acts of union, generation,
affinity, and death."[16]

The award-winning family history appears in books written by great-
great-granddaughter Shannon Applegate, entitled *Skookum: An Oregon Pioneer Family's History and Lore* and *Living Among Headstones: Life in a Country
Cemetery.*

Applegate home,
circa 2000

"Wedding Dress" Quilt.
*Collection of Shannon
Applegate, Yoncalla*

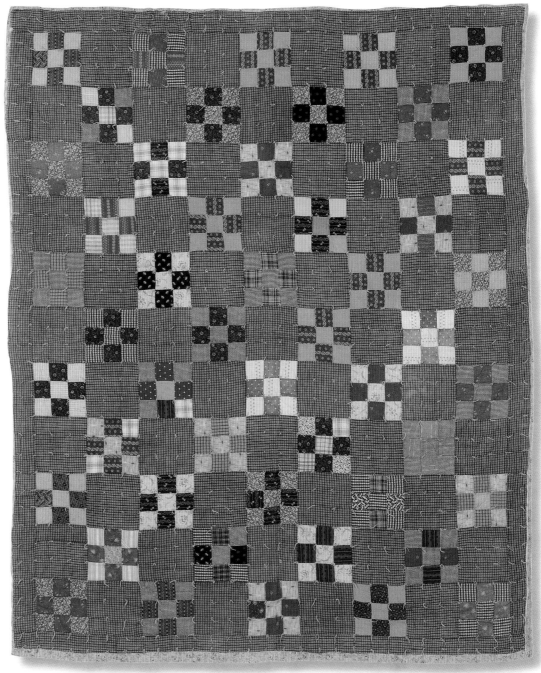

A-3

Quilt: Wheel of Fortune
Category: Pieced
Size: 82.5" x 72"
Date: circa 1880
Maker: Lavina Elizabeth Frazier Wright
　　(1829-1912)
Year Over Trail: 1843
Came: As a daughter with stepfather and mother
　　William and Sarah Russell McHaley plus
　　two brothers and one sister
County Where Settled: Marion County, then
　　Clackamas County, Oregon

Lavina Elizabeth Frazier
Wright (1829-1912)

This popular nineteenth-century pattern is one with a variety of names reflecting the area or purpose for which it was made. The name Wheel of Fortune calls to mind the migration experience and life experience of Lavina Elizabeth Frazier Wright. Traveling with the Applegates (Quilt A-2), she found the 1843 journey especially long and difficult since it was necessary to clear the route as the group traveled. It was particularly harrowing to be stranded on the edge of the Columbia River for four or five days with no food or shelter until rescued by Dr. John McLaughlin from Ft. Vancouver.

The quilt, pieced of solid colors, has several interesting features. The reds are two different shades, indicating that the maker ran short of the first fabric and carefully placed the second in the upper left and lower center so it would not detract from the visual affect of the quilt. Two colors of quilting thread are used, a red and an aqua. Sometimes, in quilts of this era, the quilting thread will pick up the dye of the fabric and change colors; however that is not the case here, where the colors are in the white areas of the quilt. The quilt has elbow quilting in rows one inch apart and a flower quilted in the center of the white area.

Lavina Elizabeth Frazier was born March 16, 1829 in Bloomfield, Monroe County, Indiana to Randall and Sarah Russell Frazier. Her ancestors had come from Virginia. Her father died in Bloomfield, and her mother married William McHaley. The family joined the wagon train led by Jesse Applegate.

Lavina married Harrison Wright on February 22, 1847, settling on his donation land claim in Clackamas County near Molalla. After the birth of their first son, Harrison Wright went to the gold fields of California in 1849. He returned not with gold, but with a herd of Spanish longhorn cattle that he used to start a cattle business. He also raced horses and built his own racetrack, as did several other pioneers of this era. Over

The Old Wright Farm House, circa 1876

the years, Lavina and Harrison had eleven children; the second youngest, Elizabeth Wright, to whom the quilt was given, was born in 1865.

Harrison was a public oriented citizen and held many minor political offices while Lavina cared for her home and family. He secured the post office for the Molalla area and became the first postmaster. He operated the ferry over the Molalla River. While attending the Legislature in Salem in 1870, Harrison unknowingly contracted smallpox. Upon his return home, he exposed the disease to his family. Fortunately, a knowledgeable neighbor and former slave, Sam Oakley, knew how to culture a cowpox vaccine that countered the effects of the smallpox. In the end, the father and the youngest child, a baby, died of the disease. Sam Oakley helped the three older sons to build a coffin for Harrison. He was buried in the dead of night in an unmarked grave in the Dibble Cemetery. The baby died two weeks later and was buried next to his father. The others all survived.[17]

Family lore states that after the disease subsided, everything in the house—including all the bedding, newly woven rag rugs, and straw rug padding—was burned, and the house fumigated. It is very likely that the quilt was not made until after this time. Clues supporting that date include the difficulty in dating solid color fabrics, the parallel lines of quilting, and the chronology of events in Elizabeth's life.

Wheel of Fortune Quilt. *Collection of Molalla Area Historical Society, Dibble House, Molalla, #68.17*

A-4

Quilt: Red and Green Tulip
Category: Appliqué
Size: 82" x 70"
Date: circa 1840
Maker: Sarah "Sally" Hull Perkins (1789-
    1876)
Year Over Trail: 1844
Came: As a wife with husband Eli, four married
    children, and one unmarried son Joel
County Where Settled: Yamhill County, Oregon

Sarah "Sally" Hull Perkins (1789-1876)

The simple appliqué tulip pattern was common in the mid-nineteenth century. The solid colors, although damaged by an unknown stain, appear to be home-dyed, with perhaps the blue intended to be green, a result of over-dyeing. The dye pot results were difficult to control. The orange fabric was produced commercially by the 1840s with mineral dyes.[18] The appliqué technique appears to be the "dogtooth," where the edges are slashed and turned rather than carefully cut.[19] The evidence is the variation in the template shapes and placement. The quilting pattern of lines grouped in threes uses the format known as fan or elbow quilting. According to Sally's great-granddaughter Iona Westerfield, who gave the quilt to the Yamhill County Museum, Sally made the quilt before she came to Oregon and brought it with her in 1844.

Sally Hull was born October 3, 1789 in Vermont. According to family history, her father, Matthew Hull, was kidnapped by British sailors off a beach in Dublin, Ireland and, with a school chum, was brought to America, where he was compelled to fight for the British. Sally married Eli Perkins (1786-1869) on March 6, 1809 at Warsaw, Genesee County, New York. His father, Joel Perkins, was the immigrant ancestor, having come to America from Wales in the 1760s. This Joel Perkins served in the Revolutionary War and received a government land grant in Genesee County for his service. Eli and Sally had seven children born between 1811 and 1828 while living in New York state. In 1832, they moved to Tippecanoe County, Indiana.

The Perkins family were part of the two thousand people who made the trek to Oregon in 1844. Coming at this time, they found a lack of housing and few people in Oregon.

The winter of 1844-45 is recorded as being particularly difficult.[20] With two business partners, Eli Perkins built the first sawmills and gristmill in Yamhill County. The Perkins' son Joel was the typical adventurous young man of the mid-nineteenth century. He filed for one of the first Oregon donation land claims in 1845. The next year, he founded the town of Lafayette, the first town on the western side of the Willamette River above the falls at Oregon City, and petitioned successfully to have the town made the county seat for Yamhill County. Joel went to the gold fields and conducted merchandise and ferry operations up and down the West Coast. Unfortunately, he was murdered by a hired hand named John Malone on July 24, 1856. According to Yamhill County historian Ruth Stoller, his family never fully recovered.

Red and Green Tulip Quilt. *Collection of the Yamhill County Museum, Lafayette, #YC-2-188*

A-5

Quilt: Tufted White on White
Category: Whole Cloth
Size: 86" x 73.5"
Date: circa 1825
Maker: Mary "Polly" Greene Scoggin Chambers
(1809-1890)
Year Over Trail: 1845
Came: As a wife with second husband James Washington Chambers, five children; his parents Thomas McCuthcheon and Latitia Delzel Chambers and six children; and his brother and wife David and Elizabeth Chambers
County Where Settled: Washington County, Oregon

The earliest quilt found that connected to the Oregon Trail was this white-on-white quilt, a rare find today, especially in the Northwest. These were made during the first decades of the nineteenth century in the East. From the published sources available, they are found in the major East Coast collections. One in the Metropolitan Museum is similar to a number of whitework pieces with drawnwork panels that were from Kentucky.[21]

This quilt has several unusual features. It is made of a whole cloth with no seam lines. Fine white fabric of this quality was available in a wide width.[22] The featured technique is tufted candlewicking, using a thick thread. One aid in dating this quilt is that thread-intensive quilting was dependent upon an inexpensive and plentiful supply of cotton thread that became available around 1810.[23]

The classic design is a central medallion of leaves and flowers with a center bloom and four radiating blooms and leaves in each quadrant. This is surrounded by a vine of grape clusters and leaves. Then, towards the edge, centered on each of the four sides is a star. The stars on the sides and top match with a small circle in the center. The star at the top has a bird beside it. The fourth star, on the bottom, is composed of diamond segments. These motifs are similar in style and format to those used on bed rugs in the seventeenth and eighteenth centuries in Europe and America. The major difference is that the bed rugs are a form of needlepoint with the surface entirely covered by rich textile stitches, while the quilt has just the outline of the design in running stitch that is tufted. The simple explanation is that the need for a heavy bed rug was not felt in the warmer climate of Kentucky as it was in New England.[24]

The quilting design is an outline, or echo, where one to three lines of stitching surround each of the motifs. There is also a gridwork of diamonds filling in various open spaces of the quilt.

A marking of initials, or extra motif that was stitched in the quilting thread in the lower center

Mary Green Scoggin
Chambers (1809-1890)

front, may be an identification clue. Because of the age and wear of the quilt, it is hard to interpret.

Machine-stitched lines along the edges of the quilt were added later as a means of stabilization. The replacement binding is a commercially made tape.

The quilt's maker, Mary Greene, was born in 1809 to Reverend John and Rachel Mackey Greene in Kentucky. She was married in 1828 to Woodson Scoggin; her sister Sarah married Woodson's brother James. Both were sons of John Scoggin of White County, Tennessee. Woodson and Mary Scoggin settled in either Cooper or Morgan County, Missouri in the early 1830s.[25] Woodson died January 25, 1840, leaving Mary with five children under the age of eleven. She married James Washington Chambers in 1844.

Both the Greene and Chambers families have a long history in this country. Mary descended from the Greenes and Whitfords of Rhode Island, who emigrated before 1700. James' parents, Thomas and Latitia Delzel Chambers, were married in Belfast, Ireland in 1795. Latitia was a sister of Andrew Jackson's mother and Thomas served as plantation overseer and an officer with General Jackson. James was born at the Hermitage in about 1815.

According to family lore, James, in his teens, was a companion of western fur trading Mountain Men and French voyageurs visiting Indian bands across the Missouri River Valley. He maintained "only loose connections" with his parents. He arrived at his parents' home as plans for the western migration were underway and offered to lead his father's wagon train. Two versions of the story exist. One is that Thomas Chambers, the father, explained to this wayward son that he wasn't mature or civilized enough for the position. What James needed was a wife and Thomas had chosen the widow for her "settling influence." The other version is that James responded he was already courting Mary before "being ordered to marry her."[26]

The couple came west in 1845 with his extended family, arriving in December two weeks before their first child was born. According to the Oregon Territory 1850 Census, they were living with her five children, their two children, and five other unrelated men between the ages of eighteen and forty-five in Washington County, Oregon.[27] James was identified as a farmer. In the 1860 Census, the family was still residing in Washington County with an unrelated laborer and the schoolmistress.[28] But by 1870, James had relocated to eastern Oregon's Butte Creek Valley with his daughter Mary Jane and her husband Thomas Hoover, plus a couple of the Scoggin men. The men were stock raisers and the Hoovers were the founders of the town of Fossil, named for the area's fossil beds.[29] Again, according to family lore, Mary Greene Chambers reportedly visited once, declared it "the most God-forsaken place she'd seen," and returned to the Willamette Valley where the couple were listed in the 1870 Census as living in Washington County.[30] She preferred to be with other family members on Chambers' Prairie in Washington Territory.

A museum donation record states the quilt was given to Martha P.I. Scoggin as a wedding present when she married C.B. Comstock in 1853. The quilt was given to the Lane County Museum in Eugene, Oregon by LaVella Young Gilbert, granddaughter of Mr. and Mrs. Comstock.[31]

Detail of bird
and star

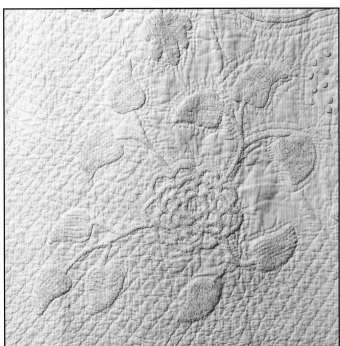

Detail of flower and leaves

Tufted White on White Quilt.
Collection of the Lane County Historical Museum, Eugene, #848

A-6

Quilt: Basket
Category: Pieced/Appliqué
Size: 82" x 70"
Date: circa 1850
Maker/Owner: Jane Summers Coyle (1841-1922)
Year Over Trail: 1845
Came: As a daughter with parents Thomas and Elizabeth Summers and younger brother William
County Where Settled: Linn County, Oregon and Walla Walla County, Washington Territory

This treasured heirloom has been handed down through five generations of family. The hand-piecing and quilting indicate a labor intensive project. There are several factors that create a question of who may have made the quilt and the possible date. First, the pieced triangle Basket pattern with appliquéd handles is of solid indigo-blue cotton fabric. Unlike the probably home-dyed fabric in the Perkins example (Quilt A-4), this fabric was unusual as either a successful home-dye or early American commercially produced. The consistency in the color quality is the clue. Fabrics in solid colors were produced starting in the late eighteenth century. In America, eighteenth-century printers were not demonstrating the technical expertise or design skills needed to create other than elementary procedures in dyed or printed textile production. In contrast, even in the infancy of the textile printing industry in Europe and India, polychromatic combinations and simple design motifs were printed on the fabric to appeal to the customer and to show the manufacturer's skill.[32] Yet, often fabrics such as this require a careful study because there can be a motif printed in a slightly lighter shade on the dark fabric during this era of 1830-1860.[33] Assessing an accurate date is a challenge without more thorough study of the quilt's thread and fabric construction.

Second, the quilt uses an "on point" block set format with the plain white blocks between the pattern blocks. This format for quiltmaking became popular in the mid-nineteenth century when quilters began to showcase their piecing skills by assembling hand-stitched triangles into patterns. The plain blocks would emphasize the pieced ones. This block was set on point to accommodate the basket width. The forty-two eight inch blocks can be read from either side of the bed. The quilting is a gridwork pattern with lines three-quarters of an inch apart. There are two hand-stitched borders, a blue one that is one-inch wide and a white one that is an-inch-and-a-half wide. The binding has been replaced.

The main characteristics of the quilt place its construction sometime between 1830-1860. Yet,

Jane Summers Coyle, Nina Coyle Timmons, Jack Timmons

knowing that Jane Summers was born August 22, 1841 in Burlington, Iowa to a young Irish bride of twenty-one suggests that the quilt may have been made by some other adult and given to the Coyle family upon their migration west in 1845, or made as a wedding gift for either Jane or her mother Elizabeth. Little is known about Jane's mother except that she was born in Ireland in 1820. After giving birth to five children and settling in the Willamette Valley, Elizabeth disappeared in 1864, leaving no verifiable trace. Her father Thomas Summers never remarried.

The family traveled west with the Hackleman and Holliday wagon train from St. Joseph, Missouri. They were among the group that chose to lay over at the Whitman Mission during the winter of 1845-1846. Family lore says Jane attended the school conducted by Narcissa Whitman that winter.

The following spring, the family completed their journey and settled near Sodaville in Linn County. The Summers claimed 640 acres of land that included a mineral water spring. The water became popular with the neighbors and a lawsuit over ownership of its surrounding land lasted eighteen years. In the end, Thomas was declared the owner. In return, he deeded the state of Oregon the land for a public area that became known as Sodaville Spring Park. It became the first dedicated public park in the state dating from 1871.[34]

On July 17, 1859 at Sand Ridge, Jane married James Bunch Coyle who had emigrated from Peoria County, Illinois in 1851. At age nineteen, he traveled with his widowed mother Elizabeth Stringer Coyle, four younger sisters, his widowed grandmother Delila Owen Springer Coyle, age seventy, and his uncle and aunt and their family. The grandmother died on the Trail and was buried at Farewell Bend on the Snake River. His older brothers, William and Reuben, had come out with their families in 1847. The immigrant ancestor was Patrick Coyle, who had come from Ireland, and at one time, was married to Delila Owen Springer, his son's mother-in-law.

In 1866, James and Jane Coyle moved east to the Walla Walla area in Washington, Territory. They settled on one hundred and sixty acres of fertile land in the Mill Creek area, not far from the Whitman Station. They acquired more land until they had approximately six hundred acres. They raised hay and grain and later operated a dairy farm.

James and Jane became the parents of ten children, nine of whom lived to adulthood. Jane was a charter member of the Whitman Congregational Church and active in community affairs. She was friendly with the Indians and knew enough Chinook jargon to converse with them.

After James died at his plow in 1901, Jane continued to operate the farm with the help of her sons until her death in 1922.

Detail of basket

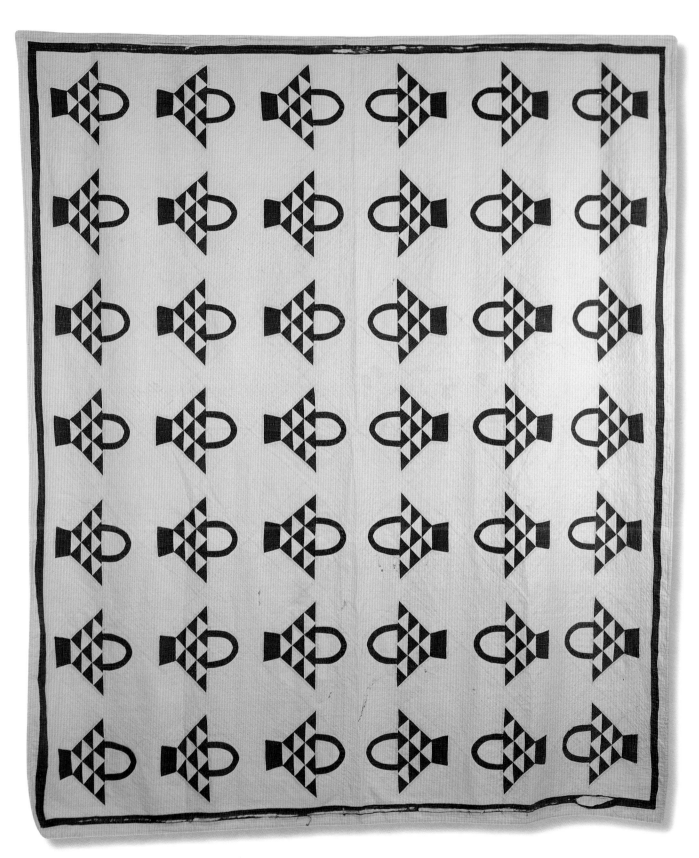

Basket Quilt. *Collection of Susan Queen, College Place, Washington*

A-7

Quilt: Tulip in Vase variation
Category: Pieced/Appliqué
Size: 72" x 65"
Date: circa 1890
Maker: Susan Mary Officer Vaughan (1833-1911)
Year Over Trail: 1845
Came: As a daughter of parents James and Evaline
 Cooley Officer and their seven other children
County Where Settled: Clackamas County, Oregon

This quilt was made long after the maker traveled to Oregon and lived a full life. It shows several common practices of late nineteenth-century western quiltmakers. Combining the pieced flowers and appliquéd vases was an opportunity for quiltmakers to show their technical skills. This is a variation of the Tulip in Vase pattern because Susan included handles on the vases.[35] Here the flowers are hand-pieced with some stems and vases hand-appliquéd and others machine-appliquéd. The blocks are set square so the quilt reads from either side rather than the foot.

The dark color thread used to appliqué the ten-inch blocks indicates it most likely absorbed the color from the fabric before it faded, or the fabric faded and the thread remained the darker original color. The reasons for this would be the thread's ability to absorb and hold the original dye while the fabric's dye was weaker and faded.

The quilting patterns are horizontal parallel lines and diagonal lines placed two to two-and-a-quarter inches apart. This was a common method to be able to complete quilts within a relatively short time. It was much faster to draw parallel lines than to quilt around each pattern piece or to create a separate quilting pattern in each block. This method was also used by older women whose eyesight and quilting skills may have started to decline. There are six stitches per inch.

This is a utilitarian quilt made to be used by a woman who enjoyed quilting. There is a possibility that the quilt was cut down in size as the edges began to wear. Two clues are there are no borders and the edges are turned to the inside and machine stitched.

Susan Mary Officer was born in Clay County, Missouri on March 3, 1833. Her parents were James Officer of Tennessee and Evaline Granville Cooley of Kentucky. In 1845, the family with their eight children traveled west in four covered wagons with the Solomon Tetherow wagon train. The train was large with five companies in four hundred and eighty wagons. James Officer was a member of the train's Executive Council. After the train arrived at Ft. Hall, an alternative quicker, safer route directly

Detail: Family photo at her seventieth birthday celebration, 1903

across Oregon was proposed and Stephen Meek volunteered to lead the two hundred families who agreed to try it. This train, later known as "The Meek Cut-off Wagon Train of 1845" or "The Blue Bucket Mine Train," became lost in eastern Oregon because the supposed route had not been marked.

On August 26, 1847, fourteen-year-old Susan married William Hatchette Vaughan (1822-1906) in a double wedding ceremony with her older sister Martha at their parents' home. William came to Oregon with the first wagon train in 1843 after his father refused to allow him to attend West Point Military Academy. His parents, James and Nancy Hatchette Vaughan, were natives of Virginia and had Scotch-Irish ancestry.

The couple settled on William's Molalla Prairie land claim in Clackamas County. His was the first permanent land claim in the area. Between 1849 and 1876, they became the parents of eleven children, whose names reflect William's Scotch-Irish ancestry and places where the family had resided. Among the daughters were Nancy Virginia, Mary Tennessee, and Susan Florida.

According to family lore, Susan was "always busy." First, caring for her large family and later, caring for her father, who lived with her until his death at ninety-one. She earned money by operating an egg and butter sales route in Molalla. She would regularly drive her buggy the three mile distance to deliver her products to her customers. She also chewed tobacco for health reasons.

William was a farmer and livestock rancher working on his nine hundred and sixty-acre farm. In 1883, the family moved into their Italianate-style country home built by William between the years 1882-1885. The State of Oregon designated the land as a "Century Farm," honoring the family ownership of the remaining one hundred and eight acres of land. The ten-room house is now on the National Register of Historic Places and owned by descendants. This continuing ownership by descendants is symbolic of the emigrants' successful achievement of migrating and settling in Oregon.[36]

On August 26, 1897, the couple celebrated their 50th wedding anniversary with many family and friends. One of those to attend was Elizabeth Frazier Wright (Quilt A-3). She had attended the wedding as well and was recognized in the weekly newspaper as one of the few to attend both celebrations.

The family photo celebrates Susan's seventieth birthday, a time when all eleven children returned home. Susan passed away at the age of seventy-eight.[37]

Detail: Machine stitched appliqué block

Tulip in Vase Quilt Variation. *Collection of Champ and Maria Vaughan, Molalla*

Elizabeth Currier Foster   A-8

Elizabeth Currier Foster, circa 1850

The next four quilts, made by Elizabeth Currier Foster over a span of almost seventy years and change of location, offer a uniquely complete history of one woman's experience as expressed in her needlework. The time span represents a return to quiltmaking after her family was raised and her major responsibilities for home and family lessened. Her life and work have been meticulously recorded by her youngest daughter, Lulu Foster Schminck, and lovingly treasured at the Schminck Memorial Museum in Lakeview, Oregon. These completed quilt projects and others represent the joy and satisfaction quiltmaking brought to one specific woman, a pioneer of 1846.

After a study of the collection and its individual fabrics, it appears Elizabeth brought this legacy of quilts and quilting in her trunk to Oregon in 1846. The Poke Stalk (Quilt A-9) and a fragment of Star (Quilt A-8) were brought as completed quilts. A Rose of Sharon (Quilt A-10) was brought as a partially completed project. A set of fabric templates for a Mexican Lily (Quilt A-11) and additional fabrics that would appear in other quilts were packed away.

The Schminck Memorial Museum has an extensive quilt collection, a well-documented family history, scrapbooks, and collections of more than five thousand artifacts representing the life span of two Oregon families. This was a life's project of Lulu Foster Schminck and her husband, Dalpheus, a retail clerk in the local general store for over fifty years. The museum is administered by the Oregon State Society of the Daughters of the American Revolution.

The family history is related here in segments illustrated with the quilts and family photos. Their story is divided among the quilt presentations.

Quilt: Star
Category: Pieced
Size: 86.5" x 67" fragment
Date: circa 1840
Maker: Member of the Currier family
Year Over Trail: 1846
Sent: With Elizabeth Currier Foster and her brother and sister
County Where Settled: Polk County, Benton County, then Lake County, Oregon

This fragment of an old quilt is included because it represents the interest of Elizabeth Currier Foster and her daughter to retain a quilt treasure, in spite of its tattered condition. It had long been a non-inventoried item until the connection was made to another quilt in the collection. The vivid indigo blue triangles along the edge are the same fabric as the Double Irish Chain made in 1852.

The six large stars and the smaller eight-pointed four-inch stars in the quilt's ground are pieced of fabrics from the early nineteenth-century textile production in New England, where the family was living.

The early history of the Currier family in America identifies the many descendants forming three direct lines. This Currier family descends from Jeffrey Currier (circa 1635-1680s) of the Isles of Shoals, off the New Hampshire coastline.[38]

Detail of Star

Further study reveals a tragic life for a young girl. Elizabeth Currier Foster was born on June 18, 1832 in Irisburg, Orleans County, Vermont. Soon after, the family moved to Massachusetts and New York. In 1844, they moved from New York to Andrew County, Missouri, where her mother, Elizabeth Smith Currier, died suddenly of a flu-like ailment. A year later, in 1845, her father, Jacob Currier, died of a broken heart and lost spirit.

In 1846, three young Currier adults, Sarah Currier Humphrey (age twenty-four), Jacob Manley Currier (age nineteen), and Elizabeth B. Currier (age fourteen), along with Sarah's husband, A.L. Humphrey, started for Oregon. Traveling via wagon and ox team, they crossed the Missouri River on May 10, 1846. The record of Elizabeth's Trail experience is fairly complete through her reminisces and mementos as well as journals of others on the trip. She had time to enjoy her friends, and to appreciate the places she saw. She did her westering tasks with her family members including herding cattle by riding horseback.

For the last part of their journey, they were members of the first wagon train Jesse Applegate (Quilt A-2) led over the proposed southern cut-off across the Black Rock Desert of Nevada and the Goose Lake Valley in northern California. It avoided the dangerous raft and canoe trips down the Columbia River and mountain crossings of the Blues and Cascades. The trail become known as the Applegate Trail (now as the California National Historic Trail), turning south and west at Ft. Hall and coming into the southern end of the Willamette Valley.[39]

Star Quilt. *Oregon State Society of the Daughters of the American Revolution Schminck Museum, Lakeview, #92.5512*

A-9

Quilt: Poke Stalk
Category: Appliqué
Date: 1845
Size: 82" x 76"
Maker: Elizabeth Currier Foster (1832-1921)

This second quilt, Poke Stalk, is a unique original design indicating a sense of migration. The plant, more commonly known as Poke Weed or Pokeberry (*Phylatocca decandra* or *Phylatocca americana*), was a tall herb native to the eastern part of the North America but not grown in the west. It was readily used in early homes for many purposes. The reddish purple berries and purple root were used in medicine. The young green leaves and shoots were edible and used in salads. The roots and berries provided a weak dye, which tended to stain rather than dye. The red color also faded towards brown.[40]

The reason why Elizabeth chose this plant for her quilt design is not recorded but speculation would indicate that it had special meaning for her family and was something she wished to record with her needle. Her work is realistic, including the use of pink for the stems.

The quilt does reveal two personality traits she is known to have shown: a sense of self-discipline and determination, and a joy of whimsy. There are 554 small raised red berries. The appliquéd Turkey red fabric baskets, laid on the intersections of blocks, show a whimsical sense with regard to the placement of the stems.

The quilting patterns include outline quilting around the appliqué work and a repeat of the appliqué leaf radiating from the stems or scattered over the quilt's surface. There are also six traditional ten-inch wreaths quilted at regular intervals not far from the vine border. The workmanship in the quilting varies.

Elizabeth was thirteen in 1845, leading to speculation that the quilt may have been quilted by family and friends in celebration of her work or in preparation for their leave-taking.

Continuing with their migration story, an accident happened during their time spent on the Applegate Trail that had a lasting impression upon Elizabeth, and later, her family. The younger sister of her friend Lucy Henderson died after overdosing on a bottle of medicine. Elizabeth was so saddened that she cut a beaded flower from her bag and laid it on the grave.★

She noted waiting sixteen days for the Applegate Trail to be cut through the Calpooia Mountains of southern Oregon. She and her sister were the first women through the Cow Creek Canyon, not an easy task for anyone. They finally arrived in Polk County on December 5, 1846, where they spent the winter sheltered by a family in Rickreall.

Detail of vase

Detail of stalk

Detail of wreath

★An account of the accidental death of Salita Jane Henderson is included in Appendix B.

Beaded bag

Polk Stalk Quilt.
*Oregon State Society
of the Daughters of
the American Revo-
lution Schminck
Museum, Lakeview,
Oregon, #69.2331*

A-10

Quilt: Rose of Sharon
Category: Appliqué
Date: Begun earlier; 1854 Finished
Size: 90" x 80"
Maker: Elizabeth Currier Foster (1832-1921)

This quilt, Rose of Sharon, is another illustration of quilts as representative of a woman's migration experience.

My thesis is that the blocks were started "while in the States," packed away, and brought out to complete in 1854 after Elizabeth had been in Oregon for eight years. The clues and reasons are as follows:

The large roses in the nine blocks have the same Turkey red fabric as the 1845 Poke Stalk quilt, indicating the fabric was probably acquired at the same time and place. Supplies and stores were not that prevalent in the 1840s.

Of the nine blocks, four were completed with the *same* four fabrics throughout. These four also have eight floral blossoms with seven fully shaped petals each.

A fifth block almost matches except for four leaves done in a second green print and the centers of three of the eight blossoms are a different pink print. It also has a mixture of the five fully sculpted blossoms and three more rounded blooms. This may indicate it was almost completed before Elizabeth ran short of fabrics and had to change the style of bloom. It may also indicate she had less time to devote to appliqué work. The fully developed blooms would be more difficult and take more time to complete.

The remaining four blocks have a significant amount of the second green fabric appearing in the stems and leaves of each of the blocks. With two exceptions, they have buds instead of blooms at the ends of the stems. One block has a single pieced and appliquéd flower. The other block has seven appliquéd stems and buds, with the eighth being quilted.

The placement of the quilting designs reveals much the same format as the Poke Stalk quilt. Outline, or echo, quilting is combined with additional leaves along the stems, and designs of circles, crescents, and flowers are scattered whimsically over the surface.

The border and the binding are machine stitched while the blocks are hand stitched together. Elizabeth Currier Foster's small sewing machine at the museum has the earliest patent date of Mar. 7, 1854 and the last of Nov. 18, 1867, indicating it was purchased after the 1867 date. The possibility exists that a sewing machine came into her home at the

Elizabeth Currier Foster and her young daughters with the Newhouse sisters, circa 1869

earlier date, since machines were extremely popular and available in the Philomath area of Benton County where she was living.

Elizabeth married James Foster in 1848 at age sixteen in Benton County. A year later, her sister Sarah Currier Humphrey died. In 1850, her brother Jacob Manley Currier married Maria Foster, Elizabeth's sister-in-law.

At this time, as a young wife and mother, she returned to making quilts. She finished a Double Irish Chain quilt in 1852. In 1854, she completed this Rose of Sharon and started work on the Mexican Lily (Quilt A-11), only to be interrupted by family needs.

By 1869, Elizabeth had had eleven babies. The three surviving girls are in the accompanying photo along with the Newhouse sisters, neighbors of the family. Four sons had survived, although one died at age twelve in August 1869. A twelfth baby, Luvia was born in November 1869.

In 1873, the Foster family of ten moved to southeastern Oregon to a dryer climate for health reasons. Here, on Summer Lake in Lake County, they built a ranch known for its fine produce, cattle, and racehorses. Their ranch was one of the most magnificent in the valley, producing nearly every variety of fruit. Here, Elizabeth's last two children, Ralph and Lulu, were born and raised. Lulu is the daughter who started the family museum with her husband in the 1930s.

Block of eight blooms with five fully developed while three are less defined

Block with two patterns of green cloth, stem and leaf motif quilted but not appliquéd

Rose of Sharon Quilt. *Oregon State Society of the Daughters of the American Revolution Schminck Museum, Lakeview, #69-2330*

A-11

Quilt: Mexican Lily
Category: Appliqué
Date: 1854 Started; 1915 Finished
Size: 86" x 84"
Maker: Elizabeth Currier Foster (1832-1921)

Examination of the appliquéd vase and flowers reveals two clues that connect this quilt to the period before the Currier migration and lead to the conclusion that the templates for the pattern were cut before leaving and brought over the Trail. There is one pattern

Elizabeth Currier Foster, circa 1915

piece for each element of the design in the same green and Turkey red fabrics as the Poke Stalk quilt. However, the fact that these pattern pieces are not on the same block leads to the conclusion that a block was not constructed. Instead the individual pieces were cut and used for a pattern when the additional pieces were cut and assembled in 1854, at the time recorded by the family. In the process of cutting and stacking the pieces for the appliqué work, the two fabrics were mixed in and ended up on different blocks. The appliqué work also shows a whimsy in the shaping of the stems and flowers that adds personality but also, perhaps, reveals less attention to detail by Elizabeth, who was now a wife and mother of two young boys.

Sarah Currier Humphrey's death in 1849 may also factor in this quilt. If the pieces were cut as a pattern design reference when the women lived in Missouri, perhaps before their mother died, Sarah may have helped to appliqué the pattern. By 1854, Sarah was gone and Elizabeth was left to do the work and set the blocks together.

A finish date of 1915 is reflected by the mitered corners of the single border. The primary quilting design is an outline of the appliqué work, with the secondary pattern being a grid of lines drawn in pencil. Both features would have taken considerable time to complete.

There is an additional quilt top of five Mexican Lily blocks with four solid white blocks

interspersed between them at the Schminck Museum. It contains the same red and green fabrics.

At this time in Elizabeth's later life, her husband of sixty-one years had died in 1909 at their Summer Lake ranch home.

Elizabeth continued to visit her ten surviving children and shared her past with friends, family, and at pioneer reunions. A 1913 newspaper clipping from the Schminck scrapbook describes a trip she took alone at age eighty-one from her home in southeastern Oregon to Portland to attend a reunion and visit family. It reads in part:

> Notwithstanding her advanced age, Mrs. Foster enjoys traveling and is perfectly able to take care of herself among strangers. She is a great reader and is more familiar with national politics than many of the younger generations, and discusses modern events with the same intelligence and enjoyment as she does those happenings of the earlier history of Oregon.[41]

Block comparison of fabric placement and whimsy

Mexican Lily Quilt. *Oregon State Society of the Daughters of the American Revolution Schminck Museum, Lakeview, #3144*

A-12

Quilt: Lily
Category: Appliqué
Size: 81" x 73"
Date: circa 1850
Maker: Sarah Hammond Buell (1800-1885)
Year Over Trail: 1847
Came: As a wife with husband Elias and seven children, two sons-in-law, and several grandchildren
County Where Settled: Polk County, Oregon

Elias and Sarah Hammond Buell

This quilt of solid red and green prints in a pieced and appliqué lily pattern offers early evidence of a migration motif. The wheel design quilted in the solid white blocks is represented by four circles surrounding a center circle with double lines bisecting the centers of each. Also in the blocks are little hearts quilted in each corner. Symbols like hearts have long been used in wedding quilts and other needlework to connote sentiments of love, whereas wheels represent divine guidance during "leave taking" or migration.

The quilt is carefully made with attention to detail. Each of the stems is folded to fit the space of the block and to shape the design. There are three narrow borders of each of the quilt's colors on two sides and a wide green border on the other two sides.

Family history indicates Sarah made the quilt as she journeyed across the Plains. This may be true, but a comparison with quilts of the period suggests the careful piecing and appliqué work would have been hard to plan and place while moving or in the temporary location of a camp. The number and size of borders indicate she had time to handpiece each of them in place. The amount of quilting in each block is more like that of quilts completed in the East before coming West. The quilt probably was completed before the trip and brought with the family.

Sarah Hammond Buell was born January 22, 1800 in Liberty, Frederick County, Maryland and died in Sheridan, Polk County, Oregon in 1885. Her family was of New York ancestry. She married Elias Buell on October 19, 1817 in Allensville, Switzerland County, Indiana. Robert Buell was the immigrant ancestor of the family, having come to America in the early 1600s and settled in the Hartford, Connecticut area. After arriving in Oregon in 1847, Elias went to the California gold fields. He returned with $2,000 and built the first sawmills and gristmill on Mill Creek near Buell, Oregon by 1855.[42]

According to family history, the quilt was a wedding gift to Sarah's daughter Melissa, who met her future husband, Isaac Hinshaw, on the wagon train en route to Oregon. He and his nine-year-old son, Sanford, were coming to Oregon for a new start after the death of his wife. Melissa Buell and Isaac Hinshaw were married in Gooseneck Valley, Polk County, Oregon. They eventually had eight children.

The quilt remained with Melissa Buell Hinshaw Vanhorn throughout her life, and then passed through her family to a great-granddaughter, JoAnn Wiss. In 1982, realizing the value of the antique quilt to historians, she donated it to the Horner Collection of the Benton County Museum.[43]

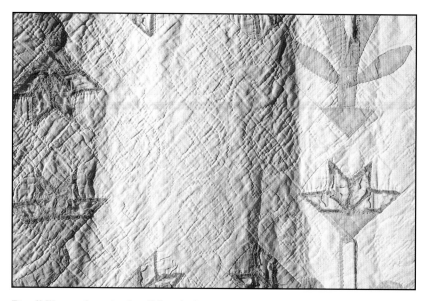

Detail illustrating wheel quilting design

Lily Quilt. *Horner Collection at the Benton County Museum, Philomath*

A-13

Quilt: Flashing Minnow
Category: Pieced
Date: 1852
Size: 79.5 x 70"
Maker: Lucinda Cox Brown Allen Spencer
 (1816-1888)[44]
Year Over Trail: 1847
Came: As a wife with husband Elias Brown and three children, her father Thomas Cox, and other family members
County Where Settled: Marion County, then Benton County, Oregon

This brown and white quilt reveals the extraordinary needle skills and project commitment by a talented woman. It is labor-intensive, entirely hand-pieced and hand-quilted. There are six narrow borders of no more than an inch wide with mitered corners, showing a further time commitment to completing the planned design.

The name is derived from the white diamond piece darting around the brown square, as a minnow flashes in water. Quilt historian Lenice Bacon referred to the pattern as "Darting Minnow."[45]

The use of just three fabrics in construction indicates there were sufficient quantities available to Lucinda so that she could design the quilt using a set number of fabrics. Her father, a merchant in the Midwest, had decided to come to Oregon to establish a business to serve the many emigrants. The quilting is extensive, with straight lines one-fourth inch apart and grid work of squares one-half inch apart.

Lucinda Cox Brown Allen Spencer was an example of the young married woman, who, through her loyalty to husband and family, agreed to come west, leaving behind her twin sister and the graves of her three infants. Additional tragedy soon faced her. As a result of swimming and herding the teams across the Platte River, Elias Brown became ill and died. He was buried in the middle of the Trail, and the wagons driven over his grave to hide it from predators.

Arriving in Oregon as part of the first wagon train to use the Barlow Road along the south side of Mt. Hood, the family settled in Salem. Their journey took eight months and sixteen days, terminating on October 16.[46] The father built a two-story building, with the store on the lower level and living quarters above.

To support her family, Lucinda used her sewing skills to make silk hats. She also plaited wheat straw for bonnets and hats and decorated them with ribbons. By 1849, she had purchased her own claim of land outside of Salem. According to the U.S. Census 1850, she was married to Hiram Allen, whose wife had died crossing the Plains. They had four children. After Mr. Allen died of typhoid fever in 1858, she married George Washington Spencer, whose first wife had died coming to Oregon. The last of her eight children, Nettie, was born in 1861.

Lucinda was active in her community and in her church, the Methodist Episcopal and later, the United Brethren. While living near Corvallis, then called Marysville, she helped to make two hundred pies for the town's first Fourth of July celebration. July Fourth was the outstanding social event for many early settlers. They would gather for the day beginning with a parade, a community-wide outdoor dinner, speeches, and close with toasts: "Will Amette and Miss Issippi—may they speedily be united by the iron bond of a railroad, and may President Buchanan perform the ceremony."[47]

Within her family, Lucinda and her daughter, Elvira, fostered the image of the pioneer mother. To honor his mother Elvira and all pioneer mothers, Lucinda's grandson, Burt Brown Barker, commissioned The Pioneer Mother sculpture.★

Lucinda's descendants have a long record of contributing to historic activities, especially historic preservation in Oregon.[48] This quilt was recently donated to the Oregon Historical Society by Board member and great-great grandson John Herman.

★See Postscript.

Detail of corner treatment with six borders

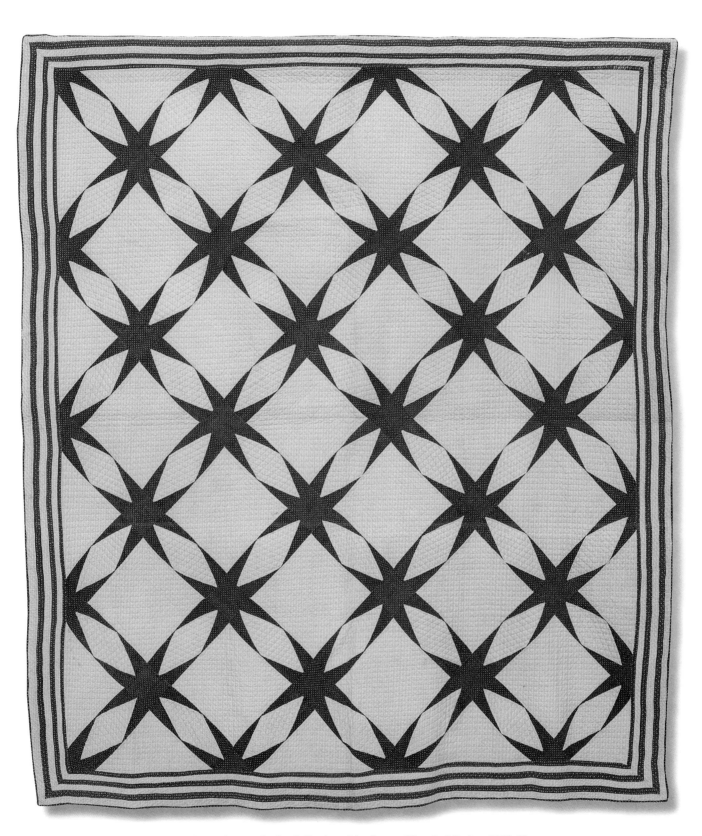

Flashing Minnow Quilt. *Collection of the Oregon Historical Society, 2005-49*

A-14

Quilt: Pin Wheel
Category: Pieced
Size: 81.75" x 77.5"
Date: 1849
Maker: Sarah Koontz Glover (1803-1885)
Year Over Trail: 1849
Came: As a wife with husband, Philip Glover, and eight of their children, including James Nettle Glover, who would later found Spokane, Washington; his brother John Glover; and sister-in-law Matilda Glover Koontz, wife of Nicholas Koontz, who had come in 1847.
County Where Settled: Marion County, Oregon

This quilt is the first of two by Sarah Koontz Glover. Attached to the quilt is a penciled note by Mabel C. Glover Root, the maker's granddaughter, which says it was made "while crossing the plains in 1849."[49] The pieced blocks are primarily brown with some greens and blues. The pinwheels and wheel quilting motif give a sense of movement as might be experienced in the slow-moving wagons and by the blowing wind. It is particularly effective with the blocks set "on point." The quilting further reflects the Trail and nature in the simple vinelike design of flowers and leaves.

Sarah Koontz was born April 13, 1803 in Missouri, the daughter of Nicholas and Rebecca McConnell Koontz, who had migrated from Pennsylvania. Her immigrant ancestors were Robert McConnell from Scotland and Peter January of France, who both came to America in the 1700s.[50] She met Philip Glover at her father's tavern on the Boonslick Trace, west of St. Charles, Missouri. He was a native of Maryland, veteran of the War of 1812, and participant in the Great Migration of 1818 over the Cumberland Road. The family story about their first meeting says Sarah was so overcome by the appearance of the handsome, distinguished-looking Philip that she had to retire to the rear of the cabin where she sat down on a wine cask and cried. The couple were married in November 1819. They lived in a flint rock house built on the line between Lincoln and Warren Counties in eastern Missouri.

Theirs was a prosperous farm, with fertile fields, substantial orchards and buildings, and a "great swarm of slaves." The flint rock house had the slave quarters nearby and a large open fronting space where, family history relates, Philip Glover would walk bareheaded in the violent storms carrying his Bible. It was said that his presence and calm, reassuring words would allay the fears of the slaves that the world was coming to an end.

This ability was again recognized when, in 1849, he was chosen leader of the train of fifty wagons to leave the racial strife of Missouri and head for Oregon.

They traveled with three wagons, coming into the Willamette Valley by way of the Barlow Road after a journey of six months and a day. Their oldest son, William, having come in 1848, was there to meet them. The area they claimed was between the Salem Prairie and the Waldo Hills of Marion County.

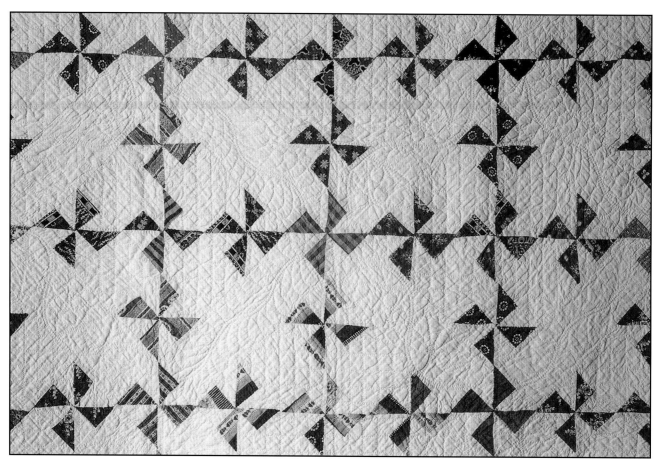

Detail of block

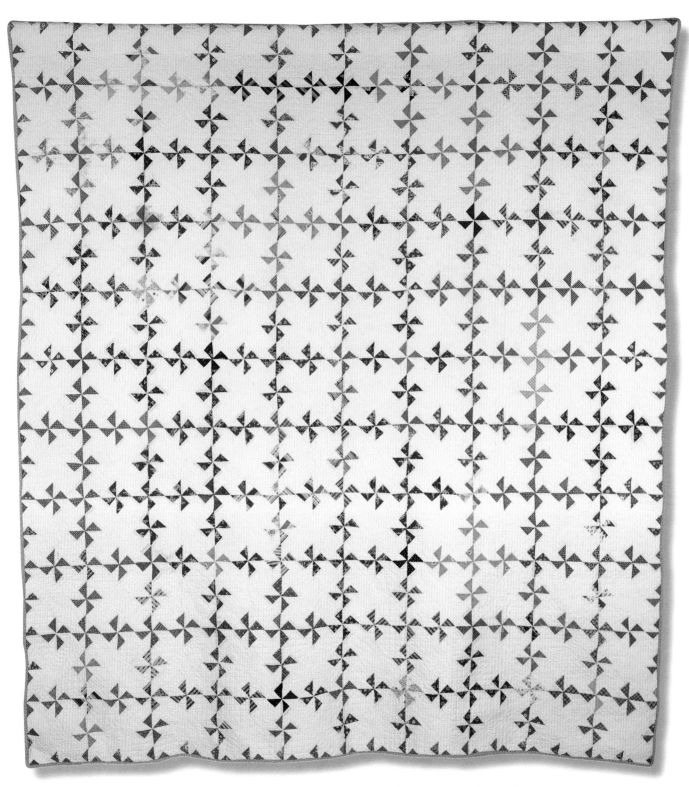

Pin Wheel Quilt. *Collection of Oregon Historical Society, Portland, #88.80*

A-15

Quilt: Wheel Pattern
Category: Pieced
Size: 83.75" x 71.5"
Date: 1849 began; Finished later
Maker: Sarah Koontz Glover (1803-1885)

Sarah Koontz Glover
with her youngest son
Wiley

This is Sarah's second quilt. The family believes this quilt was also pieced while crossing the Plains in 1849. From study of the quilt, the family history, and discussions with the current owner, my opinion is that it was finished later—perhaps after her husband died in 1872. She was known then to have spent time on her needlework while staying at her daughter's home.

The quilt's most significant fact is the identification of the pattern as being a wheel. This accords with the thesis that quilts were made to reflect the women's experience of migration. The placement of the red and green colors gives the sense of circular movement.

As noted above, after Philip Glover died in 1872, Sarah Koontz Glover spent much of her time in the home of her youngest daughter Lou Glover Culver, west of her old homestead. Sarah was described as neatness and dexterity personified, always making sure that things were done just right. Because her eyesight remained strong, she was able to do much needlework. As quoted in the family history, "Some of the prized possessions in our family being quilts in beautiful designs which she 'pieced' and quilted. I have one in a wheel pattern in green, red, and white which she gave to Father."[51]

Although, generally this is referred to as a star pattern, it is a widely produced pattern with at least twelve names.[52]

Detail of block

Wheel Quilt. *Collection of Louise Godfrey, Portland*

A-16

Quilt: Sun and Hexagon Quilt Blocks
Category: Pieced
Size: Unfinished
Date: 1850
Maker: Mary Helen Venable Medley (1817-1851)
Year Over Trail: 1850
Came: As a wife with husband John Medley, their seven children; her parents Nathaniel and Mary Venable, their two children; her sister and husband Martha Frances and Harrison Pinkston and her family
County Where Settled: Washington County, then Umpqua County, area later named Douglas, Oregon

This museum gift consists of two sets of blocks. One is a small set of a sun pattern that appears to have been taken apart from a project because there are needle holes along the edge seam lines. The fabrics appear to be early prints.

The second is a larger set of pieced hexagons in various stages of completion representing a broader range of fabrics. Prior to the family's departure from Daviess County, Missouri, John Medley had a general store. It is also interesting to note the very tiny fabric pieces in the center hexagons. This indicates the importance of these fabrics in the life of the maker. They, no doubt, served to trigger memories of the people and activities associated with the tiny pieces.

The acquisition document states that these blocks were pieced by Mary Helen Venable Medley while crossing the Plains. During the journey, tragedy struck the family on June 11, 1850. Mary Helen's mother, Mary Venable, and her sister, Martha Frances Pinkston, both died, probably of cholera. They were buried along the Trail.

Within a year after their arrival, Mary Helen died in Washington County on July 24, 1851. John Medley took his family to the Umpqua River in southern Oregon, where the other members of the Venable family had settled. Later, John Medley worked as a druggist in Oakland and lived with his oldest son Oscar.[53] His brother-in-law Harrison Pinkston eventually married his deceased wife's sister, Maria Louisa Venable.

It is an appropriate tribute to Mary Helen Venable Medley and, possibly, to her mother and sister, that the blocks were left unfinished and given to the Douglas County Museum of History and Natural History in Roseburg, Oregon.

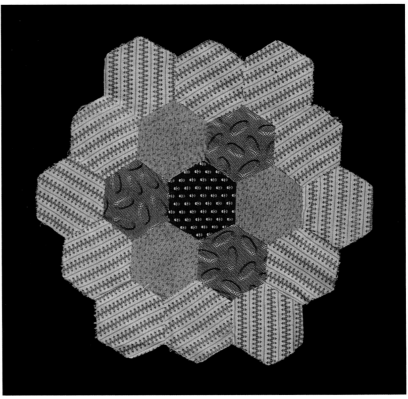

Hexagon Blocks. *Collection of the Douglas County Museum of History and Natural History, Roseburg, #68.78.8-9*

Sun Blocks.
Collection of the Douglas County Museum of History and Natural History, Roseburg, #104.2

Hexagon Blocks

A-17

Quilt: Harlow Album Quilt
Category: Pieced
Size: 86" x 69.5"
Date: 1898
Maker: Frances Burris Tandy Harlow (1815-1911)
Year Over Trail: 1850-1851
Came: As a wife with husband Mahlon Hall Harlow and six children; her mother Sarah Snelling Tandy; her brothers William and Robert Tandy; and her sisters Jemima Tandy, widowed Sarah Tandy Benson and her four daughters, Ann Tandy Henderson and her husband Henry M. Henderson and their four children. Also Caleb Harlow and his family
County Where Settled: Yamhill County, then Lane County, Oregon

Mahlon and Frances Burris Tandy Harlow and their family, circa 1890

This album quilt contains the names of thirty-one family members of Francis Harlow embroidered on the ten-inch blocks. All the names are female except one, Joel H. Abshier—a grandson and only child of her daughter Juda Joanna Harlow Abshier, who had passed away in 1894. Mrs. Harlow's name appears in the center with the notation "Pieced by Grandma Harlow Age 83." Her daughters' blocks are immediately surrounding hers. Then come the granddaughters and great-granddaughters, each grouped near their own mother's name. One name refers to a non-family member. It is Nellie Pogue, who was the hired girl living with and caring for Grandma Harlow at the time the quilt was made.

The presence of these names on the quilt reflects the importance of community and family to this pioneer woman. The quilt also represents a definite time in the history of the family. The family continued to expand after the date of the quilt, as many members do not appear on the quilt but do appear on a genealogical family tree. The family history was celebrated annually at Harlow-Tandy reunions, with shared and recorded reminiscences.

One person wrote the names on the quilt, which were then embroidered with white thread in a stem stitch. The quilt is hand-pieced and hand-quilted in diagonal lines.

Francis Burris Tandy was born near Hopkinsville, Kentucky in 1815. She married Mahlon Harlow on August 19, 1835 in Lafayette County, Missouri. They had six children born between 1836 and 1848. They started west in the spring of 1850 with a large party of extended families and Jerome B. Greer as the captain. They traveled with covered wagons and loose stock. Frances Harlow drove her own carriage pulled by horses.

At Fort Bridger in western Wyoming, the wagon train divided, with some going to the California gold fields and the rest heading to Oregon

but forced to winter over in Mormon country, near Ogden City, because the grass along the route needed for the livestock had been burned. When the Mormons tried to impose a tax for using their land, the party was forced to leave their temporary camp in the winter's deep snow and move on toward Oregon. At this point, Mahlon Harlow was arrested and accused of being part of the Missouri militia company who had driven the Mormons out of Far West, Jackson County, Missouri in the late 1830s. He was released when word spread that he was a man of influence back in Missouri.

When they reached the John Day River in eastern Oregon, the high water forced them to use their wagon boxes as flat boats to haul their supplies across. Mrs. Harlow's carriage became caught in the river current and was lost. After arriving at The Dalles in early May, Mahlon Harlow took a contract to build culverts and bridges for the portage railroad being built around the Cascades of the Columbia River. After the work was completed, the party hired a keelboat to take them to Portland, leaving a couple of young men to tend the livestock. The party was met by Vincent Snelling, a brother of Sarah Snelling Tandy and pioneer of 1844, who took them to Yamhill County. Some of the men returned upriver to bring the livestock down the Barlow Road to Oregon City, arriving there on July 4, 1851.

Later, Mahlon traveled south into the Willamette Valley, where he traded five dollars and an old pistol for the rights to a land claim in Lane County.

Frances Harlow and her extended family were active members in their community. Their cabin was the organizing site for the Willamette Forks Baptist Church of Jesus Christ, the forerunner of the First Baptist Church of Eugene. Francis and Mahlon Harlow, along with Sarah Tandy, brothers William and Robert Tandy, sister Sarah Tandy Benson

Detail inscribed "Pieced by Grandma Harlow Age 83"

Harlow Album Quilt. *Collection of the Lane County Historical Museum, #77-63*

and Joseph Meador, were the chartering members on July 1, 1852. Mahlon was the church's first deacon.

The Harlow family played a part in the story of the Lost Wagon Train of 1853.★ Frances Harlow was one who rushed to get supplies organized to send out to the stranded emigrants.

Mahlon Harlow operated the first hotel in Lane County's Eugene in 1856. Later, he helped to build the first courthouse and was elected the county assessor.

The Harlows eventually had ten children. The names of their sons illustrate the nineteenth-century tendency to name sons after famous men. Their first and second sons were Anderson Jackson and Henry Clay. Their tenth and last child was Mahlon Hall Harlow, Junior. According to the 1880 Census, the family was living on their farm near Springfield, Oregon with three unmarried daughters working as dressmakers, one son helping to farm, and Mahlon's maiden sisters Juda and Joanna, who arrived in 1871 to live with them.[54]

A number of places are named in honor of the family including Harlow Crater on the North Sister of the Cascade's Sisters Mountains and Harlow Road in Eugene.[55]

★An account of Lucinda Ann Leonard Worth's experience can be found in Appendix B.

A-18

Quilt: Hovering Hawks and Peonies
Category: Pieced and Appliqué
Size: 69.5" x 68"
Date: Circa 1865
Maker: Sarah Amanda Ann Hazelton Gilfrey
    (1844-1884)
Year Over Trail: 1850
Came: As a daughter with parents Royal and
    Mary Ann Hazelton and family
County Where Settled: Lane County, Oregon

This predominantly red and green quilt celebrates nature and the outdoors and, very likely, the maker's Trail experience, in a mixture of large pieced and appliquéd blocks measuring eighteen inches square. Although the motifs of pieced triangles and peonies and themes of nature and migration are common in nineteenth-century quilts, this design is original.

The carefully placed dark triangles create the effect of dark Hovering Hawks above the brown earth in three blocks and the blue river in the other two. The peony represents "healing" in the nineteenth-century floral lexicon. After a Trail experience, the pioneers truly needed healing, rest, and recovery. The quilting patterns include feathers in the peony blocks and on the borders. The borders match on opposite sides of the quilt, giving variety and interest to the original interpretation of the appliquéd phlox flowers.

Sarah Amanda Ann Hazelton, known as Amanda, was born in Green County, Missouri in 1844 to Royal and Martha Ann Reynolds Hazelton. John Haseltine was the immigrant ancestor from England to Massachusetts in the mid 1600s. Royal went to the California gold fields from Missouri in 1849. Unsuccessful in mining, he learned of settlement opportunities in the West. So, in 1850, he and his family joined a train, where he served a wagon repairman. They first settled west of Skinners Butte in what is now Eugene. A year later, the family moved twenty miles south to Hazelton Creek, near Creswell, where he built a sawmill and gristmill and created the village of Royal. When construction of the Oregon and California Railroad bypassed the settlement in the 1880s, the mills moved south to a new location, Slabtown, now known as Cottage Grove.

Family history relates that while Royal Hazelton was away, busy with his hotel and toll road ventures, a peddler offered Martha a bolt of silk material. Eager to have the fabric and short of cash, she traded a pig to get the cloth. After that, Hazelton Creek was called Silk Creek.[56]

In 1874, Amanda Hazelton married George Gilfrey, a pioneer of 1853 with his family. The couple had one daughter, Nellie, before Amanda died in 1884. This Hovering Hawks and Peonies quilt was a treasured heirloom owned by Nellie. Before her 1906 marriage, Nellie worked as a saleslady and resided with relatives in Eugene, the Hendricks family, who donated the quilt to the Lane County Historical Museum.[57] The quilt was a focal point of a national traveling exhibit entitled "Webfoots and Bunchgrassers: Folk Art of the Oregon Country" in 1980, part of the continuing celebration of Oregon pioneer women.[58]

Detail of piecing

Phlox growing in Wyoming

Hovering Hawks and Peonies. *Collection of the Lane County Historical Museum, #63-96*

PART II
1851-1855

Approaching Chimney Rock, painting by William Henry Jackson. *National Park Service/Scotts Bluff National Monument, Gering, Nebraska, SCBL25*

The Trail

Gradually, as the journey progressed and knowledge about the realities of the Elephant became known, the challenges of the terrain and the economies of the trip began to disrupt women's lives and rob them of a sense of control and routine. Although they traveled with published guidebooks suggesting locations to camp, by the late 1840s many of these were out of date or the resources of a site had been exhausted when a family sought them out. As water and grass supplies diminished, travel days were lengthened in an effort to find the necessary water and feed. All of these obstacles created frustration among families.

On occasion, to ease the work of the starving oxen by lightening the wagonloads, possessions were abandoned. Then it might be necessary to jettison those treasures that bound women to families and friends back East. When forced to leave behind some of her cargo, one woman penned a note inviting others to help themselves to "five good quilts."[1]

At Ft. Laramie, Wyoming, the first major opportunity to regroup after experiencing the Elephant of the Great Platte River, the scene was described as the following:

> Yesterday [May 30] being a rainy day and most trains laying by having nothing else to do, a general destruction and devastation appeared to take Place—in almost every train—I thought I had seen destruction of property but this morning beat anything I had ever seen. … Trunks, clothes, Matrasses [*sic*], Quilts, Beef, Bacon, Rice, Augers, Handsaw, Planes, Shoes, Hats, Thread, Spools, Bass [*sic*] Soap, Mowing sythes [*sic*], etc. These were thrown out yesterday by one train in order to make their loads lighter…
>
> We found a number of emigrants here [at Fort Laramie]—many with broken down teams, some preparing to pack, others turning back, not being able to procure the necessaries for packing, and less able to proceed farther with their present teams. This appears to be a place of general renovating amongst travellers. Most stay a day or two for the double purpose of resting their mules and repacking their loads—Good wagons here bring from 4 to 30 dollars. Mules from 100 to 150 dollars. … Everything you buy cost four times as much as it is worth and every thing you sell being perhaps one tenth its value.[2]

The second part of the journey (from Ft. Laramie to Boise) often became one of monotony and hard work. The routine of travel was established after the preparations for getting underway were accomplished: a drive of nine to twelve miles moving at an average of three miles an hour; a "nooning," or stop for dinner and rest; an afternoon of continued travel; and then the stop for the night with evening activities of rest and relaxation.

Often at the end of the day, there would be an hour or two of socialization in the form of visiting, dancing, singing, and game playing. Most of these activities by now were a combination of pain and pleasure—involving physical tiredness along with the joy of accomplishment and satisfaction of achievement.

As they continued across the high plateaus toward South Pass City in Wyoming at an eight-thousand-foot elevation, the trip became more strenuous. Difficulty in finding food and potable water meant that unknown distances must be traveled. As illnesses began to set in, additional needs and requirements were placed on women's time. These changes in schedules and activities forced them to abandon some of what they valued.

Traveling Across the Desert

When the weather was very hot, as it could be in the high plateau areas of Wyoming, Idaho, and eastern Oregon, wagon trains would travel all night and make a rest stop during the day. If this meant going through sand, people would carry as little extra water and wood as possible because of the extra weight. Night travel was particularly hard because of the difficulty of keeping track of the animals or trying to sleep with the continuous rumbling of the wagons.

River Crossings

During the early years (1840-1850), one of the time-consuming challenges was finding a way to cross a river. Depending on the speed of the current, the width and depth of the water, and knowledge of previous crossings, several options were available. If a current was slow and the depth and width not too much, the wagons could be pulled across by the oxen teams. To seal the cracks of the wagon against water, each wagon carried a bucket of tar, which would be carefully and liberally applied. If the current was fast, horses would be substituted for the oxen because of their greater agility. The slower, heavier animals would have to be swum across by a man going in the water with them. The young husband of Lucinda Cox Brown Spencer (Quilt A-13) died as a result of getting sick after swimming the animals across the Platte River. If a river was considered too dangerous, then a raft or canoes would be built to carry each wagon across. This took time and caused significant delays in travel. If members of a party could do so, as with the Riddle family (Quilts B-2-3), they would stay behind and ferry others across using their raft to earn extra money.

In the middle years (1851-1855), journeys were shortened when bridges and rafts were more readily available. These would be set up by the Indians or individuals hoping to make money by charging inflated tolls.

Presence of Federal Government and Escort Services

In order to ease the strain on pioneers, interest was expressed to the federal government early in the trail years for some form of military presence, either as escorts on the Trail or in established military posts. In 1846, an act passed by Congress provided money to support and equip a regiment of mounted riflemen, "military stations" on the route to Oregon, and to compensate the Native Americans for land where stations were established. Unfortunately, this action was delayed by the Mexican War, so the mounted riflemen did not travel the Trail until 1849.

During the 1850s, the army established a permanent presence in the West with a number of forts along the Trail at Ft. Leavenworth, Ft. Kearny, Ft. Laramie, Ft. Bridger, and Ft. Hall, as well as in the Pacific Northwest with Ft. Vancouver, Ft. Steilacoom, Ft. Lane, Ft. Umpqua, Ft. Hoskins, and Ft. Yamhill. Their purpose was to protect the emigrants and quell the raids by curious Native Americans through a show of strength. This launched a new era of relationships between the federal government and both parties. It is estimated there were 206 battles throughout the West between the soldiers and Native Americans between 1848-1861.[3] The reaction to this support by overland travelers was mixed. Some wanted more military while others wanted more government services like workshops and supply stations, better guidebooks, wagon trains to support stragglers, and surveyors and road builders. Many were dismayed at the treatment the Native Americans received. Quiltmakers of this study who extended the hand of friendship and interest to the Native Americans included the Applegate women (Quilt A-2) and the Riddle women (Quilts B-2-3).[4]

With the onset of the War Between the States and the federal troops needed on the battlefronts, men with overland trail experience volunteered to serve for the Emigrant Escort Service. Two of the people commissioned to lead wagon trains between 1862-1864 were Medorem and Leroy Crawford, husband and son of Adeline Brown Crawford(Quilt A-1). Medorem received the position of Captain in the Quartermaster Corps and was assigned as leader in the Service. His troop of one hundred and fifty mounted and armed men was equipped with four head of livestock, extra rations, and a mountain howitzer. They traveled the route aiding travelers, guarding livestock so men could track down others run off by Indians, and repairing the road in advance of the approaching wagons.

As an example of Crawford's leadership decisions, he chose to follow the Lander Road, a newer route in Wyoming developed for access to grass and water for livestock. Then, he chose to head for Walla Walla, Washington via the old Whitman Mission route, rather than proceeding along the regular trail to the Willamette Valley.[5] Crawford repeated his assignment in 1863 and it is very likely that some of the pioneers who were a part of the Aurora Colony (Quilt C-2), the Wingville families (Quilt C-3), and the Lieuallens (Quilts C-8-9) might have been assisted by his train's services. It is possible but confirmation is difficult because public lists of wagon train families do not exist.

An advantage gained by later wagon trains was having an experienced leader who knew the route, the best places to camp, rest, and cross the rivers and mountains, as well as possible dangerous places to avoid. Not only did such leaders help to shorten the travel time, they also helped to avoid the high priced tolls.

Although there were other ways to find the best routes and camping places, word of mouth was always a source as were the messages and notes found scribbled on dried bones and animal skeletons.

Fears

Mixed in with this life of monotonous routine would be the other extreme—moments of sheer fright or violence. Dealing with illness, whether of oneself or one's family, the death of a loved one, accidents that would occur, runaway wagons being pulled by frightened oxen, complications of pregnancy and birth, and rapid changes of weather all had to be faced and endured. Dr. Peter D. Olch ranked the order for the cause of death: first, run over by wagon wheels; second, firearms accidents; third, stampede by livestock, followed by attacks by other emigrants, lightning strikes, gun powder explosions, and suicides.[6]

Fear of Disease

The increased number of people traveling the Trail resulted in a deterioration of the water supply and an epidemic level of illness and disease, especially cholera. The worst years were between 1849 and 1854. Cholera had arrived on board ships from Asia and Europe at the seaports along the coasts, striking in the Midwest where it had been carried by Mississippi River steamers from New Orleans to St Louis and up the Missouri River. It followed the emigrants as they began their overland journeys along the Missouri and Platte Rivers.

The disease and death levels were so high that President William Henry Harrison declared a national epidemic. He issued a call for ministers and religious leaders to pray for help in controlling the spread of disease. The Reverend J.H.B. Royal (Quilt B-13) included in his writings a prayer he offered in response to this request.

Fear of the Indians

The fear of Indian attacks was one of the much-publicized concerns about the Trail experience. Reports were common of coming upon sites of raids and attacks, but there is no evidence that actual difficulty and brutality occurred to the families whose stories are included in this project.

Generally, the greatest difficulty came through misunderstanding and lack of respect shown to the Native Americans by the whites. Several of the family histories and related stories report instances when Indians were fascinated with the young white girls. They made comments about their beauty and attractiveness. There are several stories about how Indian men sought to trade horses for the daughters of traveling families.

In the Daniel Bayley family, eighteen-year-old daughter Caroline was kidnapped by Indians but was rescued by a member of the train. A party of Sioux had visited their wagon train near Fort Laramie, and the chief had asked how many horses Mr. Bayley would take for his daughter. Jokingly, he said ten. The next morning, the Indian returned with thirty horses in exchange for the girl. Not understanding Mr. Bayley's humor, the Indians became annoyed. Leaving unhappily, they later kidnapped the young girl as she wandered from camp. She was returned only after successful negotiations by Bosh Rickner, a young man who had traveled the West before and knew the language and culture well enough to explain the situation to the Indians.

Fear of Weather

Thunder and lightning storms along the Platte River through Nebraska and into Wyoming are some of the strongest weather occurrences anywhere. The wagon cover, being made of soft cloth, did not provide much security in a driving rainstorm, but many wagon covers were actually made like quilts, having cloth placed on either side of a rubber sheet that served to insulate and waterproof the interior. In 1900, pioneer L. Jane Powell reminisced about the severest rain and hailstorm she had ever witnessed while traveling along the Platte River:

> Peal after peal thunder shook the ground as though it was tearing the world to pieces. The continual lightning occasionally struck the wagon tires and ran around them, presenting the appearance of great balls of fire. The wind shook the wagons until they felt as though they would upset, and the rain sifted through the heavy lined wagon covers like Oregon mist.[7]

Reports like this have shaped the perceptions of the Oregon Trail experience. Although the image of lightning circling the tires is dramatic, its actual happening is not possible.[8]

Fear for Children

Women traveling with children faced the additional challenges of keeping track of them, tending to them during illness and accident, and suffering through their births and deaths. The problems of pregnancy were increased by not knowing when or where they would deliver or what help would be available.

Six-year-old Eliza Dibble Sawtell (Quilt B-14) was bitten by a rattlesnake on the Trail, permanently injuring her leg. Lucinda Ann Leonard (Quilt B-17) was a constant worry to her family while on the Trail because of sickness. They feared she would not survive the journey, especially after being part of the Lost Wagon Train of 1853.

For Elizabeth Currier Foster (Quilts A-8-11) the accidental death of Salita Henderson during a layover left a lasting impression on her. The child died of a medicine overdose, after seeing her older sister Lucy as well as Elizabeth taste laudanum, which was used medicinally. She was buried in a black walnut coffin made of boards that had been a table. Elizabeth was so guilt ridden, she cut a flower from her beaded bag and placed it on the grave.

Fear of Stampede and Run-away Wagons

Another fear voiced by women like Lucinda Cox Brown Spencer (Quilt A-13) was the possibility of buffalo herd stampedes. There were so many animals during her 1847 journey, the emigrants were aware that anything in their way would be trampled.

A greater fear occurred when the oxen pulling a wagon were spooked into a stampede. This was especially scary for older women and younger children, who were usually riding in the wagons. It could be caused by anything, including loose stock being driven too close to a yoked team, the smell of water to a thirsty team, or Indians masquerading as animals on the Trail. This risk was always present, as one would never know when or how the animals might be frightened.

Fear of Losing Role and Responsibility

As physical conditions began to deteriorate, changes had to be made; one of these often involved the practice of observing the Sabbath as a day of worship. For women, this change could have been a threat to one of their major roles, that of maintaining moral authority and religious responsibility. A study of sixty-six female diarists on the Overland trails reveals that most were busy with other responsibilities, accepted the conditions and circumstances that prevented a Sabbath day religious practice, or encountered obstacles that prevented a rest day. Yet, evidence shows that women discussed the importance of honoring the Sabbath before and after their journeys and many became active, contributing members of their congregations once settled.[9]

At the beginning of the journey, Sunday was regarded as a day of worship and rest for some. As one woman wrote:

> Men needed 'physical rest,' so they lolled around in the tents and on their blankets spread on the grass, or under the wagons out of the sunshine, seeming to realize that the 'Sabbath was made for me'...[Yet] women, who had only been anxious spectators of their arduous work, and not being weary in body, could not fully appreciate physical rest.[10]

For the Royal family of Methodist ministers (Quilt B-13), preserving the Sabbath was a defining goal of their journey. On the way west, they invited or joined with other parties only if they would observe the Sabbath. Reverend J.H.B. Royal regularly recorded the number of Sundays they were able to uphold this ritual: "This is the 29th Sunday from Randolph's Grove, McLean County, Illinois and we have not yet traveled on Sunday even once. I hope we may get through without doing so, have found no necessity for it yet."[11] A short time later, a demand for a change in this ritual occurred at the Humbolt River on the Applegate Trail. Late in their journey, the family's supplies were extremely low. They were using borrowed oxen to pull their wagons. The leader of the train was demanding that all move forward. Mary Ann, wife of Thomas Fletcher Royal, was expecting the birth of a baby at any moment. The only physician in the party would be moving out on Sunday. All these were legitimate reasons to break tradition and travel. Mary Ann was allowed to make the decision for the family. She chose to put her trust in God that He would protect the family if they observed their ritual. The family kept the Sabbath and survived.[12]

B-1

Quilt: Star
Category: Pieced
Size: 91" x 70"
Date: circa 1830
Maker: Jane Lieb Riggs (1814-1874)
Year Over Trail: 1851
Came: As a wife, with husband Zadoc S. Riggs and five children
County Where Settled: Polk County, Oregon

Early fabrics and family history combine to make this a special heirloom quilt. The fabrics represent the period between 1800 and 1830, the early stages of the textile printing industry in America. There are the roller-process brown prints, the indigo-blue-and-white discharge print, the pink geometric, and the early Turkey red print with evidence of rotting caused by the dye process. The fourteen-inch blocks are set together with three-inch sashes. At the intersections, feathered wreaths are quilted in fine detail.

Jane Lieb was born in Tennessee on August 21, 1814. She married Zadoc S. Riggs on December 27, 1832. He was the son of Scott and Hannah Berry Riggs of Tennessee. Both the Berry and the Riggs families were early colonists in this country. John and Elizabeth Berry came from Germany around 1720, while Edward and Elizabeth Riggs came to Massachusetts from England in the 1600s.

Zadoc and Jane Riggs were living in Scott County, Illinois when he left for the gold fields in 1849. He returned home enthusiastic, and the family started for Oregon in 1851 with Zadoc as the wagon train's captain. Then, tragedy struck—he died at the Sweetwater River crossing in Wyoming on July 5th. In addition, their daughter Cynthia died September 15th at The Dalles, Oregon. The rest of the family arrived in the Willamette Valley, where they stayed with James Berry Riggs, a brother-in-law who had come the previous year.

In 1853, Jane Riggs and her three young sons staked a claim on Salt Creek in Polk County. There they built a house of logs they harvested and dragged to the site. In 1861, the young men built their mother a four-room house with a double fireplace that caused the neighbors to marvel at their accomplishment.[13]

Jane Lieb Riggs (1814-1874).
*Oregon Historical Society, Portland,
CN#017763*

Her life and her family have been celebrated annually at a family reunion. A newspaper clipping refers to the quilt and the reunion:

Highlights of the dinner and the afternoon were stories connected with the antique dishes, furniture and other old possessions of the family, which the group enjoyed viewing. One of the family heirlooms of great interest was the quilt pieced by Jane Lieb Riggs and handed down to her granddaughter Jane Baxter, who in turn presented it to her great granddaughter, Jane Woods...on the occasion of Jane's graduation from the eighth grade last year.[14]

Detail of quilt block

Star Quilt. *Collection of the Oregon Historical Society, Portland, #76.13.52*

B-2

Quilt: Birds in Flight variation
Category: Pieced
Size: 86.5" x 76"
Date: circa 1850
Maker: Members of Maximillia Bousman Riddle Family
Year Over Trail: 1851
Came: As a wife with husband William Riddle; three daughters, including Artenecia and her baby boy, Isabella, Ann-Maria; five sons, William, Abner, George, John, Tobias Stilley; her half-sister Lucinda McGill, age forty-five; and an orphaned niece Anna Hall, age eleven.
County Where Settled: Umpqua County, area later named Douglas County, Oregon

William and Maximillia Riddle. *Douglas County Museum of History and Natural History, #N1622*

Triangles in quilts have long represented birds in flight, thus the pattern name connects to a migration and outdoor theme. The forty-two pieced blocks each contain forty-nine triangles, for a total of over two thousand pieces hand-stitched together. The many varieties of brown, yellow, and blue fabrics date from the 1840s and earlier. The placement of the butterscotch-yellow prints in the four corners and the single strip of indigo-blue-and-white triangles in the center show the thought the maker put into placement of her blocks.

There is a possibility the quilt was pieced on the Trail because of the many small triangles and the large number of women traveling together in the Riddle family. A second quilt in the collection, a Star variation pattern from the same donor (a descendant of Ann-Maria "Mollie" Riddle Beal), shows the same love of piecing. It has fifteen blocks, each having fifty-seven pieces and four borders.[15]

Maximillia Bousman was born to John and Rebekah Stilley Bousman in Champaign County, Ohio on January 13, 1809. Her mother's family came from Sweden to Delaware in the late 1600s. Maximillia married William H. Riddle in 1826. The couple lived in Logan County, Ohio before moving west to Sangamon County, Illinois in 1839. They were lured to Oregon by high praise of the territory from a respected Illinois neighbor, Isaac Constant, who had returned from the Northwest. In the company of a large party of forty men and a few women, the Riddle family traveled with three wagons, each drawn by three yoke of oxen; one large carriage pulled by four horses; and forty head of cattle, cows, and heifers. They abandoned the carriage along the Platte River.

They chose the Applegate Trail, the southern route into Oregon across Utah and Nevada. Following a friend's recommendation, they settled one of the first claims on Cow Creek in southern Douglas County, near Canyonville. The Riddle daughters complained about having to leave their Illinois friends and endure the journey's hardships, only to locate in an isolated valley. They spent the first winter living in a large and a small tent, using the wagon boxes with covers arranged on the ground for sleeping and a canvas over the cook stove brought from Illinois.

This was the home of the Cow Creek Indians, with whom the extended family had excellent relations. William Riddle and Chief Miwaleta respected each other. Young George Riddle played with many of the Indian boys. In the early spring of 1853, Sam, one of the chief's young grandsons who was weak with a contagious illness, was left behind when the band left for their summer grounds. Maximillia welcomed him into her home and George cared for him until he died. Because of this kindness, Maximillia once negotiated a cease-fire with the Indians during a time of conflict. In 1855, while under the threat of attack from the Indians and grieving from the recent death of daughter Clara, whom she wanted to bury under safety, Maximillia was able to bring the threatening group of Indians together with the neighbors. She did this by riding alone to the Indians' camp and convincing them to talk. Respect was re-established with the local Indians, and nothing was destroyed in the white neighbors' homes they had deserted for safety.

William Riddle was an ambitious settler. The first log home he built was larger than most—a story and a half in height and eighteen feet by thirty feet in size. Working as a blacksmith, he also established a freighting service, hauling farm equipment from Portland to southern Oregon during the summers of 1852-1854. Maximillia Riddle demonstrated her commitment to building her home and community by accompanying her two sons, Abner and George, ages twelve and fourteen, on one trip to Portland without her husband. They went by wagon to purchase agricultural equipment, especially plows, to sell in southern Oregon. The three camped out along the four-hundred-mile round trip.[16]

During the winter of 1855-56, the family lived in Roseburg. There, William ran his blacksmith business and Maximillia took in boarders, her son George assisting her.[17]

Maximillia died in 1868 at the age of fifty-nine.

Birds in Flight Variation Quilt. *Southern Oregon Historical Society, Medford, #62.3.6.1.*

B-3

Quilt: Single Irish Chain
Category: Pieced
Size: 90" x 80"
Date: 1846
Maker: Artenecia Riddle Chapman Merriman
    (1830-1917)
Year Over Trail: 1851
Came: As a young widow and daughter with
    parents William and Maximillia Riddle and
    family; and her baby son John Chapman
County Where Settled: Umpqua County, area
    later named Douglas County, then Jackson
    County, Oregon

Riddle sisters, 1902: (left to right) Artie Riddle Merriman and Mollie Riddle Beal. *Southern Oregon Historical Society, Medford, #5682*

The Double Nine Patch set of this quilt, making the Single Irish Chain, creates a sense of movement across the surface. In this quilt, as well as in the similar Double Irish Chain pattern, this can be interpreted as a migration pattern when the design element of line is considered. The line defines and connects two dots and creates a sense of visual movement because the eye is carried across the surface by the diagonal line formed by color and placement of the squares.

The quilt was hand-pieced of three-inch blocks of early blue and white fabrics, which place it as perhaps the early work of a young woman learning to sew. These fabrics became readily available during the 1840s and sewing a straight line was one of the first lessons taught to young sewers.

By comparison, the quilted wreaths with the grid of intersecting lines show a count of fifteen stitches per inch. This indicates that the work may have been finished later as the maker became a more talented needleworker, or that a different, more experienced quilter completed it. Stitching a curved line while catching fifteen stitches on a needle requires a great deal of needle skill.

Artenecia Riddle was born in West Liberty, Ohio in 1830. At the age of eighteen, she married John Chapman and lived in Springfield, Illinois. He died in 1851, just a few days prior to her parents' planned depar-

ture for Oregon, leaving Artenecia a young widow and mother. She had little choice but to immigrate with them, leaving Illinois in late May. Although traveling with her family, she had her own wagon and three teams of oxen.

An incident on the journey was vividly recalled by her brother, George W. Riddle. After a gunshot shattered the bone in the arm of a member of their train, Artenecia Chapman bravely forced the bone fragments out and dressed the wound. The patient recovered well. "I witnessed the operation and it made such an impression upon my mind that at times I can visualize the operation. My sister Artenecia was a brave girl."[18]

In 1853, she married widower William H. Merriman, a member of an 1852 wagon train also from Sangamon County, Illinois. They had fourteen children of their own, in addition to one each from their former marriages.

In 1857, they moved to the Rogue River Valley, where Artenecia became an interpreter between the government and the Indians because of her ability to speak Chinook. She, no doubt, learned the language through the close friendship her family had with the neighborly Cow Creek Indian band.

By 1870, they were in the Jacksonville area of Jackson County with ten of their children.[19] Artenecia's sewing machine was the first in the Rogue Valley, producing considerable interest from the people of the area.

As an Oregon pioneer, she was one of those receiving recognition in her adopted state. Her participation in an early silent promotional film called *Gracie Visits the Rogue Valley* was featured at the 1915 San Francisco Exposition's Oregon Building.[20]

For forty years after her husband's death, Artenecia celebrated her life by traveling extensively to visit her children, grandchildren, and great-grandchildren until her death in 1917.

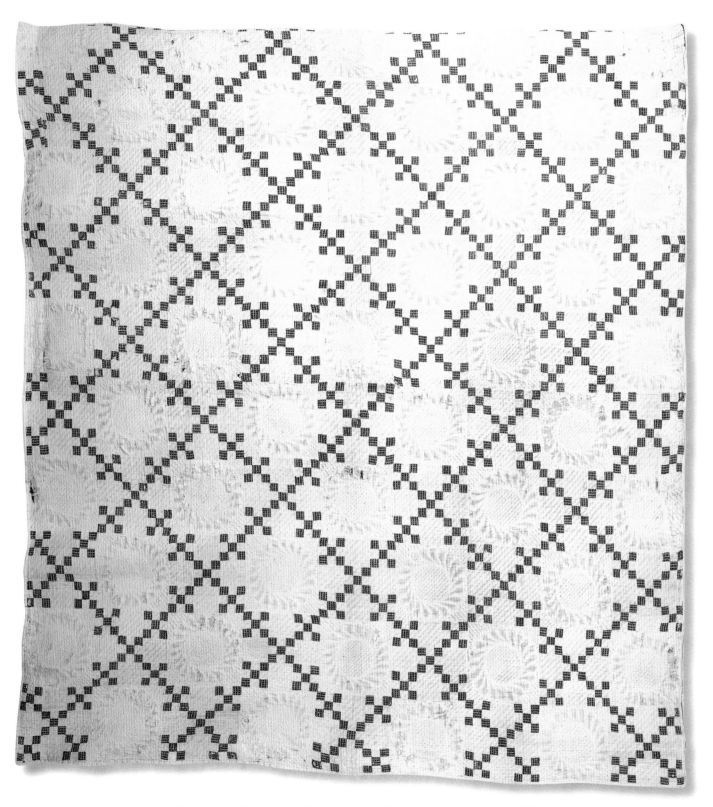

Single Irish Chain Quilt. *Southern Oregon Historical Society, Medford, #582*

B-4

Quilt: Wandering Foot
Category: Pieced
Size: 82" x 74"
Date: 1852
Maker: Almedia Grimsley Morris (1826-1912)
Year Over Trail: 1851
Came: As a wife with husband Joseph Hooker Morris, and daughter Mary
County Where Settled: Benton County, Oregon

Almedia Grimsley Morris (1826-1912)

Each pieced block of indigo-blue-and-white fabric with some additional yellow is fifteen and a half inches in size. According to family history, the solid blocks are made of fabric that was brought as a bolt over the Trail and used for baby clothes for the infant born in April 1852. Originally the color of this fabric was purple, but it has turned brown over the years. The instability of color, common at that time in fabrics of this hue, was caused by exposure to heat and light. Advanced technical skill was required to piece the blocks so the fabrics would lie flat and be consistent. The lines of elbow quilting are spaced five-eighths of an inch apart in the solid blocks. The quilting in the pieced blocks echoes that of the pattern. There is a two-inch border of a pink print fabric on all sides of the quilt. The choice of this color probably reflects the limited range of fabrics available at this early time in Oregon.

The quilt was completed in the winter of 1852 after the family arrived in November 1851. Knowing that the fabric had been bought for baby clothes, and understanding the significance of the Wandering Foot quilt pattern to the theme of migration, this quilt was probably pieced on the Trail as the couple moved westward. The pattern's significance is described in Appendix A.

Almedia Grimsley and Joseph Hooker Morris were married in 1847 in Washington County, Iowa. Joseph was a native of Virginia and Almedia had been born in Kentucky. Joseph farmed in New London township of Henry County, Iowa before leaving for Oregon. Almedia's preacher father and mother, John and Mary Scott Grimsley, and their four other children, Robert, Pamelia, Malinda, and Mary E., had migrated west in 1847. The young couple moved to the Grimsley's home in Benton County late in their first winter, before daughter Sarah was born in April 1852 . By November, they had

Detail of fabric and quilting

secured their own land claim in Benton County. The couple farmed until Joseph's death in 1888. Almedia then moved to Idaho to live with her son, where she died in 1912.

Wandering Foot Quilt

B-5

Quilt: Floral
Category: Appliqué
Size: 86" x 74"
Date: 1875-1900
Maker: Susannah Goode Morris (1822-1915)
Year Over Trail: 1851
Came: As a wife of husband Eliam S. Morris, and their five children
County Where Settled: Yamhill County, Oregon

Dr. Henry Morris of Salem, Oregon, described his grandmother's quilting as follows:

> My grandmother pieced quilts and quilted them. She always had a quilt in the quilting frame. I think every grandchild has a quilt that she quilted especially for them. Money would not buy mine. My personal impression is that she had pieced and quilted well over a hundred quilts; perhaps all of which she gave away with the exception of those that she used in the house. That was no small number, as I think there was never less than ten people that made their home there, the family and others. As I remember, there were ten double beds besides the two or three couches that could be used in an emergency.[21]

Susannah Goode
Morris (1822-1915)

Often, in these settlers' homes, there were two double beds in a room sleeping up to five people. W.B. Chandler described the sleeping arrangements in his home as, "two large boys fitted very comfortably in one end and a small boy in the other end."[22]

The thirty-five inch size of the block is an example of the scale of things in this woman's life. Unfortunately, the colors have been faded by direct sunlight. The quilt's intricate appliqué work shows excellent craftsmanship, except for quilting thread knots showing on the quilt's top. These may indicate the work of two different people or the work of the same person done at two different periods of her life.

There is another quilt of this same pattern owned by a great-great-great-granddaughter, showing that Susannah enjoyed her quilting and indicating she repeated using her quilt patterns.

Susannah Louisiana Goode was born in Missouri on December 6, 1822, the daughter of Richard Goode and Sarah Adams. On March 11, 1839, in Mineral Point, Wisconsin, she married Eliam Small Morris, who was a native of Pennsylvania. They had eleven children born between 1840 and 1866.[23] The family settled in Yamhill County, where they purchased Donation Land Claim #1330 with a log house and five acres of cleared land for five hundred dollars from Charles Hubbard. Eliam Morris spent a few months of 1852 in the gold fields near Yreka, California.

Susannah and several members of her family lived into their nineties, with one man living to 111 years. As noted above, her home had rooms large enough to hold a total of ten double beds. The garden was planted with shrubs and vines that grew and grew. One ninety-year-old grape vine was over 240 feet long. On Sundays, she would faithfully prepare dinner for an average of thirty-five to forty people.

In 1951, the Morris family celebrated the ownership centennial of the land they called "The Farm," marking the successful achievement of their family to obtain and retain the land.

The Yamhill County Museum owns this quilt and also has a supply trunk brought across the Plains and a bed made soon after the family arrived.

Floral Quilt. *Yamhill County Museum, Lafayette, YC-2-73a*

B-6

Quilt: Setting Sun
Category: Pieced
Size: 86" x 71.5"
Date: 1840
Maker: Margaret Hamilton Greer (1808-1895)
Year Over Trail: 1852
Came: As a wife with husband James and four
 of their nine children
County Where Settled: Benton County, then Polk
 County, Oregon

The accession information states the fabrics came from the baby dresses of George Hamilton Greer (1836-1928), a religious leader in the Pacific Northwest for many years. Study of the quilt reveals these to be the centers of the sun motifs and possibly the indigo-blue-and-white print of the sun's rays. It was the practice of the period to use fabrics left over from making adult clothing for that of children. Also, young children wore gender-neutral clothes of the same style, so a floral print might be expected to appear in a boy's dress. Since they lived in Philadelphia, a textile production center, this family had access to the early checked, striped, and overlaid prints.

The triangle motif across the bottom may be a ground for the sun units, either as mountains or waves. Triangles were used to represent both.

James and Margaret Hamilton Greer were born in Ireland and emigrated in 1831. Settling first in Philadelphia, James used his trade as a hand-weaver to work in the mills of the area. With the advent of the power loom and the steam process of weaving, his job was eliminated.

Turning to farming, the family lived in Indiana and Missouri between 1837 and 1852. In 1850, James went to the California gold fields, returning with $1,000 and "Oregon Fever." In the spring of 1852, the family started for Oregon with four oxen yoked to the wagon. They settled in the King's Valley area of Benton County and were actively involved with the Methodist Episcopal Church, "cordially despising" whisky, gaming, and slavery. Their home was free of tobacco smoke except when needed to drive away mosquitoes. A memorial window in the old Methodist Episcopal Church building in Dallas, Oregon honored James and Margaret.[24]

As an only son, George Hamilton Greer clerked in a Camden, Missouri general store while his father was at the gold fields. Later, in the West during the 1850s, he taught school in Oregon and California. In the 1860s, he was

James and Margaret Hamilton Greer family, circa 1888. *Oregon Historical Society, Portland, #46*

Detail of floral print

ordained a Methodist Episcopal minister and served in Oregon and western Washington. He left the church and turned to farming full time until 1883, when he became a student at the Unitarian Theological College in Meadville, Pennsylvania. Returning to the Pacific Northwest, he established Unitarian societies in Seattle, Olympia, and Tacoma. While in Tacoma, his wife Cornelia Jane Spencer, pioneer of 1852, was elected Pierce County Superintendent of Schools.

Returning to Oregon after 1893, the couple settled on her father John Spencer's 320 acre donation land claim, the site where the James Greer family had spent their first Oregon winter in 1853.[25]

Setting Sun Quilt. *Oregon Historical Society, Portland, #3013*

B-7

Quilt: Wandering Foot
Category: Pieced
Size: 85" x 67"
Date: circa 1840
Maker: Celia Hargrave (1799-1850)
Year Over Trail: 1852
Sent: With daughter Nancy Jane Whiteaker and her husband John
County Where Settled: Yamhill County, then Lane County, Oregon

This indigo-blue-and-white quilt, which came to Oregon as a gift, is unusual for several reasons. The pieced pattern is white on a blue ground rather than the more common blue on white. The design is one that appears either appliquéd or pieced. At this time, there was a transition from mostly appliquéd to more pieced quilts.

Indigo was a popular dyestuff in the mid-nineteenth century because of its colorfastness. Prior to this, home dyes usually resulted in fugitive colors of browns, golds, and muddy greens, commonly referred to as "drab." With the development of the textile industry in America, including improved dyeing and printing processes, new colorfast textiles featuring interesting design elements were produced and were readily available to quiltmakers. These fabrics were sold with a premium price. Natural indigo dyestuff was $2.35 per pound while fugitive logwood blues cost only six cents per pound.[26] Having access to fabric that would retain its color was a boon to the quiltmaker.

The technical skill required to piece the thirty-one blocks is advanced. The curved edges of the narrow pieces required an experienced hand to get them to lay flat and be consistent.

The theme of migration is evident in the name of the pieced pattern block, Wandering Foot, and the triangles in the border. The pattern is described in Appendix A.

At the museum, the quilt's accession information states, "Mrs. Thomas Hargrave gave this to her daughter Mrs. John Whiteaker, on her 16th birthday."[27]

Nancy Jane Hargrave was born in 1829 in Indiana. Her parents were Thomas and Celia French Hargrave. William Hargrave of England was the immigrant ancestor, arriving in the Carolinas sometime before 1750. Nancy was eighteen when the family moved from Illinois to Putnam County, Missouri in 1846. In 1847, she married John Whiteaker, a carpenter and cabinet maker.

Leaving his wife with her parents, John Whiteaker went to the gold fields in 1851. Attracted to the West, he returned to Missouri to bring his wife to Oregon in 1852. Serving as captain of the wagon train, he guided them to Yamhill County by October. Moving to Lane County in 1853, he first staked and improved a claim at Spencer Butte. Selling that land six years later, he invested in another farm at Pleasant Hill. In 1859, he was elected first governor of the State of Oregon and served until 1862. He then returned to his farm until 1885, when he was appointed by President Cleveland as the collector of internal revenue, based in Portland. He retired to Eugene in 1889.[28]

John and Nancy Whiteaker had six children. Their first daughter, Frances, was born while crossing the Plains and died at The Dalles on the Columbia River. Their second daughter, Ann, a teacher, retired to devote her time to administering her father's estate and caring for her invalid mother. According to the 1870 Census, the family had an eleven-year-old Native American boy named Jake living with them.[29]

The Lane County Historical Museum has two other quilts in their collection also brought west by the Whiteakers.

Detail of block

Wandering Foot Quilt. *Lane County Historical Museum, Eugene,#705*

B-8

Quilt: Wandering Foot
Category: Appliqué
Date: circa 1840
Size: 87" x 72"
Maker: Member of Arsenone Patterson family
Year Over Trail: 1852
Came: With family of Cabell and Arsenone Tureman Patterson
County Where Settled: Washington County, then Lincoln County, Oregon

Although in poor condition, this red-and-green appliqué quilt illustrates the third variation of the recurring pattern among these Oregon Trail quilts—Wandering Foot. The pattern is important because of the connection to migration. It is described in depth in Appendix A. On this quilt, the eleven-inch blocks of older fabrics indicate a date of around the 1840s. One block stands out on the quilt; it may have been an early repair. The quilt is completely hand stitched except for a replacement binding put on with a sewing machine. There is extensive quilting in wreaths and grid lines. There are four borders to add width to the quilt.

The quilt came from the estate of Hester Hill Coovert Rogers and is at the Lincoln County Historical Society. The museum has an extensive collection of Rogers family items. Even though the quilt is in poor condition, it is valuable as a research and material culture object.

Hester Hill was the daughter of Samuel and Harriet Patterson Hill. Samuel Hill was the son of Phillip and Nancy Watters Hill of Kentucky. He was orphaned after his parents went to the California gold fields. Harriet Elizabeth, born in 1847, was the only daughter of Cabell Adair Breckenridge and Arsenone Tureman Patterson. Cabell's mother, Lovey Truett, was a Welsh Quaker from Pennsylvania. Arsenone Tureman was from a large German family in Illinois. The family crossed the Plains by wagon in 1852 and

Harriet, Hester, and Samuel Hill, circa 1905. *Lincoln County Historical Society, Newport, #1986.21.3*

filed a claim on November 1, 1852 on land in what is now the Tigard area of Washington County.

Harriet Patterson completed high school and attended college in Portland before joining her only brother, Caleb, in the newly opened land for white settlers in Indian territory on North Beaver Creek in Lincoln County near Ona. They were the first whites to move to the Beaver Creek area. After her brother's accidental death, Harriet was alone in the wilderness and nearly lost her mind with grief. Soon after she married a neighboring bachelor, Samuel Hill. At the age of forty, she gave birth to her only child, Hester, on November 27, 1887.

Hester began her career as a schoolteacher at the age of seventeen. In 1909, she became a charter member of the Lincoln Grange #395, an important community resource in rural Oregon. She served as Master for seven terms, a record still standing. In 1915, at the age of twenty-eight, she married John R. Coovert. He died in 1926, leaving her a widow without children. She continued to teach elementary grades in the rural districts of Lincoln County along the Oregon coast. She often hiked, rode horseback, or drove her Model I Ford to reach the schools. In 1941, she married Jack Rogers. She died in 1966 in Arizona.

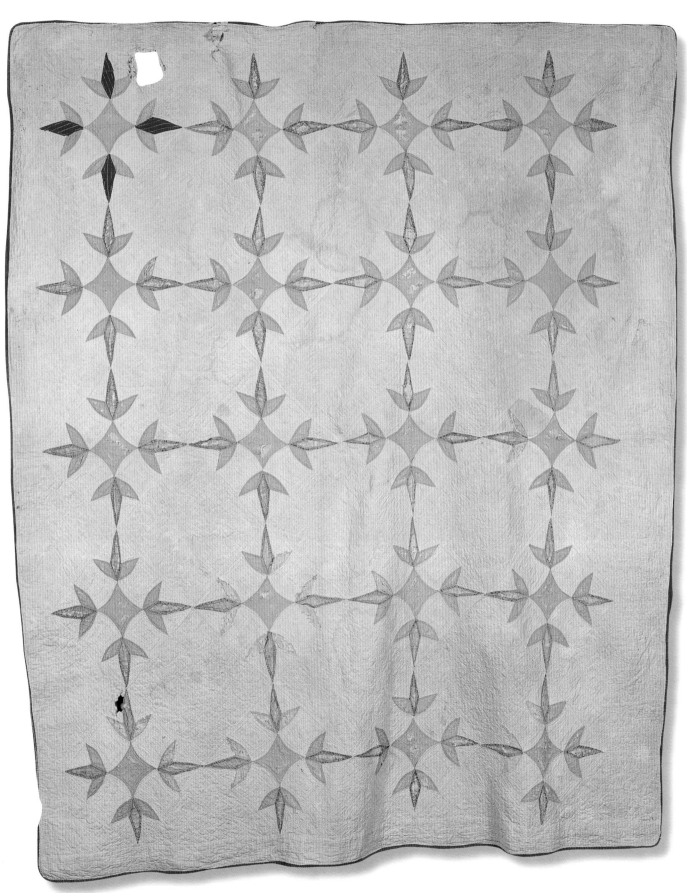

Wandering Foot Quilt. *Lincoln County Historical Society, Newport, #1966-100*

B-9

Quilt: Peony with Flying Geese Border
Category: Pieced and Appliqué
Size: 80" x 78"
Date: 1848 dated
Maker: Grace Weaver (1815-1885) or Susanna
  Weaver (1787-1872)
Year Over Trail: 1853
Sent: With Family of Hans Weaver, Jr.
County Where Settled: Douglas County, Oregon

The Turkey red and green pieced and appliquéd peonies alternate with blocks of white stuffwork wreaths in this classic Ohio quilt. Turkey red was the colorfast dye used to create the expensive prints imported from England. These fabrics were not produced in America because they involved a time-consuming and labor-intensive process of thirteen to twenty steps over a very long time frame, making them very expensive. This primary palette of red and green reflects the Pennsylvania Germanic influence present in Ohio at the time. It was popular for these quiltmakers to use such colors in an effort to bring the beauty of garden flowers inside their homes year around. As is common with these fabrics, the centers of the print's flowers have deteriorated.

The peony is a flower that often appears in floral appliqué quilts. Its meaning in the nineteenth-century lexicon of flowers is "healing."[30] The stems and leaves have been appliquéd in place.

The pieced green-print triangles in the border, known as Flying Geese, are a migration motif. The way the geese trail off two of the edges adds a bit of whimsy and sense of the unknown.

This is a beautiful, richly decorated master-piece that probably took months, if not years, to complete. Placing the plain white blocks between the patterned blocks was an effort to lengthen or widen the quilt, as well as to offer the quiltmaker a surface to demonstrate her quilting ability. Here, there are eight stitches per inch and the lines are one-quarter inch apart.

The quilt was meant to be treasured as an heirloom showcasing the maker's ability. Women without the responsibility of managing a home and family could spend countless hours focusing on their needlework. Young single women did piecing and quilting for hope chests prior to marriage, and maiden aunts made quilts for other family members. The quilt could have been a gift for the young niece Grace Weaver would rarely see. Or, an older woman named Susannah, who had nine adult sons and daughters, could have made the quilt for a granddaughter who was her namesake. The quilt has the initials "S.W." with the date of "1848" on the front above the lower right border. The name and date generally refer to the woman who made

Susannah Weaver Hall. *Douglas County Museum of History, Roseburg, #N11547*

the quilt and the date it was completed. Placing them on the front signals that the maker was proud of her skills and wished to be identified to the viewer. The quilter also was giving the young daughter a sense of place and value within the family of mostly boys, and highlighting the concept that needle skills were something to be learned and valued by children.

Studying this quilt has led to opportunities to learn additional Weaver history through their extensive family of descendants. The history compiled by A.C. Seely states, "My wife has a quilt made by Grace Weaver for her niece Susannah Weaver. A beautiful piece of very complicated needle work, hand made." The accession record states, "made for Susannah Weaver, b.1818 in Philadelphia, by Grace Weaver, b. 1814 in Ireland." There is no information about their lives or their deaths.[31]

The history states that Susannah Weaver was born to Hans Weaver, Jr. and Harriet Bigham Weaver on July 19, 1842 in Washington County, Illinois. Her parents had married August 26, 1841 in Guernsey County, Ohio, where the Irish immigrant ancestor Hans Weaver, Sr. and his wife Susannah Cleland had settled and raised their seven sons and three daughters.

The younger Weaver family came across the Plains in 1853. Her father objected to her marriage, so Susannah left home to marry the man of her choice, John Hall, in 1862. He had left Ohio to seek his fortune in the California gold fields and then came to Douglas County, Oregon where he mined, farmed, and milled wheat flour. Successful in all endeavors, John and Susannah Weaver Hall purchased 320 acres for $2,500 at the mouth of Myrtle Creek in 1862. They platted the town of Myrtle Creek in 1864 and operated a livery stable and the Overland Hotel. Susannah advertised her meals using the slogan "All You Can Eat for Two Bits."[32] They became the parents of seven children before she passed away in 1896.[33]

The quilt passed through her family until donated to the Douglas County Museum of History and Natural History in Roseburg, Oregon in 1969.

Detail with "S.W.1848" quilted

Peony Quilt with Flying Geese border. *Douglas County Museum of History, Roseburg, #69.154.1*

B-10

Quilt: Road to California
Category: Pieced
Size: 73" x 63"
Date: circa 1850
Maker: Nancy Gates Ensley Drain (1817-1892)
Year Over Trail: 1852
Came: As a wife with husband Charles Drain and family
County Where Settled: Marion County, then Douglas County, Oregon

Charles and Nancy Gates Ensley Drain, circa 1860. *Douglas County Museum of History, Roseburg, #N9051*

"Road to California"[34] was most likely a conscious choice of pattern for the indigo-blue-and-white nine-inch blocks of this quilt. The pieced triangles represent the "wandering" of Charles Drain, who left his wife and family in Iowa in 1850 to go to the gold fields, returning in 1851.

Nancy Gates Ensley was born in Venango County, Pennsylvania on May 20, 1817 to John and Catherine Gates Ensley. Her German grandfather, Johan Georg Goetz, was the emigrant ancestor to America in 1729. Her immediate family moved to Bartholomew County, Indiana, in 1824. In 1839, she married Charles Drain, a Lancaster, Pennsylvania native, who had been orphaned at the age of five along with his brother and sister. According to family history, his parents, a member of the working class in love with a "high-born maiden," had eloped from Ireland about 1810. They settled eventually in Indiana in 1823, where both died. After their marriage, Charles and Nancy moved to Van Buren County, Iowa, where he farmed.

In 1850-1851, Charles was in the California gold fields mining and operating a mercantile business from a tent. He returned to the Midwest via Panama after learning of Nancy's ill health and the death of two daughters. Impressed with the mild climate of the Pacific Coast, he brought his family to Oregon in 1852. He was elected captain of their wagon train. Their two-year old daughter, Josephine, died of cholera as the family arrived in Marion County.

They settled for eight years on a farm in Marion County, where Charles was elected to the Territorial Council and State Senate.

In 1860, the family moved to Douglas County, where they acquired over 2000 acres of land in the Pass Creek Canyon, including the Goodell Donation Land Claim near Elk Creek from Jesse Applegate.[35] They established "Drain's Station," a resting place on the Oregon-California route and the Umpqua River trail from the coast to Roseburg. In 1872, Charles donated land to the Oregon and California Railroad Company for a depot and renamed the town Drain. The town's first school and Methodist Church were both built on land he owned. He also partnered with his sons in a mercantile business and a gristmill.[36]

Charles and Nancy Drain celebrated their fiftieth wedding anniversary in 1889.[37] Nancy Drain was the key figure in a piece of Oregon's early pioneer lore as the owner of a darning needle, the only one in the valley. The other key figure in the darning needle story was Aaron Meier, founder of the Meier and Frank Department Store, another Oregon tradition.★

★The darning needle story can be found as Triumph #8 in Appendix B.

Road to California Quilt. *Collection of Joanna Stewart Nelson, Roseburg*

B-11

Quilt: Oregon Rose
Category: Appliqué
Size: 88.5" x 84"
Date: 1851
Makers: Friends, neighbors, and relatives of Robbins Family
Year Over Trail: 1852
Sent: With Jacob and Sarah Robbins and their nine children; his cousin Nathaniel and Nancy Robbins with five single children and three married children and spouses
County Where Settled: Marion County, then Clackamas County, Oregon

This red and green appliqué is the quintessential Oregon Trail quilt. It was made for the Robbins family as they prepared to leave for Oregon. Inscribed on the quilt is "Jacob and Sarah Oregon Rose!" the year "1851," and initials "R," "S," and two "Ns." Other designs randomly placed and quilted are wheels, hearts, and grapevines. The theme is migration, in the pattern name and quilting designs.

The floral designs of this quilt brought by immigrating Anglos over the Trail have been substantiated as one of the sources influencing the stylistic designs used by Native Americans living in the Columbia River Plateau area of eastern Oregon. Their beadwork florals, which date to the 1860-1875 period, have been directly connected to the arrival and association with white settlers from the Midwest.[38]

Jacob Robbins (1809-1896) and Sarah Spilman (1812-1865) were both natives of Kentucky. He was the son of Jacob and Nancy Hanks Robbins, but little other information is available. Sarah was the daughter of Thomas and Mary Love Spilman. The couple was married March 23, 1833 in Decatur County, Indiana, and became the parents of nine children. A tenth was born in 1857 in Oregon.

Because of a well-researched family history, the story of their migration and the extended Robbins family in Oregon is quite complete. One reason why they wanted to migrate was the large number of people in Decatur County with the last name of Robbins. According to the history, this Jacob was called "Little Toe Jake," "Oregon Jake," and "Redhouse Jake."[39] He and his wife were encouraged to make the move West by his cousin. They sold their farm and gathered the necessary equipment and supplies, with Sarah and her helpers quickly making woolen clothing and bedding for the journey.

As the family traveled westward, they often experienced bad weather, swarms of bugs, lack of timber, lost or stampeding livestock, insufficient food, and bad water. The water may have been the cause of cholera, the highly infectious illness that ultimately resulted in the deaths of three of Nathaniel Robbins' daughters and one son-in-law. Nathaniel reportedly told his wife Nancy that nothing in Oregon would be worth the lives of their three daughters. Reference is made of the girls being buried together on a mattress in a wagon box covered with quilts and blankets.[40]

Death also struck the Jacob Robbins family when two of their sons died: Aaron, age five, at the Sandy River near the end of the Trail, and Theodore, age eight, just after they had arrived at Sam Barlow's place and their destination near Oregon City.

After spending the winter in a large two-story house in Linn City, Oregon, Jacob Robbins filed a claim on land in Marion County and later on Salem Prairie. In the early 1860s, they moved to the Molalla area in Clackamas County. Sarah Robbins died on Christmas Day 1865. According to her son Harvey, she had always prepared a big Christmas dinner for the family by working hard the day before Christmas. She went to bed feeling as good as usual but woke her husband with her struggling. By the time, he was able to raise her up, she had died at the age of fifty-two.[41]

Sarah Spilman Robbins (1812-1865)

Jacob Robbins (1809-1896)

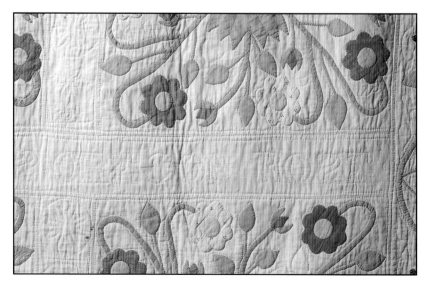
Detail of Oregon Rose in quilting

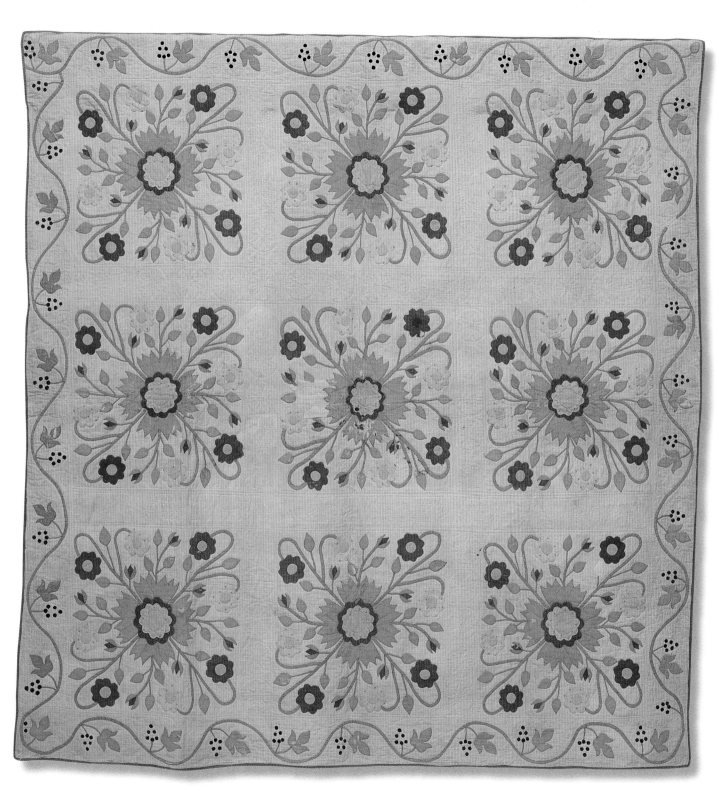

Oregon Rose Quilt. *Molalla Area Historical Society, Dibble House, Molalla, #78.3.3*

B-12

Quilt: Tulip
Category: Appliqué
Size: 85.5" x 77"
Date: 1851-1852
Makers: Relatives and friends of Lucinda Powell Propst (1817-1852)
Year Over Trail: 1852
Sent: With family of Andrew Propst and Lucinda Powell Propst, their five children, and nephew Franklin Propst
County Where Settled: Both parents died on the Trail; children raised by uncles in Benton and Linn Counties, Oregon

This quilt has been a treasured heirloom from the fateful journey of the Propst family. It was handed down to Wanita Propst Haugen when she was a child by her great-grandfather, John Wesley Propst, the eldest orphaned child of Andrew and Lucinda Powell Propst.[42]

Its fabrics of soft-shaded Turkey red, yellow, and green are those of the 1840s. In the lexicon of symbols, the appliquéd tulip means "renown, fame, spring, and dreaminess," all possible references by friends to a woman who "dreamed" of being with her family and brothers in the Northwest.[43] The simple swag border on three sides with the primitive bow appliqué adds an element of delight. Rows of infill quilting complete the body of the quilt with rows of echo quilting in the border.

Lucinda was the fifth daughter of Joseph and Sarah Alkire Powell, born February 19, 1817, in Champaign County, Ohio. The Powell family had emigrated to America from Wales in the 1600s. These descendants moved to Sugar Grove, Menard County, Illinois in 1825. Lucinda married Anthony Propst in 1836, and they became the parents of six children born between 1837 and 1849.

Eager to join her parents and brothers John, Noah, and Alfred and their families, who had migrated in 1851, Lucinda persuaded her husband to make the journey to Oregon. They sold their Illinois farm and started with an outfit of two wagons, nine yoke of oxen, a two-horse light wagon, and thirteen head of cattle. Among their personal items was this quilt.

The journey went well until they reached the Blue Mountains in eastern Oregon. There, Lucinda's dream of joining her family ended when she became ill and died August 19, 1852 on Butter Creek near Echo in Umatilla County. An official historical marker is on the former site of her grave along the Trail on the Madison donation-land-claim ranch.

Later, while crossing the Cascade Mountains, Anthony Propst became ill and died at Philip Foster's place in Clackamas County.* The Powell uncles arrived expecting to greet the family, but soon learned they needed to bury their brother-in-law. The five children were taken to the uncles' homes, where they were raised in the Willamette Valley's Benton and Linn counties.[44] The extended family of Powells made a positive influence on their lives as they contributed to their communities of Albany and Monmouth, helping to found the Christian College in Monmouth.[45]

Detail of swag and bow border

*A diary entry describing the circumstances of his death can be found as Tragedy and Triumph #5 in Appendix B.

Tulip Quilt. *Collection of Wanita Probst Haugen, Woodburn*

B-13

Quilt: Royal Presentation Quilt
Category: Pieced
Size: 87" x 75.5"
Date: 1868
Makers: Mothers and daughters of the Cowlitz Circuit of the Methodist Episcopal Church in Washington Territory
Made for: The Reverend J.H.B. and Mrs. Emma Julia Cornell Royal
Year Over Trail: 1852
Came: Reverend J.H.B. Royal came with his extended family of Methodist Episcopal ministers
County where Settled: Jackson County, Douglas County, Multnomah County, Oregon, Cowlitz County, Lewis County, Klickitat County, Washington Territory, Multnomah County, Marion County, Oregon

Studying at the United Methodist Church Archives in Salem, Oregon and Olympia, Washington, reading Violet Mumford's *The Royal Way West - Volume II*, and working with the late Ruth Stoller, a noted authority on Methodism in the Northwest history, made it possible to connect this quilt to one of the richest histories about an extended family's experience in migration, settlement, and church development in the Northwest.

The quilt was made by mothers and daughters along the Cowlitz Circuit in Cowlitz County, Washington Territory, where the Reverend J.H.B. Royal served in 1855-56 and 1866-67. The forty-one blocks are composed of six different fabrics, probably representing the different settlements where the women lived. Twenty blocks contain the same fabric and fifteen blocks have a second in common while four families are represented by each of the last four fabrics. The message communicated was that all women were part of the church's community and none were to be excluded. Prior to having churches and parsonages, Methodist ministers, called Circuit Riders, served their faithful by traveling in an area on horseback to conduct class meetings in people's homes. The Reverend Royal would row his small boat, *The Itinerant*, on the Columbia and Cowlitz Rivers and hike the trails serving the settlements of Oak Point, Rock Point, Kalama Prairie, and later Freeport (Catlin) and Monticello. This circuit was known as being a particularly hard one to travel.[46]

The daughters are those of the area's prominent citizens recognized for settling the territory and helping to develop a governmental system. Names like Catlin and Huntington appear often in the area's history. Several of the names, Laffy, Clark, and Washburn, were identified as being directly involved with supporting the church in their community.[47] As noted by historian Richard White, an important aspect of the growth of communities in the West was the stability and respectability that female "moral reformers" gave to the male investment of money, time, and energy.[48]

The presence of the daughters' names communicates a second important concept, the ritual passing of the moral responsibility for home and family from mother to daughter. The idea was that the community took care of its minister, supporting his activity and celebrating his personal as well as professional life. This minister was deservedly popular and accomplished much good in spite of the physical handicaps of impaired vision and hearing resulting from his having had measles as a baby. He was a strong supporter for Sunday schools, promoting the program as "the cradle of religion, the nursery of the Church."[49]

The Royals' emigrant ancestor, Thomas Royal, had come from Manchester, England prior to the American Revolution. The family migrated west to Illinois where J.H.B. was born in 1830 in Sangamon County. The Reverend Mr. Royal came to Oregon with his extended family at age twenty-three in 1853. The father, William Royal, three sons, and one son-in-law were all Methodist ministers coming to help develop the church. Family members fondly remembered one late journey incident. As the family was gathered around the campfire, J.H.B. removed the patched overalls he had worn crossing the Plains. He made an eloquent speech to them saying they had served him well, pronounced their service honorably completed, and gently placed them on the flames, assuring them they would be held in affectionate remembrance.

The Reverend Mr. Royal was married to Carrie A. Hall in 1858. They had four sons prior to her 1866 death. In 1868, he married Emma Julia Cornell, daughter of William and Emily Castle Cornell and a close friend of the Royals. Her family joined their father in Oregon in 1854, traveling by ship from New York through the Isthmus of Panama. Emma Julia and J.H.B. had two daughters. She assisted him in his ministry until blindness forced him to retire in 1876. In Salem, she also had her own active role in the church and community. She was Sunday School superintendent, president of the Ladies Aid, church treasurer, and secretary of the first Woman's Foreign Missionary Society organized in Oregon. In addition, she kept boarders in their home. In 1904, the family moved back to Portland, where his extended family could assist them. Much loved and respected, J.H.B. died in 1910. Emma continued her church work until she died on April 5, 1940.[50]

The Reverend J.H.B. Royal seated with his wife, Emma Julia, behind him at Royal family gathering circa 1900. *United Methodist Archives – Oregon, Salem, OR*

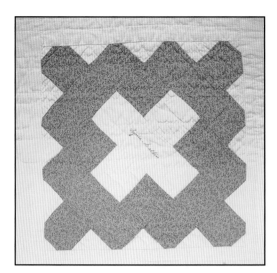

Detail, with "Agnis Catlin" embroidered

Royal Presentation Quilt. *Northwest Museum of Arts and Culture/Eastern Washington Historical Society, Spokane, Washington, #2192.1*

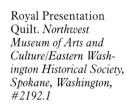

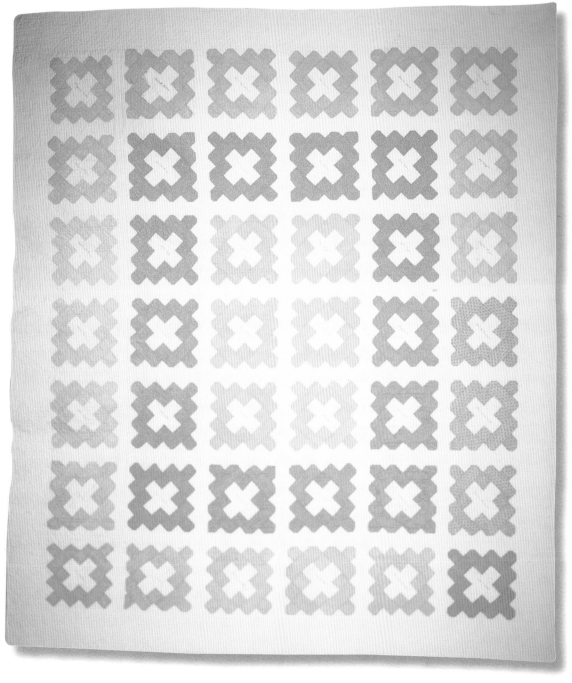

B-14

Quilt: Oregon Trail
Category: Pieced
Size: 69" x 67"
Date: circa 1880
Maker: Julia Ann Sturges Dibble (1825-1904)
Year Over Trail: 1852
Came: As a wife with husband Horace and three children: Eliza, Fayette, and Roswell (Rod)
County Where Settled: Clackamas County

Julia Ann Sturges Dibble
(1825-1904)

This pattern, called Oregon Trail, is one of the many variations grouped under the general name of Drunkard's Path. Other names include Solomon's Puzzle, Boston Trail, Old Maid's Puzzle, Endless Trail, and Crooked Path. All refer to wandering or solving a challenge, such as a trail experience to "see the Elephant" would present. The design is made by cutting a curved piece from the corner of a square and then exchanging them in the piecing process. The way the seven-inch blocks are placed determines the trail of the design across the quilt surface.

This variation was listed as a pattern name by Carrie Sexton, a mail-order pattern source from Wheaton, Illinois in the 1920s and 1930s. She published pamphlets featuring old-fashioned designs from yesterday's quilts.[51]

The binding fabric is an interesting double pink print of small figures chasing other small figures. It appears to be the original binding and dates from after 1875.[52]

Julia Ann Sturges was born in New York, January 3, 1825, the daughter of Aaron Burr and Eliza Hougland Sturges. Moving to Iowa, she married Horace Dibble on July 1, 1845. He was a descendant of an early New England family who had come to America as early as 1630. The name was originally spelled Deeble, meaning "beansetter," a common garden tool. The Dibbles had resided in Connecticut for over one hundred years before Horace's parents moved west to New York and then to Iowa in 1837. Horace and Julia came west in 1852 with their three small children, including Eliza Emily Dibble (Quilt B-15).

In 1856, Horace Dibble contracted for a builder to build a salt-box house, reminiscent of the homes from his New England boyhood. The work took three years. The exchange was 320 acres of land for the labor of building the six-room house of handmade bricks and hand-planed lumber. In her later years, Julia Ann used the small south bedroom for her bedroom-sitting room.

The property continues to serve as a symbol of the early Oregon settlers. It is now the museum house of the Molalla Area Historical Society, where the quilts, including the Wright, Robbins, Dibble, and Sawtell ones in this survey, are exhibited each Mother's Day weekend.[53]

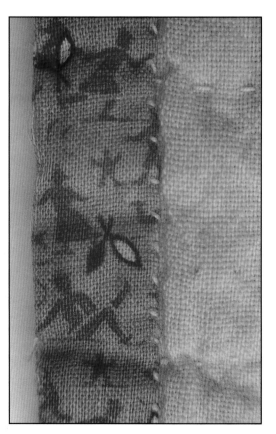

Detail of double pink fabric binding, circa 1880

Dibble House, Molalla, Oregon

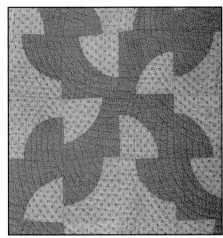

Detail of fabric
and quilting

Oregon Trail Quilt.
*Molalla Area Historical
Society, Dibble House,
Molalla #68.16*

B-15

Quilt: Double Nine Patch
Category: Pieced
Size: 83" x 74"
Date: 1856
Maker: Eliza Emily Dibble Sawtell (1846-1927)
Year Over Trail: 1852
Came: As a child with parents Horace and Julia
      Ann Sturges Dibble and two brothers
County Where Settled: Clackamas County, Oregon

Eliza Emily Dibble Sawtell (1846-1927)

The small three and one-half inch blocks are grouped in larger squares of nine blocks each, creating the pattern Double Nine Patch. It is a traditional pattern used by young children to learn simple running stitches used in needlework. Such was the case with this work, done when Eliza Emily Dibble was ten years old.

The blocks are predominantly indigo-blue-and-white prints of the mid-nineteenth century. The center of each small block is a different print, which serves to create a secondary design of lines across the surface.

In setting the blocks together, there appears to have been a conscious decision by the maker to place the ones with all the same fabrics near the center of the quilt. The blocks on the edges tend to have a variety of blue-and-white prints in each one.

The quilting designs in the solid blocks are wreath patterns, some with double lines of grid work and others with feathers. Again, tradition has it that sometimes these early piecing projects, when completed, would be celebrated by having older adults assist in quilting.[54] This may well have been the work of adult women to support the young girl's early piecing effort.

According to family history, Eliza was born to Horace and Julia Ann Dibble (Quilt B-14) in Van Buren County, Iowa, on May 25, 1846. Eliza was six years old when her family left for Oregon.

On the Trail, she was bitten on her leg by a rattlesnake. As a result, her leg never developed correctly and limited her activity, so she became an excellent seamstress. Perhaps, this was an added reason why the older women in her family encouraged her early patchwork.

She married Alfred Sawtell on March 23, 1869 and had one daughter, Iva May. Sawtell owned a commercial teasel ranch. He hired Chinese workers to plant, cultivate, and harvest the 150 acres of teasels, which were dried and attached to wooden holders, then used to raise the nap on woolen blankets woven in the area's mills.[55] In 1892, his sales increased when a large New York woolen manufacturing center learned

that domestic teasels were available instead of having to import them from France.[56] But by the turn of the century, Sawtell lost his market when metal nappers were introduced and replaced the teasels.[57]

The Molalla Area Historical Society owns a second quilt attributed to Eliza in a Snowball pattern.

Detail of fabric and quilting

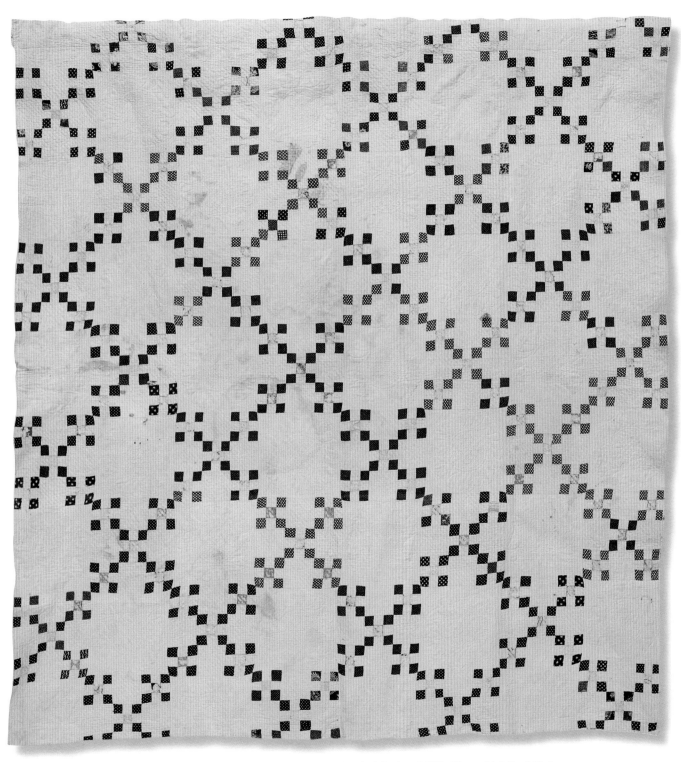

Double Nine Patch Quilt. *Molalla Area Historical Society, Dibble House, Molalla #82.6*

B-16

Quilt: Hexagon
Category: Pieced
Size: 80.75" x 60"
Date: 1869 Started (dated); 1900 Finished
Maker: Abigail Scott Duniway (1834-1915)
Year Over Trail: 1852
Came: As a daughter with parents, John Tucker and Ann Roelofson Scott, and her three brothers and six sisters; uncle and aunt Levi and Martha Roelofson Caffee and her sons; Cousin William Goudy and family; Cousin John Goudy; five drivers and three travelers including a photographer
County Where Settled: Clackamas County, Linn County, then Multnomah County, Oregon

In recent studies of quilt history, this silk hexagon quilt has come to symbolize the use of patchwork by enlightened nineteenth-century women. Acknowledged as not being artistically beautiful or exceptionally well crafted, it is now widely exhibited and written about as the work of Abigail Scott Duniway, business woman, journalist, and one of this country's premier women's suffrage leaders.

The quilt was begun in 1869 during her confinement after her son Ralph's birth and completed in 1900. Typewritten on an orange ribbon centered in the border of the quilt is the following documentation:

> This quilt was pieced in November 1869 by Abigail Scott Duniway of Oregon and was finished and quilted by her in November 1900, and donated to the First National Woman Suffrage Bazaar in honor of Theodore Roosevelt, the first champion of the equal Suffrage movement ever elected to a National office by popular vote.[58]

The plaid and plain silk two-and-one-quarter-inch hexagons were from materials she purchased for her millinery shop in Albany, Linn County, Oregon. The millinery shop, opened in 1866, was a respectable way for women of her time to earn an income.

Immediately, upon learning of the plan to send the quilt to the 1899 New York World's Fair as an example of the accomplishments of Oregon women, the Portland Woman's Club raised a special fund to purchase the quilt for the Oregon Historical Society, claiming it was too precious to send out of state. Abigail Scott Duniway donated the money to the suffrage campaign of 1900.

The attention given to this quilt is ironic because it is well known that Mrs. Duniway disliked

Abigail Scott Duniway (1834-1915). *Oregon Historical Society, Portland, #4146*

sewing and, especially patchwork. Writing in an editorial on quilts in her July 15, 1880, issue of *The New Northwest* after attending the Oregon State Fair, she stated:

> Any fool can make a quilt; and after we had made a couple of dozen over twenty years ago, we quit the business with a conviction that nobody but a fool would spend so much time in cutting bits of dry goods into yet smaller bits and sewing them together again, just for the sake of making believe that they are busy at practical work.[59]

Although she disliked sewing, especially frivolous handwork, she realized the successful shop was a way for her to establish contact with other women. She soon learned the vast range of experiences shaping their lives, and used that background to focus her work for women's rights, especially the right to vote.

Abigail Scott was born the second daughter of John Tucker and Ann Roelofson Scott on October 22, 1834 in Tazewell County, Illinois. The only known emigrant ancestor was a William Terry, who came from England to Virginia five generations before John Tucker Scott was born.[60] Always acknowledged as an independent spirit, her life, nevertheless, was influenced by experiences inflicted by family and societal demands.

Abigail Scott Duniway was assigned by her father the task of keeping a record of their journey west, with the intention being future publication. As a younger sister, Harriet, later noted:

> I still can "see" her as she was, a slight young girl, evenings after the weary stretches of travel with that old book in her lap—sitting either by the tent—or perchance one of the wagon wheels—or sitting on the ground—while our father was giving her commands to lay the Diary correct!—she was too weary at times to write—But always did her best.[61]

This record was the basis for several of Abigail's publications, including her 1859 *Captain Gray's Company, or Crossing the Plains and Living in Oregon* and her 1905 *From the West to the West: Across the Plains to Oregon*.

Arriving in Oregon, she taught school but soon married Benjamin Duniway in 1853 and settled first in Clackamas County. The couple eventually had six children born between 1854 and 1869.

Abigail Scott Duniway's words and actions have become banners for rallying behind in recent years: "When woman's true history shall have been written, her part in the upbuilding of this nation will astound the world."[62]

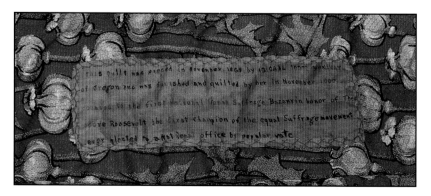

Detail of typewritten documentation on quilt

Detail of fabric and piecing

Hexagon Quilt. *Oregon Historical Society, #1721*

B-17

Quilt: Delectable Mountains
Category: Pieced
Size: 87" x 66.5"
Date: circa 1840
Maker: Katherine Purdom (1786-1860)
Year Over Trail: 1853
Sent: With daughter Mary Purdom Leonard, her husband Joseph Leonard, and their four children: Catherine Jane, Cyrus, Lucinda Ann, and Joseph
County Where Settled: Linn County, then Polk County, Oregon

The family of Lucinda Ann Leonard Worth, the granddaughter of the maker, treasure this Delectable Mountains quilt as a symbol of her survival of The Lost Wagon Train experience in 1853. As evidence of the importance of the Oregon Trail in their lives, this quilt has been cherished for six generations, from the maker to the great-great-great-great-granddaughter.

As a twelve-year-old, Lucinda Ann suffered severe illness and exposure on the journey. According to family history, there was concern she would not survive until they reached Oregon. This is thought to have been the reason why she forbid any of her family and friends to talk or ask about her experience. This was the opposite of her older sister, Catherine, who wrote extensively for publication.*

This non-communication is a very strong confirmation of the use of quilts as visual yet silent objects of life's passages. Their existence is known while they remain quietly stowed in a family trunk, hidden away but not thrown away.

A study of the quilt's sixteen-inch pieced blocks shows the variety of fabrics and dyes available in the mid-nineteenth century. There are fifteen different indigo-blue-and-white prints and sixteen different pink-and-brown prints in the blocks, indicating a significant number of available fabric choices. Family history reveals that the Purdoms were living along the Mississippi River in Clark County, Missouri, an area well serviced by commercial river boat transportation.

The Delectable Mountains pattern has a long tradition connected to migration through John Bunyan's allegory *Pilgrim's Progress*. The reference is, "They went then till they came to the Delectable Mountain ... behold the gardens and orchards, the vineyards and fountains of water..."[63] Unfortunately for the Leonard family, this was quite the contrast. They found cold, rain, hunger, and starvation in the mountains of central Oregon on their journey toward Lane County.

After finally arriving in the Willamette Valley in November, the family took up a donation land claim of 320 acres at the foot of Peterson's Butte on the Calapooia River in Linn County. Lucinda married John C. Worth in 1864. Together they farmed in Linn County and raised two children. At the time of her husband's death in 1900, Lucinda was living at Monmouth in Polk County, where she took in boarders, students at the Christian College. This was a common practice among her neighbors.[64]

Katherine Purdom
(1786-1860)

Lucinda Leonard Worth (1841-1931) with children, Vida Ethel, born 1869 (left), and William Leonard, born 1865 (right)

*A copy of Catherine Jane Leonard Jones' letter describing her family's experience on the Lost Wagon Train of 1853 can be found as Tragedy #6 in Appendix B.

Detail of fabrics

Delectable Mountains Quilt.
Collection of Patricia Leicher,
Piedmont, California

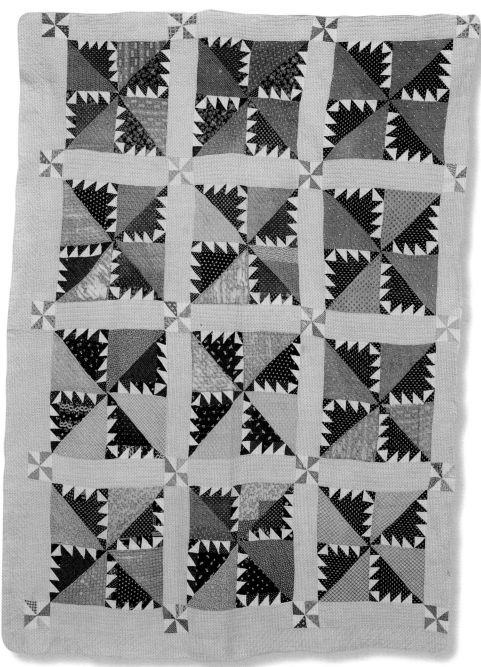

B-18

Quilt: Rose Variation
Category: Appliqué
Size: 90" x 90"
Date: circa 1850
Maker: Zeralda Carpenter Bones Stone (1822-1914)
Year Over Trail: 1853
Came: As a wife with second husband Samuel Stone and two children: Sarah Jane and John W.
County Where Settled: Polk County, Oregon

This Rose Variation appliqué quilt is now thought to have an earlier date than the previously assigned 1880. Recent research has brought forth new information on dating fabrics and styles of quilts. The red and green colors of the twenty-four inch blocks are mid-nineteenth century. The construction of the sewing thread appears to be wrapped, as were the earlier threads. The randomly placed quilting designs were more common in the mid-century than later. The designs of this quilt are different from the large number of Zeralda Stone's other later quilts. The unique border with pairs of doves on perches suggests the possibility of a wedding quilt.

Zeralda Carpenter was born in Cass County, Missouri on September 25, 1822. Her parents were William D. and Mary "Polly" Warren Carpenter. His father, Adam Carpenter, was one of three sons of George Carpenter, Sr., who traveled from Virginia to Kentucky in 1780 to establish Carpenter's Station, one of the first permanent stations built after the American Revolution.[65] Zeralda first married John Bones on March 1, 1844. They had two children, Sarah Jane born in 1845 and John W. born in 1849. After John Bones died in 1848, her younger sister lived with her before Zeralda married her English neighbor, Samuel Stone, on December 22, 1851.[66] They crossed the Plains in 1853.

Settling in Polk County near Buell, they registered Donation Land Claim #3611 on March 17, 1854.[67] Two of their three children died in infancy, with the third, Thomas Buford, born September 1, 1857.

"Grandma" Stone, as she is now referred to by people who know her quilts, was an active member of her community and was one of early members of the Christian Church near Sheridan. She also provided a home for eleven motherless children and served as a comforter and an aid to the sick and needy. In both the 1860 and 1900 Census of Polk County's Douglas District, a minor child is listed as living in her household.

She is one of the women who came relatively early to Oregon, established a farm, worked to serve her community, and stayed with or returned to quilting. Her quilts have become a celebration of life. Quilting was obviously important to her, as she fulfilled her role as caregiver and community member. According to her great-grandson, Silas E. Starr, she made many quilts that she gave to relatives and friends. In 1967, he donated at least seventeen of them, representing a long career of quiltmaking, to the Oregon Historical Society. It has been noted that she never wore glasses, although she made quilts continuously over a seventy- year period.

Grandma Zeralda Carpenter Bones Stone (1822-1914). *Collection of Oregon Historical Society, Portland, #11017*

Detail of pair of doves on perch

Rose Quilt Variation. *Oregon Historical Society, #67.500*

B-19

Quilt: Running Squares
Category: Pieced
Size: 81" x 77"
Date: circa 1870
Maker: Emma Wagner Giesy (1835-1882)
Year Over Trail: 1853
Came: As the only woman in a party of ten Bethel, Missouri scouts to find an Oregon site for their communal society
County Where Settled: Pacific, Washington Territory, then Marion County, Oregon

This wool quilt, a treasure from the Aurora Colony, is an outstanding example of life within the communal society in the Willamette Valley's Marion County between 1855-1877.

The pieced quilt of eight-and-three-quarter-inch blocks is made of woolen fabric totally produced in the communal society. The wool for fabric and batt were from sheep raised by the Colony. The rich colors were natural dyes of black, red from madder root, blue from indigo, and green from the area's peach tree leaves.

To produce the cloth, the women did the preparing and spinning, while the men did the dying and the weaving. Each member of the Colony had training in a particular trade. Yet, all were expected to assist each other when needed.[68]

The quilting pattern is a unique arrangement, a possible variation on the traditional elbow/fan. The parallel lines come together, forming a deep V shape. The eight-and-one-half inch border has a zig-zag arrangement of straight lines placed one and one-quarter inches apart. There are two other quilts in the museum collection with a similar quilting pattern, showing a sharing of patterns and styles.

The quilt is marked with the cross-stitched initials of "C. G." in the same quilting thread. The marking appears in the middle of one of the solid red blocks near the bottom of the quilt. Its casual placement suggests perhaps a laundry marking, needed for purposes of identifying personal property within the communal housing.

In 1835, Emma Wagner was born in Missouri to David and Catherine Wagner, natives of Württemberg, Germany. In 1853, when her husband Christian Giesy was chosen to lead a party of scouts, she, as a young bride, would not be left behind, reportedly saying "What trials of the wilderness trail you face I will face, what privations and dangers you face I will face."

Arriving in the West in October of 1853, they wintered at the Puget Sound Military Post at Ft. Steilacoom, Washington Territory, It was there that Emma gave birth to her first son, Andrew Jackson Giesy, later in October.

The following spring, Christian Giesy and some others of the party staked claims in the Willapa Valley along the Willapa River and Bay. There, the Giesys lived in a canvas covered log house. According to Clark Will, an Aurora historian, Gen. Ulysses S. Grant, stationed at Fort Vancouver, may have been the one to suggest the party go to Ft. Steilacoom, where there was a cow, and to consider the Willapa Bay area for settlement. This was the site that Colony President Dr. William Keil rejected once he got to Oregon as too isolated and moved instead to the Aurora location.[69]

Christian Giesy drowned in 1857 while crossing the bay. Seven months later, Christian Giesy, Jr. was born. Emma brought her two sons and a daughter to Aurora in 1861.[70] In the 1870 census, Emma and daughters Catherine and Ida were living in the Beaver Precinct of Clackamas County with her parents David and Catherine Wagner. Her teenage sons were living in Dr. Keil's Colony "Grose Haus," along with twelve single men, five housekeepers, four cooks and Keil's wife and three teenage children.[71] That explains the need for a laundry mark on the quilt. It is also a validation of how Dr. Keil chose to direct the lives of the Colony's residents.

By the 1880 census, Dr. Keil had died but the Colony had not formally ended and many of the residents still resided in Aurora. Emma was now living there with her son Christian, a miller, and younger daughter Ida. She died in 1882 at the age of forty-seven. The assets of the Colony were distributed in 1883.

Often, quilt history research leads to themes and content for other writers. Award-winning historical fiction writer Jane Kirkpatrick has written a series of three books entitled *Change and Cherish*, based on Emma Wagner Giesy's life in the Pacific Northwest.

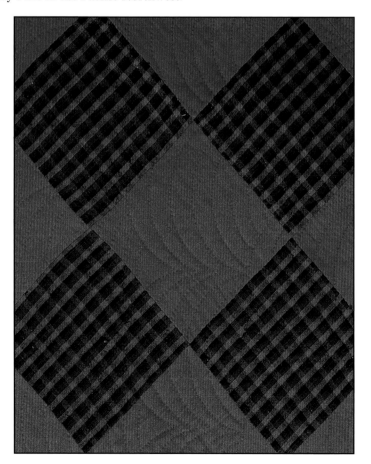

Detail of fabric and quilting

Running Squares Quilt. *Old Aurora Colony Museum, Aurora, #A69-591*

B-20

Quilt: Log Cabin
Category: Pieced
Size: 54" x 36"
Date: 1875-1900
Maker: Grace Jane Simpson Skeeters (1839-1924)
Year Over Trail: 1853
Came: As a daughter with parents, Francis and Sarah Linder McIntire Simpson, and eight brothers and sisters
County Where Settled: Multnomah County, then Jackson County, Oregon

The nine-inch wool squares of red and green are built around a center of green. This is unusual, because the centers of log cabin quilts of this period were either red or yellow, a practice thought to reflect the hearth or the light within the log cabin.

The quilt was donated to the Southern Oregon Historical Society in the mid-1970s during a time when volunteers were in charge of the textiles. Both the teal green twill binding and the synthetic backing are twentieth-century materials added to a nineteenth-century piece. Of course, this is unacceptable by today's standards, but the piece has special interest because the maker compiled a sixteen-page typewritten autobiography reminiscing about her life's experiences.

Grace Jane Simpson was born in Nelson County, Kentucky in 1839, the seventh child of Francis and Sarah Simpson. Sarah's first husband, Charles McIntire, was killed by a runaway horse, leaving her with two small boys. She married Francis Simpson in 1825. In 1841, the family moved to Adair County, Missouri. The father and second oldest son James went to the gold fields in 1849. Francis returned in 1852 to bring the rest of the family to Oregon. James traveled directly to Oregon to join his half-brother Horace and Narcisa McIntire on their northwestern Oregon land claim on Sauvies Island.

Grace Jane Simpson Skeeters (1839-1924) with the quilt. *Southern Oregon Historical Society, Medford, #11917*

After the family had finished equipping themselves for their westward journey, their home burned, destroying many of their supplies and melting the remaining gold and silver into two large chunks. These were weighed and traded for other money. They left for Oregon with two big covered wagons.

Grace was fourteen years old at the time her family traveled over the Trail. She thoroughly enjoyed the experience of walking or riding her pony. Her history includes memoirs of trail landmarks like Chimney Rock, Court House Rock, Soda Basin, and the Grand Ronde Valley; gathering buffalo chips; seeing graves; and encountering Indians. She was flattered by the attention they gave her.

One common Trail experience took place in the Grand Ronde Valley, when the family came upon a pile of household goods along the Trail. A note was attached to a chair asking Francis I. Simpson to carry a bundle to a little boy as far as the nearest trading post. He gladly did so and returned it to the young family further along the Trail.

A second common experience also occurred—the theft of livestock, including milk cows, cattle, and their best oxen. Happily, soon after a day of despair, their son James arrived from Sauvies Island to guide them the rest of their journey. At the Columbia River, they sold their remaining wagon and team and boarded the steamer, *Fashion*, which took them downriver to the McIntires' Sauvies Island home, where they spent the winter.

After relocating to nearby Portland, Grace's family operated a boarding house. In 1858, the family followed James to the southern Oregon gold fields, settling in Sterlingville, a mining town near Jacksonville. Here her stepfather started another boarding house.

In 1859, she married Isaac Skeeters, a member of the Hillman party who discovered Crater Lake in southern Oregon. Over the years, they lived on a number of ranches, eventually trading the last for several lots in the town of Medford and about an acre of land with a large eight-room house. It was here that Grace lived with her youngest daughter Addie, celebrating her extended family.[72]

Log Cabin Quilt. *Southern Oregon Historical Society, Medford, #76-27*

B-21

Quilt: Crazy Quilt
Size: 82" x 81.5"
Date: 1894 dated
Maker: Annis Parsons Bonnett (1814-1902)
Year Over Trail: 1854
Came: As a wife with husband Samuel Jasper Bonnett and family
County Where Settled: Lane County, Oregon

The Bonnett Crazy Quilt displays two styles of construction used in this type of silk quilt. The center is "uncontained," meaning the design flows freely over the surface of the quilt, while the borders are "contained" by blocks, in which geometric shapes and fans give the sense of containment and control to the design.

This style of quilt became popular after the nation's Centennial Exposition of 1876, when the public was introduced to a stunning display of Japanese art and artifacts. Interest peaked in the mid-1880s, when women's publications were still promoting the concept of the "sphere of domesticity" and the creation of a pleasant home environment to raise a family. Publications were printing how-to instructions, commentary on appropriateness, and advertisements for fabrics, kits, threads, and patterns.[73]

When compared with the many richly decorated and heavily embellished crazy quilts, this one has a special attraction. The simple marks and symbols stem-stitched on the pieces and the feather-stitched seam lines create an appropriate background for drawing attention to the central feature of the quilt—the pink ribbon with the maker's name, date, and age in black thread: "Mrs. Annis Bonnett Age 72 1894."

Crazy quilts were made to celebrate people's lives and often included fabrics from their silk clothing. Without documentation, it is impossible to validate the fabrics in this quilt, but it definitely can be said that it honors the life of a woman who came to Oregon in 1854, survived the journey, and successfully established her family.

Annis Parsons was born in Virginia about 1814. She married a fellow Virginian, Samuel Jasper Bonnett, in Van Buren County, Iowa in November 1840. Little is known about her ancestors, but the first from his family were Jean Jacques Bonnett and his wife, who came from Germany around 1730. Samuel and Annis traveled to Oregon in 1854 and became the fourth family to settle in the town of Eugene in 1855. In 1857, they settled on a claim on the McKenzie River, outside of Eugene. In the 1870 census, they were living in Springfield, Oregon with eight of their eleven children.[74]

Detail with "Mrs. Annis Bonnett Age 72 1894"

Crazy Quilt. *Lane County Historical Museum, Eugene, #1833*

PART III
1856-1870

Old Fort Kearney, painting by William Henry Jackson. *National Park Service/Scotts Bluff National Monument, Gering, Nebraska, SCBL276*

The Trail

After crossing the Continental Divide near South Pass City, the Trail continued on toward the West. At this time, exhaustion, starvation, and the rugged terrain ahead were the main challenges. Food and water supplies for the company were diminished just when it was necessary to muster as much strength as possible to cross the rivers and mountains ahead. These depleted resources were often the deciding factor in choosing the route to follow for the last third of the journey.

As they traveled onward toward the most challenging and difficult part of the Trail, the trains came to the dividing points for other trails and routes, requiring the pioneers to make decisions from which there was often no return. Information posted or passed by word of mouth would give the latest knowledge about the route conditions ahead. Sometimes it was accurate and up to date, but other times it was not.

As the years of the Trail experience continued, new and better routes were always under consideration. Almost from the beginning in 1843, alternate routes were sought to avoid the difficult crossing of the Blue Mountains and the challenging float by canoe and raft down the Columbia River toward the primary destination of Oregon City, the territorial capital.

Crossing the Blue Mountains

After crossing the Snake River and Grande Ronde Valley, the wagon trains came to the first set of difficult mountains to cross. The Blue Mountains in eastern Oregon, named by David Thompson in 1811 because of their azure hue, were not as spectacular and scenic as the later Cascades but were more difficult to handle because of the continuous series of ridges with deep draws and few good passes between.[1] L. Jane Powell, part of the extended family of Lucinda Powell Propst (Quilt B-12), wrote of their experience:

> The road through the Rocky Mountains was a gradual ascent and descent, and not very bad except for big rocks in the road, but when we struck the Blue Mountains, we found the road rocky and steep. The teams were very much jaded, and it looked very much like cruelty to animals to goad them on.[2]

Coming out of these mountains, the pioneers then faced the sandy soils of the high desert areas of eastern Oregon. The burden would be to move the wagons through the soft ground as they sank under the weight of household goods and people. It was here in 1852 that Lucinda Powell Propst (Quilt B-12) died at Butter Creek, a popular location for rest and regrouping.

Floating the Columbia River

The river trip from the Methodist Mission at Wascopum (The Dalles) was a costly and dangerous navigation through the narrowest part of the river and over some of the largest falls. There were delays while people waited for opportunities to get on the river. Supplies would become scarce and the prices would be high.

The difficulty experienced by Lavina Elizabeth Frazier Wright's family (Quilt A-3) as they rafted down the Columbia River with the Applegate family (Quilt A-2) was due to severe wind and rain that prevented them from being able to land. Finally landing and unloading, William McHaley found a fresh cowhide that he singed over the fire to remove the hair and then used to make soup. Although it resembled glue in appearance, no one refused to eat it.

During the early years and as areas became settled, competition evolved over alternative routes from Ft. Hall to the Willamette Valley.

The parents of Susan Officer Vaughan (Quilt A-7) chose to be a part of the Stephen Meek Cutoff Wagon Train of 1845. Rachel Bond and the family of Lucinda Worth Leonard (Quilt B-17) were members of the Lost Wagon Train of 1853. They were rescued by the family of Francis Harlow (Quilt A-17). The Meek Cutoff Wagon Train, later known as "The Blue Bucket Mine Train," became lost in eastern Oregon because the supposed route had not been marked. The blue bucket refers to the bucket found with gold indicating a mine somewhere in the area. Years later, in the 1880s, interest in the mine's location was renewed by wagon train members' stories. This interest, stimulated by newspaper coverage, encouraged others to explore the area of eastern Oregon, resulting not in the discovery of the gold mine but in awareness of available resources such as timber, range, and mineral.[3] Many of those who came in the 1860s ended their journeys by claiming land in eastern Oregon.

Two of the most popular options to the Columbia River route became the Applegate Trail and the Barlow Road. (See map in Introduction).

Applegate Trail

After the Applegate family's devastating loss on the Columbia River in 1843, Jesse Applegate (Quilt A-2) and others sought to find a southern route to Oregon by leaving the main trail and following the Humbolt River. In 1846, his was the first wagon train, which included the parties of Elizabeth Currier Foster (Quilts A-8-11) and Tabitha Moffett Brown (Triumph #1 in Appendix B), to try and successfully complete a different route. The group turned south on the California road at Ft. Hall, heading west until they got to the place where Reno is today, then turning north toward Oregon. They laid over sixteen days in the area of High Rock Canyon while the men of the train worked to clear the route over the Calapooia Mountains. It was during this time, that Elizabeth got to ride horseback and help drive the cattle. She and her sister were the first white women through the Cow Creek Canyon of southern Oregon.[4]

On the Applegate Trail in the southern Cascades, George W. Riddle, pioneer of 1851 (Quilts B-2-3) described the crossing as the worst ten miles he had been through since leaving the Missouri River. He told of having to brace the wagons against trees by blocking them with ropes and pulleys to prevent them from overtaking the teams, overturning, or sliding. Then, once on the valley floor, the walls of the canyon would be right down to the water's edge, forcing the wagons to be driven through creeks often blocked by fallen logs and boulders. It was a slow and strenuous ordeal coming near the end of the long, exhausting journey.[5]

In spite of the challenges, the Applegate Trail became popular and was used as the fastest way to southern Oregon and the lower end of the Willamette Valley. It avoided the dangerous raft and canoe trips down the Columbia River and mountain crossings of the Blues and Cascades. The trail is now known as the California National Historic Trail.[6]

Barlow Toll Road

For those following the northern route over the Blue Mountains, the next challenge was the falls of the Columbia River, west of The Dalles. The only options were to travel by raft or canoe on the dangerous river float or by wagon over the steep wooded slopes of the Cascade Mountains. As an alternative, in 1846 Sam Barlow was granted a license by the provisional legislature to construct a toll road east from Philip Foster's place in rural Clackamas County to The Dalles. By the fall of 1848, the two men, working in partnership, cut through thickets, and over streams on the south side of Mt. Hood to create an eighty mile road passable in its entire length by "wagon train" time in the fall of 1848. The pay station for tolls was about midway along the road on the western side of Mt. Hood, because it was thought pioneers would better understand and accept making a payment after having used the "improved" road, the only section of the entire Trail to charge a toll. Between 1846 and 1849, a total of 1,150 wagons with 5,770 people came in over the Barlow Toll Road to Foster's place, where many rested and camped until moving out into other areas of the Willamette Valley.[7]

Yet, pioneers often found the conditions on land were as dangerous as those on the river. On the steep slopes of Mount Hood and Laurel Hill, there were rapidly flowing streams and boulder-filled gulches. The constant autumn rains challenged all who traveled. The crossing became all the more difficult for women carrying babies and toddlers. While the women walked, the men lowered the wagons using log chains and ropes to keep them under control.

This road had a major impact on the journey of many emigrants. Two women wrote of their experience, Esther McMillan Hanna (Tragedy and Triumph #4 in Appendix B) and L. Jane Powell who reminisced:

> We must have presented a lovely spectacle carrying the babies up and down steep mountains, crossing streams and ugly gulches with the rain pouring down all day and dripping off our dirty bonnets. We kept in good spirits and at night would make a big fire of logs and half dry our clothes and some of our bedding; then go to bed and sleep soundly. Strange to say, it never hurt any of us but the little babe. It took cold and never got over it.[8]

Many of the diaries and journals refer to Phil Foster's place as a sign of having successfully completed the trail. It was a supply base, a meeting place, and a camp location. L. Jane Powell continued her reminiscence:

> We got into the valley September 3, at noon, making seven and a half days in the Cascades and five months to a day since we left Illinois. We started with four yoke of oxen to each wagon, but got through with but one or two oxen to the wagon—they were replaced by cows. All went to work for something to eat ... The women sewed and worked for vegetables and the men bought and killed some beeves.[9]

The Treasures Used on the Trail

While some quilts were packed as treasures in the trunks, to be brought out and caressed once the Trail journey was complete, others were kept at hand for immediate use: as bedding, as protection, as decorative items, as shared interaction with other women, and as part of family-life rituals. Thus, their primary function was to offer moments of peace, security, and cultural identity when their owners were faced with exhaustion, isolation, illness, and death in the vast realm of the unknown through which they were traveling.

Quilts as Bedding

The primary use of quilts on the Trail was as bedding. They were used on the beds installed in the wagons, in the tents set up each night for camping, and in the bed rolls for those sleeping on the ground. A good night of rest in a comfortable and secure place was important to the success of the journey.

In 1852, two young brothers, James M. Cornwell, age seventeen, and his older brother Francis M., age nineteen, started from Iowa on foot for the Pacific Coast with a total of five dollars between them. They signed on as teamsters for emigrants in exchange for food and wagon space to put their small bundles of clothing. After reaching Fort Boise, they were told by the leaders that because of short rations, it would be best for them to go on ahead with a party of six other men. Crossing the Alkali Flats and the John Day River, members of the starving group gradually dropped off until only the two brothers were left. Exhausted, starving, and almost delirious, the Cornwell brothers finally came upon a sheltered camp of a family. Short on food themselves, the family provided each with a quilt and allowed them to sleep in the wagon. Recovered the next morning, the brothers pushed on to The Dalles and eventually the Willamette Valley.[10]

It was frequently and specifically suggested that each traveler bring two or three blankets or comforters (quilts), indicating the importance of having enough of them for the trip. Once the pioneers arrived, they also would need them while establishing a home.[11] Textile production and quiltmaking were not among the immediately critical tasks in building a house, planting crops, or surviving the winter.

Quilts as Protection Against The Elements Of Weather

Quilts were used to line or insulate the walls of the wagons against weather, wind, and Indian raids. Nathaniel Myer, at age sixty-six, described a March day of his family's journey from Iowa's Des Moines River Valley to southern Oregon Rogue River Valley in 1853:

> M. 25th.—Clear at s.r.; white frost. The women all engaged airing the bed and other cloth which they much need. The rain and storm wetted a good many of them the two previous nights and one day.[12]

Another traveler, Andrew McClure, wrote in his 1853 journal:

> June 22nd … The morning cold and unpleasant. Overcoats, gloves, and comforts [quilts] again came into active use, and even then it was a bitter task to stand the blast.[13]

Quilts Used to Relieve Homesickness and Loneliness

Quilts and carpets were also as decorative items in tents and wagons to create a homelike setting and to help relieve the homesickness and sadness caused by leaving friends and relatives behind. In addition, they served as privacy barriers to wall off sleeping and dressing areas in the tents, much as they did in one-room cabin homes.

Quilts as Shared Cultural Identity

Women shared their lives by exchanging recipes, needlework and quilt patterns, and fabrics from their piecing bags, all extensions of the practices and routines of their life back home. Charlotte Stearns Pengra noted the following in her diary of June 1853 after she entertained a visit from a woman in another wagon: "[Mrs. Smith] woshes the pattern of my sunbonnet, which I gave her with pleasure."[14]

Quilts Used in Death and Burial

Quilts used as burial shrouds were fairly common. Because of the deterioration of water supply and an increase in the number of people traveling the Trail in close proximity, there were epidemic levels of illness and disease, resulting often in death.

Since wood was scarce for coffins, families used what was available and appropriate, both in size and meaning. Wrapping someone in a quilt was a way of preparing them for burial, but it also gave reassurance to the living that the deceased person was still linked to his or her family. The Robbins family (Quilt B-11) buried their three nieces (all victims of the cholera epidemic of 1852 within one twelve-hour period) along the Platte River after placing them together on a mattress in a wagon box covered with spare quilts and blankets.

Quilts as Commodities

Quilts had monetary value. In diaries and records of Trail activities, they are listed among items used to trade. John Boardman noted in 1843 on the Columbia River:

> Sunday, October 15th … We then determined to sell our animals at the Fort and go down the river in canoes. Sold our mules for $12 each, and horses for $10. Bought a canoe for 1 blanket and 2 shirts; traded it for a larger one and gave a blanket &c to boot, and got things ready to go.[15]

Quilts were used as toll payment for the Barlow Toll Road on Mt. Hood in Oregon. The following listing is the only complete record of the Barlow-Rector-Palmer Wagon Train, showing the drivers and number of wagons, and how much paid was paid, both in coin and in kind. The record was found in the Philip Foster Papers. One quilt was taken as equivalent to five dollars, the cost for one wagon to use the toll road.

A Sample of the 1848 Wagon Train Toll Payments

Sept. 15

Peter Hibbard	3	wagon-14# Powder		$7.95	Paid
C.P. Chatman	1	" -1 blanket		2.50	"
Hen Henningen	1	"	5.00 Due	4.95	"
Buford Smith	2	"	very sick		
Thomas Donca	1	"	Pd.Coat, pants, and shirt		
John Lane	1	"	Ran like a Turkey		
George Irwin	1	"	5.00 Due	5.00	Paid
W. Aceotty	10	horses	Order on McKinley		

Sept.20, 1848

H.V. Holmes	2	wagons	10.00 Due	10.00	Paid
J.H. Lewis	1	"	Paid 2 shirts		
Ira A. Hooker	4	"	20.00 Due	19.95	Paid
Isaac Ball	1	"	5.00 Due	5.00	Paid
Wm Porter	1	"	Paid 1 quilt		
Stephen Porter	1	"	" " "		
W. L. Adams	1	"	" " "		
J. M. Blackaby	1	"	" " "	1.50	Paid
Sam Tucker	2	"	" " Bedspread	5.00	"[16]

Quilts Made on the Journey

As women came prepared to do their sewing on the trip, it was natural that they turned to piecing and appliquéing while on the slow-moving wagons or when sharing the time of rest in the evening.

Quilts included in this study that were made on the Trail seem to show that their makers were responding to their environment in choosing designs and techniques.

Sarah Koontz Glover (Quilts A-14-15) pieced the small scraps of fabric for her Pin Wheel and the diamond segments for her Wheel while crossing the Plains in 1849. The Pin Wheel reflects her response to the wind, a very dramatic element of weather on the Plains, especially when traveling in a cloth-covered wagon or sleeping in a fragile tent. The Wheel indicates the importance the wagon wheel played in the lives of the travelers, for if it broke, they were stranded.

Isabella Fleming Mills (Quilt C-5) did the white-on-white appliqué blocks during her journey in 1863. The appliqué patterns are traditional cut-paper designs. These are examples of women using their needles on the available resources to make the blocks.

C-1

Quilt: Oregon Pioneer Ribbon Quilt
Category: Appliqué and Pieced
Size: 73" x 67.75" framed
Date: circa 1925
Maker: Elizabeth Ann Clark Kelly (1843-1930)
Year Over Trail: 1860
Came: Unknown whether she came over the Trail or by ship
County Where Settled: Portland, Multnomah County, Oregon

Plympton and Elizabeth Clark Kelly

This historic quilt was a gift of Margaret Cavigga, a West Coast quilt collector, to New York's American Folk Art Museum. There it is known as the Oregon Political Ribbon Quilt. The Oregon Historical Society archives has an extensive collection of Kelly family material, including a 1910 Kelly Clan invitation to attend the 60th year anniversary of the founding of the Plympton Kelly Homestead Farm and the 50th year anniversary of the arrival in Oregon of Elizabeth Clark Kelly.[17] The Kelly Clan held annual reunions to celebrate their heritage. Knowing of the rich history and contributions of Methodist minister Clinton Kelly and his family in Oregon, it is possible the maker desired to commemorate it in a visual record—this heirloom quilt. A more suitable name would be the Oregon Pioneer Ribbon Quilt, because most are references to social organizations serving the early settlers. This style, called a show quilt, was made of high quality fabrics and commemorative badges or ribbons and was intended for display in a home's public area or gathering place. Often, these reference an event or events in a family member's life. This style quilt was promoted in women's publications of the late nineteenth century as a way for women to showcase their needlework skills as well as their family's accomplishments or social connections. The peak of interest in this fancy patchwork was during the last quarter of the nineteenth century. But, it is recognized that popularity and interest took a while to fade out of fashion, in distance and time across the country. Older women clung to the appeal of quiltmaking as a satisfying activity in their lives.

Elizabeth Ann Clark was born in 1843 to Alexander and Nancy Hitchins Clark in Michigan. In June 1860, she was living in Portland, Oregon with her aunt and Methodist missionary uncle, the Reverend and Mrs. Calvin S. Kingsley.[18] They were early leaders of the Methodist Portland Academy, a school operating in the 1850s, prior to the advent of public schools. Elizabeth taught school in the Mt. Tabor area before her mar-

riage to Plympton Kelly, Clinton Kelly's second son, in July 1864. He was a successful farmer on his three hundred and fifty acre land claim in eastern Multnomah County. As the son of a preacher, he was active in the Methodist Episcopal Church. He organized the Sunday School for the church that met in the Lents area school in 1878 and was superintendent until 1883, rarely missing a Sunday.[19] The couple had six children, but only two survived to adulthood: Eudoxia Amelia (or Aurora), and James Garfield. Elizabeth died in 1930 after living on their farm for over sixty years.

From the badges on the quilt, Elizabeth's social activities and contributions to her community are well documented. One supporting document is her 1903 address to the Lents Elementary School in southeast Portland describing her family's settlement.

Starting at the center of the quilt, there is a commemorative handkerchief from the Midwinter Fair, 1894. This California fair, held in San Francisco, was considered the West Coast's answer to the successful 1893 Columbian Exposition in Chicago. There is very little or no information about the fair in Oregon's state archives, partly because a 1935 fire in the state capitol destroyed the major records. The only available newspaper article describes the plans for Oregon's participation in the fair as being well organized by civil leaders during this "difficult economic period." Oregon had done well in competition in Chicago and promoters felt the state should repeat "its triumphs at this West Coast event" by displaying the best the Pacific Coast could offer.[20]

Embroidered on the souvenir handkerchief surface is "Euda Aletha from E.A. Kelly." Euda Aletha, Mrs. Kelly's granddaughter, was born in 1911, the only daughter of James Garfield and Ada Ryder Kelly.[21]

Radiating around the handkerchief are the badges or ribbons of organizations important in shaping early Oregon social culture and in recording that history. Although some have frayed beyond readability, the center medallion contains twenty-four badges from the Oregon Pioneer Association for many reunion years (but not consecutively) between 1902 and 1923. Several are badges of responsibility, including one for assistant marshal in 1915. There is also a ribbon for the Women's Auxiliary Table #4 in 1924. However, since it is unknown how Mrs. Kelly came to Oregon in 1860 and she was not listed as either an assistant marshal or seated at table #4, the question becomes how did she obtain these. There are at least five guest badges for reunion years 1919 through 1923. Perhaps these were for Mrs. Kelly or for her granddaughter, Euda Aletha Kelly.

The structure of the Pioneer Association was that each pioneer would be given a ribbon (badge) with the year they traveled the Trail printed on it. Then, pioneers would be seated at tables together during the reunions and photographed by group. On the quilt are multiple ribbons for 1846 (1), 1848 (3), 1849 (2), 1850 (1), 1851 (4), 1853 (3), and 1854 (1). Since the Clinton Kelly family were pioneers of 1848 and would have received ribbons for that year, this range of years suggests that the maker collected or traded for the badges from attendees celebrating other migration years.

Forming the four corners of the medallion are badges from other associations Mrs. Kelly or her family were known to join: Women's Foreign Missionary Society of the Methodist Episcopal Church (6); the Oregon State Grange (3); Winslow Meade Circle #7 of the Ladies of the Grand Army of the Republic (Civil War veterans)(2); and Wife of the Indian War Veterans (1). They are grouped in fours, representing the different organizations, and placed so the badges were not cut when stitched in place.

Another example of the maker's commitment to religious faith is the ribbon with the "Mizpah" blessing printed on it. Mizpah comes from the Bible in the Old Testament, Genesis 31, verse 49: "The Lord watch between you and me, when we are apart one from the other." This was a popular prayer during the era, often exchanged between loved ones at weddings, anniversaries, or leave takings.

Beyond the center medallion are squares of silk, mounted on a foundation and pieced together to create diagonal lines of color. The quilt is bound with a rust colored silk binding.

Oregon Pioneer Ribbon Quilt. *Collection American Folk Art Museum, New York, Gift of Margaret Cavigga 1985.23.9*

C-2

Quilt: Tree of Life Signature Quilt
Category: Pieced
Size: 86" x 70.5"
Date: circa 1890-1895
Maker: Women of the Wingville Methodist
    Episcopal South Church
Years Over Trail: 1862-1864
Came: As extended families and friends
County Where Settled: Baker County, Oregon

According to the Michael family lore, this two-color quilt was made as a fundraiser for the Wingville Methodist Episcopal South Church in Wingville, Baker County, Oregon. It has descended through the family of Circuit Preacher Elijah Michael, pioneer of 1848, and his wife Marena Smith Michael, pioneer of 1852. They served thirty-three years in western Oregon and eastern Oregon, Washington, and Idaho.[22] The Methodist Episcopal Church South began its work in Oregon in 1866 with twelve regular ministers and twelve local preachers who organized the Columbia Conference of the M.E. South Church.[23]

On the quilt is the documentation: "W.P.H.M. Wingville, OR." According to family lore, the initials refer to "Women's Parish Home Mission." This would indicate the women's effort to support local and national social projects of the church. Often, the funds raised by a quilt-making venture would go toward the support of these projects. The quilt was made before January 1, 1896 when two named people were married.

There are one hundred and forty green triangles and fifty-six with names. Among the names are the Chandler, Osborn, Ison, and Speelman families, all pioneers of 1862. Many came with George Chandler from Trenton, Grundy County, Missouri. Joining them later were the Leonning family in 1863 and the Perkins family in 1864.

The quilt is categorized according to the years these contributors would have come over the Trail because they represent a defined segment of population moving into eastern Oregon late in the Trail era. At this time, many of the emigrants were stopping in eastern Oregon, exhausted from the long journey and aware that most of the choice land in the Willamette Valley had been claimed. Here were gold mines, rich soil, and mountain streams that would irrigate the valley fields.

Marena Michael and her daughter Mary Kirk, granddaughter Stella Robb, and great-grandson Master Robb

In the fall of 1862 thousands of emigrants came to the country and many of them were dependent upon their daily labor for subsistence. But very few of them could have found employment, had it not been for opportunity offered by the water company and by individuals who were led to build houses and engage in business through hopes for the future.[24]

The name Wingville was given to the community of southern Democrats who came to Oregon, especially Baker County, during the Civil War. While many of the counties and towns in Eastern Oregon were Republican and Union in name, this town was named derisively for the "left wing" of Confederate Army Major-General and Missourian Sterling Price's army.[25] W.D. Chandler, the grandson of two 1862 wagon train members, thought it quite accurate to say "I was born and raised in a segment of Missouri which had been loaded on covered wagons and deposited in eastern Oregon. We followed Missouri habits, observed Missouri customs, every adult was called Uncle or Aunt by all the children..."[26] A similar area in Idaho was called "Dixie" for the number of southern sympathizers who settled there from the same area of Missouri in 1864.[27]

The quilt is a whole cloth variation of the traditional Tree of Life pattern where one pieced pattern creates the entire design. This is as compared with the Pine Tree variation block-style construction (Quilt D-2). This quilt served as a banner or a backdrop for the church, drawing the people together as community in a new environment. The meaning of the Tree is important, with symbolic significance as a symbol of plenty, goodness, wisdom, and the ideal relationship of work and trust between man and God—in short, the full life.[28]

The Tree of Life theme is referenced in the creation story, in Genesis 2:9: "And out of the ground, the Lord God made to grow every tree that is pleasant to the sight and good for food, the tree of life also in the midst of the garden, and the tree of the knowledge of good and evil."[29] For these pioneers, this theme could be translated as referring to their farms, homes, and communities, as they worked to create a new life away from the social and political strife of Missouri.

Tree of Life Signature
Quilt. *Collection of
Cydney Bush, Portland*

Detail of "W.P.H.M.
Wingville, OR."

C-3

Quilt: Sunflower
Category: Pieced
Size: 101" x 85"
Date: circa 1860
Maker: Matilda Knight Stauffer (1835-1867)
Year Over Trail: 1863
Came: As a daughter with her father Joseph; step-mother Catharine; and all his family, which included seven sons and two daughters.
County Where Settled: Pacific, Washington Territory; Clackamas County, Oregon

This handmade quilt is of bright primary colors, frequent choices made by Pennsylvania German quiltmakers. The detailed hand-piecing of the quilt's thirty-two diamond segments for each of the twenty blocks and the double rows of quilting indicate the vast amount of work involved in producing this quilt. There is extensive quilting in the unbroken plume that moves around the border in a meandering curve. A hex wheel pattern is interspersed along the border at the curve of the plume.

The back of the quilt is as interesting as the front. It contains large strips of various plaid fabrics. This indicates the amount of time and desire to use available fabric remnants the young single woman had to devote to the quilt construction, and it may also be an example of the shared effort that existed within the Bethel-Aurora Communal Society because others were available to help. In Matilda's family, there were three other adult women at the time the quilt was probably made.

Matilda was born to Joseph and Sarah Gates Knight in 1835. The family had joined the Bethel Colony after being approached by Dr. William Keil in Pennsylvania. Prior to Sarah's death in 1843, they moved to Shelby County, Missouri, home of the Bethel Colony. Around 1845, the family moved into the town of Bethel, where Joseph married Catharine Bauer, a widow from Germany with five children, and they "conduced to the Bethel Fund the following in money and valuables $53.00" [30]

After Joseph Knight's two-year stay (1853-1855) in the Northwest as one of Dr. Keil's ten scouts chosen to select a new location for the colony, he returned to Bethel. The family came with the second Bethel-Aurora wagon train in 1863. Although Dr. Keil rejected the Willapa site in Washington Territory, choosing instead the Aurora site south of Portland, the Knight family went to Willapa. They joined five other families from the wagon train who chartered a schooner to take the women, children, and household goods down the Columbia River to Baker's Bay, near the mouth of the river, while four of the

Matilda Knight Stauffer
(1835-1867)

men took the cattle and mules overland on a pack trail. The family sailed by day and camped on shore at night for five days.[31] All the sons were trained in specific needed trades, in accordance with the Colony practice. One, John was a blacksmith; another Joe, a shoemaker; a third George, a miller; a fourth Will, a harness maker; and a fifth Charles, a bricklayer.[32]

At Willapa, sometime between 1863 and 1867, Matilda Knight married Jacob Stauffer. Their families had been neighbors in Bethel, Missouri. His parents had emigrated from Germany to Pennsylvania and then west to Missouri. Matilda died giving birth to twins in 1867. She and one baby were buried on the farm and later moved to the Menlo, Washington cemetery. Jacob and the other twin, named for her mother Matilda, lived with the Stauffer family where the child was raised by Jacob's five sisters. In the 1870 Census, both the Knights and Stauffers were living back in the Willamette Valley with only the Stauffers living all together in the Aurora Colony.[33] In the 1880 Aurora Census, the family unit is listed as his five unmarried sisters, his father, and his unmarried brother, and Jacob and his daughter Matilda.[34] This is evidence of dissension among Dr. Keil's followers. The Knights had left the Colony while the Stauffers had remained. The number of unmarried members of the Stauffer family is an indication of Keil's desire for celibacy and disapproval of marriage.[35] After the Colony was dissolved, on December 8, 1889, Matilda married August Will.[36] The quilt has passed through her family to be treasured now by her great-granddaughter, Vera Kocher Yoder.[37]

Detail of back of quilt

Sunflower Quilt. *Collection of Vera Kocher Yoder, Woodburn*

C-4

Quilt: Pink and Green
Category: Pieced
Size: 87" x 71"
Date: circa 1875
Maker: Women of Aurora Colony
Year Over Trail: Possibly 1863
Came: As members of the Bethel-Aurora Colony
Society
County Where Settled: Marion County, Oregon

This pink and green pieced quilt is one of at least six that exist in Oregon and are connected with the Aurora Colony communal society. The colors and pattern are representative of quilts made by the group of German religious idealists, former members of George Rapp's Harmony-Economy who were drawn together in the late 1830s in Ambridge, Pennsylvania. They approached the personable leader, Dr. William Keil, about heading an experiment in communal living and he led the group to Bethel, Missouri in 1844.

Successful in Missouri but eager to keep his group together and inspired by the dream of owning land, Dr. Keil brought the group west in four wagon caravans between 1855 and 1867. Some six hundred people of the group made their homes in Aurora and Willapa. The Colony was active until Dr. Keil's death in 1877. The assets were divided among members by 1883.

The colony was a special part of Oregon's history, becoming known for its music, food, hospitality, furniture, and clothing. Credit is given to Keil, the trained tailor, for establishing a style of dress appropriately fitting to the pioneer woman. The skirt would be gathered up to allow for freedom of movement and safety when working around open fires and hot stones. Women were encouraged to wear simple dresses of cotton calico on all occasions. To dress up, they used such simple ornaments as ribbons.[38] Under Keil's influence, the women of the commune became especially skilled in weaving, sewing, and embroidering.[39]

The quilt reflects the colonists' desire to share their patterns, their work, and their supplies. The color combination was a favorite with many quilters, especially Germans, everywhere at the time. In Aurora, a limited choice of cotton calicos would have been available in the supply store for the community. Women were discouraged from making themselves different from their neighbors and from putting undue expense upon the society.[40] This eight-and-a-half-inch pieced pattern block is common among the quilts. There is no specific record of the pattern

name used by the commune women, but Crosses and Losses and Fox and Geese are two popular ones. Wreaths quilted in the solid blocks are referred to as the "Aurora wreath."[41]

Subtly and carefully quilted within the wreaths are the letters "S" and "W," perhaps a simple identification mark. There were families by the names of Stauffer, Will, and Wolfer in the colony.

A continuous feather plume surrounds the quilt in the seven-and-a-quarter inch border, another common feature in the colony quilts.

Detail of "W" in the quilting

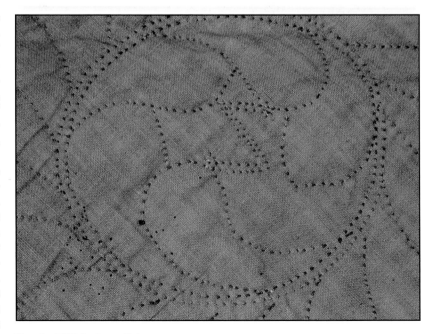

Detail of "S" in the quilting

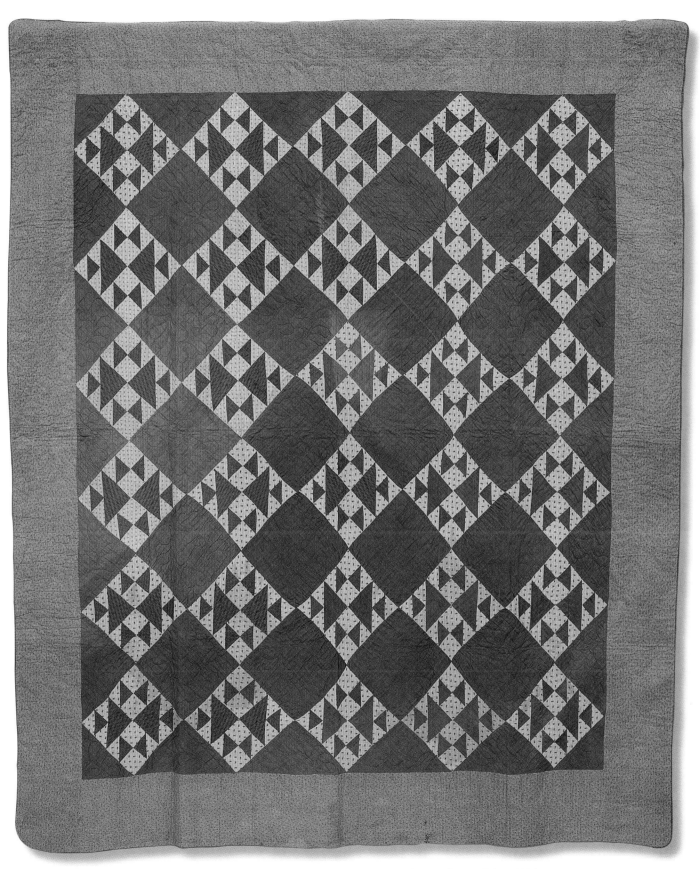

Pink and Green Quilt. *Old Aurora Colony Museum, Aurora, Oregon #A70-1145*

C-5

Quilt: White on White
Category: Appliqué
Size: 72" x 66"
Date: 1863 Started; Finished later
Maker: Isabella Fleming Mills (1835-1907)
Year Over Trail: 1863
Came: As a wife with husband George W. Mills and their six children
County Where Settled: Yamhill County, Oregon, then Thurston County, Washington Territory

George W. Mills and wife.
Early History of Thurston County, Washington

This quilt is difficult to see and study, but it is important as an example of a project started while on the Trail. However, the study of a white-on-white quilt that has been used and laundered was rewarding. Family history states the quilt was made while crossing the Plains in 1863, so the commitment was made to examine and photograph the quilt. George Champlin of the Oregon Historical Society tried to solve the photographic challenge within budget and resources.

Being made on the Trail refers to the appliqué work done on the individual blocks. The blocks are nine cut-paper designs drawn on white cloth and hand appliquéd on sixteen-inch squares of white. The set of blocks is on point, where the pattern blocks are joined at the corners rather than the edges. This more difficult arrangement, as well as the extensive amount and intricacy of quilting, indicates it was quilted after the family arrived in the Northwest when the quilt could have been placed on a large flat surface and in a quilt frame.

The quilting lines reveal four different large wheel patterns quilted over the surface. Hearts, flowers, and wheels are scattered randomly over the quilt top. A pair of open scissors appears to be in the corner of one block. In another corner is the maker's notation: "Bell Mills born Aug 11th, 1835."

Isabelle Fleming and George W. Mills were married in Illinois in 1853. Her parents had come from Ireland and his from New York and Pennsylvania. They left Illinois and migrated to Sullivan County, Missouri, where George organized Company G, 11th Missouri Cavalry for the Civil War battle at Kirksville. A war injury, along with the "bitter hard times" in Missouri and the cry of gold in California, precipitated the couple's decision to migrate West. Near the Platte River site of the Mormon Ferry, where troops of 6th U.S. Volunteers were stationed, the military officers advised them to join with larger wagon trains for safety in resisting random attacks by Indian bands.[42] The train they joined was destined for Oregon instead of California, so the Mills changed their plans. They were grateful for the advice when they came upon several scenes of disastrous raids. Because of his military training, George Mills was unanimously elected captain or military director of the sixty-wagon train.

Arriving in Oregon, they settled in Yamhill County where their son George was born. In 1865, they moved to Thurston County, Washington Territory, near Puget Sound, after receiving encouraging letters from former neighbors. When she saw the salt water before her, Mrs. Mills is reported to have said, "Well, Pa, this is the jumping off place. We haven't the money to go back; we can go no further, so we've just got to stay here."[43] Another son, Jesse T., was born here.

Eventually they purchased forty acres of land in the South Union area, six miles from Tumwater. Isabelle realized the importance of providing a good education for the children and eventually sent Mary, George, and Jesse to Olympia to board with families and graduate from the Olympia Collegiate Institute.

In 1882, when George became the industrial instructor at the Chehalis Indian school, Isabelle and the children who weren't attending school in Olympia went with him. Jesse became a popular participant in all sports and learned the native languages. When Indian parents came to inquire about their children, he was frequently asked to interpret.[44]

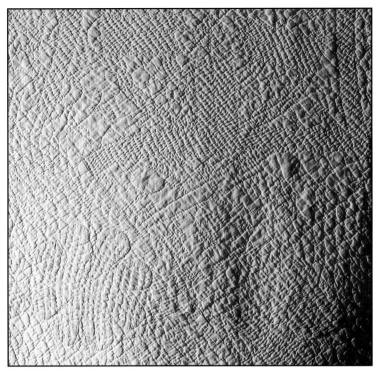

Detail with scissors motif in quilting

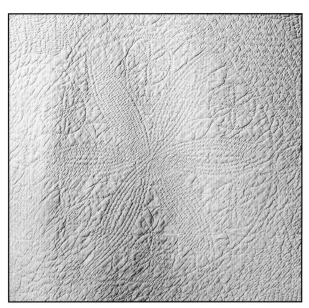

Detail with wheel motif in quilting

White on White Quilt. *Oregon Historical Society, Portland, #4475*

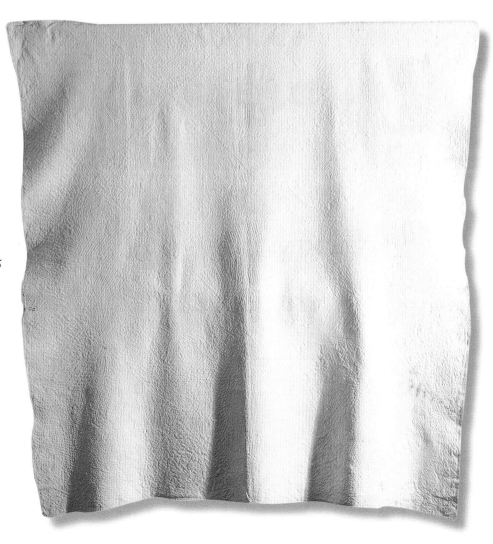

C-6

Quilt: Honeysuckle
Category: Appliqué
Size: 94" x 80"
Date: circa 1850
Maker: Great-great aunts of Minnie Robison
    Colver (1880-1960)
Year Over Trail: 1864 or 1853
Sent: With either Blin Carlos and Demaris
    McClain Goddard and family in 1864 or
    Robert Boyd and Susan Milligan Robison
    and family in 1853
County Where Settled: Jackson County, Oregon

This red and green Honeysuckle-patterned appliqué quilt is packed with meaning and sentiment. According to Elly Sienkiewicz, the nineteenth-century meaning of the honeysuckle was "devotion, generous affection, mirth, love's bond, and we belong to one another."[45]

The quilting pattern in the nine twenty-two-inch blocks is a wheel motif featuring a double circle with double lines across the center. It is likely that this wheel represents migration and the blessing of good wishes associated with leave taking. Wheels appear scattered over the surface, along with hearts, flowers and wreaths in much the same format as the project's other quilts with wheels. These expressions of affection are most often identified with wedding quilts. A rather unusual feature is the unbroken swag border appearing on three sides, with the vacant edge being one of the long sides. The swag is pieced of three diamonds set together at the high point with an appliquéd stem and three buds at the base of the loop. It is the combination of the two styles of geometric precision and free form interpretive design.

Usually, the vacant edge is either the top or the bottom, indicating it would be covered by pillows or used on a bed with a foot. Quilts with definite border construction patterns often indicate having been made for specific beds. In this case, it would be one in which the long side was against a wall or it was a bed with a wooden sideboard to be displayed, thus no need to show a quilt border. A quilt-related myth says that on a wedding quilt, a broken border vine foretells a short, unhappy married life.

The quilt was made by the great-great aunts of the donor, Minnie Robison Colver. Since two of her great-grandfathers came over the Trail, these makers would have been the sisters of either Blin Carlos Goddard (1822-1893) or John Francis Robison (1799-1870). Both Mr. Goddard and Mr. Robison had sisters whose lifespans would coincide with making a quilt in the 1840s for their brothers. Blin Carlos Goddard was born in New York and migrated West in 1837 to Missouri. His wife, Demaris McClain (1826-1893), was born in North Carolina and moved with her family to Missouri in 1835. The Goddard couple was married in 1844 and came over the Oregon Trail in 1864. Both John Robison and his wife, Susan Milligan (1806-1889), were born in Pennsylvania. They married in 1822 in Ohio, moved to Iowa in 1847, and came to Oregon in 1853. The quilt could very well have been a migration and/or wedding quilt made for either couple.[46]

Detail of swag border treatment

Honeysuckle Quilt. *Southern Oregon Historical Society, Medford, #837*

C-7

Quilt: Eight-Pointed Star
Category: Pieced
Size: 83" x 61"
Date: circa 1873
Maker: Ersula Isabelle Goddard Robison Dean
    (1856-1934)
Year Over Trail: 1864
Came: As a daughter with her parents Blin
    Carlos and Demaris McClain Goddard, her
    brothers and sister
County Where Settled: Jackson County, Oregon

The fabrics of the twelve-inch hand-pieced blocks appear to be older than the date given for construction of 1873. They appear to be of the mid-nineteenth century in the colors of brown, butterscotch, and green. The quilting designs are wreaths with clam shells.

It is unclear where or when the pattern name Eight-pointed Star was attached to the quilt. This particular pattern has a history of different names, showing the change with migration of pattern designs and names. It is also called Rolling Star, Brunswick Star, and Chained Star by Ruth Finley, who describes it as a diamond pattern.[47]

This quilt and the Colver Quilt (C-6) are from the same family and donor, Minnie Robison Colver. The two quilts illustrate the effort by the descendants to preserve their family history. The quilts are in a well-equipped museum, the Southern Oregon Historical Society. They are important as examples of the continued interest in and need for making bed quilts throughout the nineteenth century.

The common practice of piecing first, then quilting and completing the quilt later would coincide with the Goddard family history. The accession record indicates that Ersula Goddard was seventeen when the quilt was made in 1873, the year before her first marriage.

She was born in 1856 in Missouri and came to Oregon in 1864 with her family. She married Robert B. Robison, and they had two sons: Carlos, born in 1875, and Edward, born in 1878. 1880 was a difficult year for Ersula. Her daughter was born in August and her husband died later that year, leaving her with three children under five. Fortunately, her widowed mother-in-law, Susan Robison, was living with her, and other family members made their homes nearby.[48] Ersula married her neighbor Willis J. Dean in 1886.[49]

An information-rich photograph exists showing the maker sitting straight in her lawn chair in front of her home in Talent, Oregon in the 1890s. The flowering plants by the side of the house show the pride she had in her home. The planted garden in the foreground and the logged slope in the background show the fruits of the labors of Ersula and Willis Dean. He is standing proudly by his horse and buggy. He was a farmer and school teacher who wrote and gave funeral addresses for community residents. The young woman with her bicycle is Ersula's daughter, Minnie Robison Colver.

(Left to right) Willis J. Dean, Minnie Robison Colver, Ersula Goddard Robison Dean. *Southern Oregon Historical Society, Medford, #1805*

Eight-pointed Star Quilt. *Southern Oregon Historical Society, Medford, Oregon #839*

C-8

Quilt: Princess Feather
Category: Appliqué
Size: 88" x 64"
Date: circa 1860
Maker: Margaret Fuson Lieuallen (1838-1931)
Year Over Trail: 1864
Came: As a wife with husband, William T. and his brother Noah, his wife, and two daughters
County Where Settled: Umatilla County, Oregon

The next two quilts were the shared work of a daughter and her mother, Margaret Fuson Lieuallen and Sarah Moody Fuson (Quilt D-5). The red and green appliqué continued to be popular for this period of time and place. This quilt is less elaborate than many of the earlier ones, which often included intricate borders and quilting designs. Here the work is straightforward and practical: five large appliqué blocks of thirty-four inches arranged with one cut in half and placed at one end to give needed extra length. This is an unusual set.

The quilting designs are simple and practical. In and between the feathers are short chains of diamonds. The rest is a gridwork of diagonal and straight lines placed about one-half inch apart.

According to family history, Margaret Lieuallen and her mother, Sarah Moody Fuson, may have made the quilt prior to the younger woman's marriage and migration. Its unusual size, long and narrow, may indicate that the quilt was made to use on the journey west, as Mabel Lieuallen Wagner says in *Water from the Spring:*

> Beneath the tree by the spring just a year ago Margaret had promised William Lieuallen to leave her home in Kentucky and travel by covered wagon to make her home in far away Oregon. This afternoon in a simple ceremony she would become his wife and tomorrow they were joining a caravan bound for Oregon. The wagon was carefully loaded, the oxen fat, and well broken.
>
> How fast the year had passed, now so soon the dear ones would be left behind. Mother and daughter had worked long hours together, the quilts so painstakingly pieced and quilted, the heavy wool filled comforters, the homespun dresses, the simple household linens now all packed and loaded ready for the long journey.[50]

William Lieuallen's immigrant ancestors, the Llelwellyns, were three brothers from Wales who settled first in North Carolina. A disagreement regarding slavery caused them to split apart and change the spelling of their names. One took the "Lewelling" spelling while another married a French woman and changed the spelling to "Lieuallen."[51]

William was the fifth of seven sons born to Peyton and Jemima Smith Lieuallen between 1822 and 1842. Two of them, Thomas and Asbury, had come to Oregon in 1862 to explore the opportunities available there. Thomas returned to the Midwest and convinced his four brothers of the free land available in a peaceful setting, contrary to the strife in western Missouri during the Civil War years.[52] This was one family's response to the important "push" that many Midwesterners in Civil War border states like Missouri were feeling.

Since the majority of land in the Valley had already been claimed, wagon trains of this era tended to terminate in eastern Oregon or southeastern Washington Territory, near Walla Walla. Or, perhaps a knowledgeable guide or military leader traveling with the train may have advised ending the journey in eastern Oregon. The Lieuallens chose to settle in northeastern Oregon in the Pine Creek area of the Blue Mountains in Umatilla County. William chose to claim this rugged, isolated, and exposed land because of a spring of water and the open range pasture for his cattle.

Margaret and William Lieuallen had three sons born to them between 1865 and 1871. The youngest died at the age of six in 1877.

William and Margaret Fuson Lieuallen, and baby Johnny; sons Thomas and James standing

Princess Feather. *Collection of Donald and Gilberta Lieuallen, Adams, Oregon*

C-9

Quilt: Stars with Wild Geese Strips
Category: Pieced
Size: 82" x 60"
Date: circa 1880
Maker: Margaret Fuson Lieuallen (1838-1931)

Studying this quilt provides clues that date it to after the Lieuallen migration: the Centennial fabric in one star which reads "1776-1876" and the color fastness of the bright pink border fabrics as compared to the other fabrics in the quilt's center.[53] Many of the print fabrics used in the triangles and diamonds represent the years spanning before and after the maker's 1864 marriage and migration.

Since we know that Margaret's mother, Sarah Moody Fuson (Quilt D-5), came by railroad train sometime after 1884, this pattern and its fabrics may represent the reunion of the mother and daughter quiltmakers.

The pieced quilt reflects the migration theme in its sense of movement and convergence created by the diamonds and triangles. Although the family's pattern name was not recorded, a similar pattern found in Missouri at the same time was called Railroad and Depot.[54] Another name is the Spider Web, a recognition of the amount of work and effort a spider puts in to creating a place in time and space.[55]

When William Lieuallen began to suffer seizures, much of the work on their ranch was done by Margaret. She planted a garden every spring and had a cellar behind the house for storage of vegetables, canned fruits, and pans of milk. William had planted an extensive orchard with apple, cherry, pear, walnut and persimmon trees, and grape vineyards. He loved to offer someone a persimmon before it was ripe and watch the reaction to the bitter and puckery taste. After William's death in 1908, Margaret continued living on the farm, keeping a cow for milk and chickens for eggs. She sold the extra eggs for additional income.

In addition to caring for her husband and raising her sons, Margaret provided a home for his nieces and her nephews at various times over the years. She was known to all the community as "Aunt Margaret."[56]

Margaret "Grandma" Lieuallen smoked a pipe and Aunt Sarah Lieuallen used snuff, but they thought any woman who smoked a cigarette was, in their words, "a hussy." Margaret started smoking because of a digestive problem.[57]

Detail of star and triangle piecing

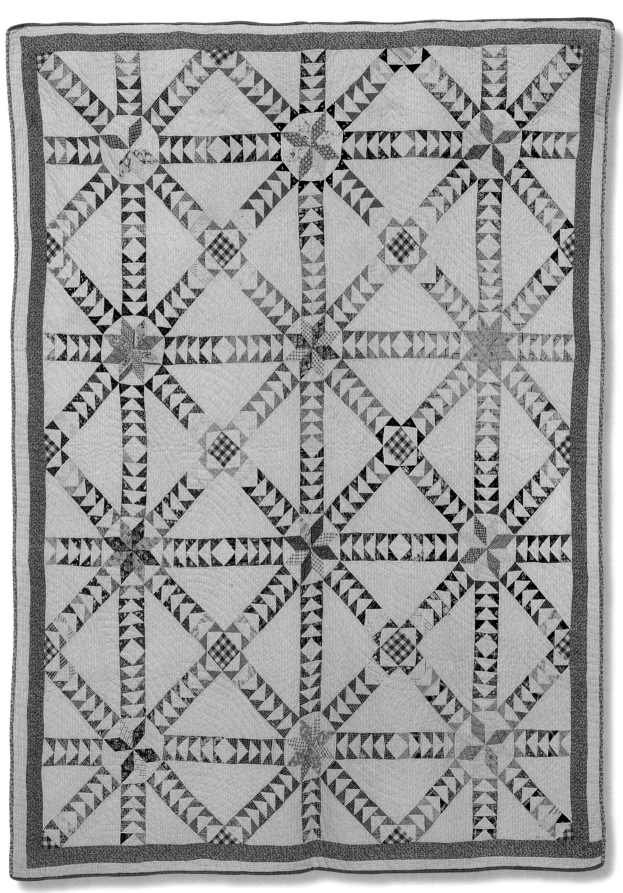

Stars with Wild Geese Strips. *Collection of Donald and Gilberta Lieuallen, Adams, Oregon*

C-10

Quilt: Bachelor
Category: Pieced and Appliqué
Size: 84" x 74"
Date: 1855 Started; 1869 Finished (dated)
Maker: Mary Jane Fairley Bryan (1839-1933)
Year Over Trail: 1864
Came: As a wife with husband Daniel Boone Bryan and two children
County Where Settled: Yamhill County, then Lake County, Oregon

The nine-and-a-half-inch pieced circles are made up of nine segments: four red, four green, and one orange. According to family history, the pattern is named "Bachelor" because the orange unit stands out in the circle; unlike the red and green pairs, the bachelor does not have a mate.[58] Probably an original name for the pattern, it fits in with the long tradition of a young woman making a quilt top for her hope chest while hoping for a bachelor. The top was pieced and appliquéd by the maker while she was living in Guernsey County, Ohio in 1855.

Another name for the pattern is "Whirl-wind," which constitutes a migration theme with its meaning of movement.[59]

Feathered wreaths surround each circle with sprays of leaves, curlicues, and grid work as fillers. Four-inch pieced strips repeat the colors in a zigzag fashion for the border treatment. The binding is a black ground with green and yellow. The quilt is dated "May 25, 1869 quilted."

Mary Jane Fairley was born to David and Mary Hyde Fairley in 1839 in Monroe or Guernsey County, Ohio. The immigrant ancestor was Thomas Farley, who had come from Worcestershire, England to Virginia in the early 1600s. Moving west to Mercer County, Missouri, Mary married Daniel Boone Bryan from Tennessee in March 1858. His family had descended from Francis Bryan, an immigrant from Ireland in the early 1600s. The Bryan and Boone families

Mary Jane Fairley Bryan (1839-1933). *Lane County Historical Museum, L77-699*

were intertwined through marriage from their early days in Yakin County, North Carolina.[60] Crossing the Plains in 1864, Mary and Daniel Bryan settled in the Sheridan area of Yamhill County. This was where she finished her quilt. They eventually had five children.[61] Later, Mary was living near her sons in Lake County in eastern Oregon, where one was a stage contractor and the other did day labor.[62] She is listed as head of the family in the 1910 census, with her son David as a farmer.[63]

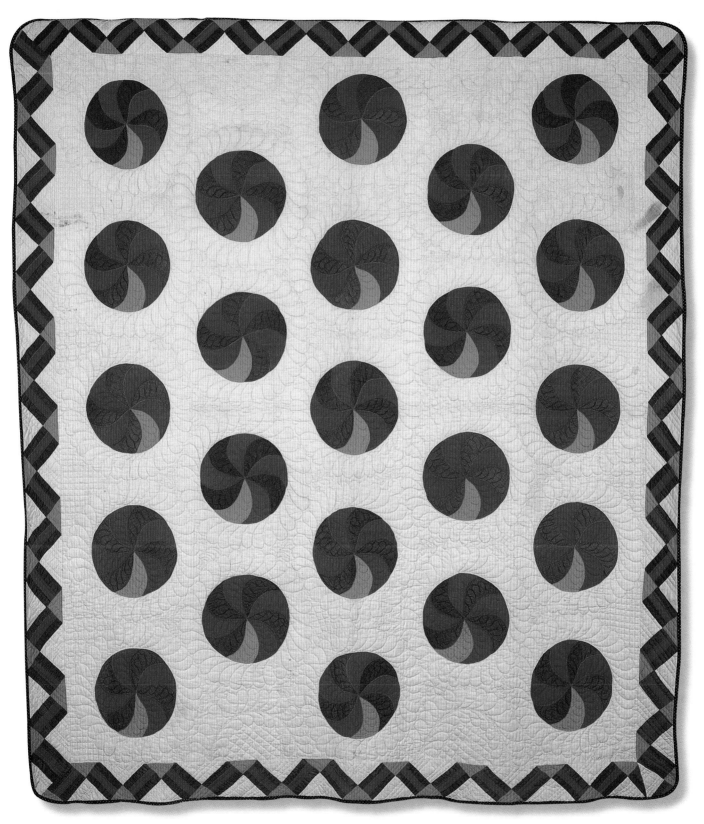

Bachelor Quilt. *Collection of Lane County Historical Museum, Eugene, #476*

C-11

Quilt: Seven Stars
Category: Pieced
Size: 85" x 82.5"
Date: circa 1875
Maker/Owner: Emma Roberts Morgan (1859-1954)
Year Over Trail: Before 1870
Came: With her parents David and Jane Anderson Roberts and family
County Where Settled: Washington County, Oregon, then Walla Walla County, Washington Territory

This hand-pieced and hand-quilted heirloom was part of a quilt legacy that descended through the maker's family in Washington State. The quilt was featured in the 1989 Washington State Centennial Tribute Traveling Exhibit and in the exhibit catalog *Women and Their Quilts: A Washington State Centennial Tribute* by Nancyann J. Twelker. Nancyann thought it was made by Emma Roberts, daughter of a Methodist Episcopal minister, when she was fourteen years old, prior to her 1877 marriage to a prominent citizen of Waitsburg, Washington. The name given for the pattern was Seven Sisters. Since then, additional important information has become available.

Recent scholarship has associated both the Seven Sisters pattern and the five strip sashings and borders with southern quilts.[64] New research indicates that most likely this quilt was either a wedding gift to the young couple or a gift to her family from someone with southern loyalties. The Seven Sisters is thought to represent the seven states that seceded from the Union at the start of the Civil War. Many unhappy southerners in the Midwest migrated to the eastern Washington area during and after the Civil War. This quilt could have belonged to one of those families.

Barbara Brackman identifies the pattern both as Seven Sisters and Seven Stars.[65] Stars had an important role in the nineteenth century. Since much of American pioneer life was spent outdoors, star gazing and the study of astronomy were popular fields of interest.

People knew their constellations and observed the changes in them.[66] Seven Stars also has a rich symbolic interpretation in the Bible. Both stars and the number seven were used in the storytelling tradition; much has been written about both. M.H. Pope's summary that seven denotes "completeness, perfection [and] consummation" is the simplest and most comprehensive generalization that can be made.[67]

The sashings are composed of five strips of one-and-a-half-inch wide cheddar yellow, red, and green. They are joined with a seven-and-a-half-inch block with a star. The skill level and attention to detail in the quilt's construction suggests an experienced quiltmaker, well beyond the age of fourteen. The three and one-half-inch stars were created by using green triangles and red hexagon centers. Then, they were connected point-to-point with pieced white background fabric to create an eleven-and-a-half-inch circle. This was set into a white block with a center circular cutout, creating the finished fourteen-and-a-half-inch block. This is a most unusual set for this pattern. Most often they are set in a hexagon pattern, not a circle.[68]

The hand-quilting accentuates the piecing, with three rows of stitches around each cluster of stars and each of the single sashing stars. There is also a double stitched heart in each of the four corners of the blocks. The stitches are small and even.

The Roberts family migrated west from Grundy County in north central Illinois, where Emma was born in 1859. Her father, David Roberts, was a wagon maker, not a minister, and had come from Wales; her mother, Jane Anderson, was the daughter of Scottish immigrants.

According to the 1870 Census, the family was located in Forest Grove, Oregon where the father continued his trade and eleven-year-old Emma was attending school.[69] The family moved to Waitsburg, Walla Walla County, Washington Territory on June 16, 1871, where David farmed and was an active member of the Methodist Episcopal Church. He served as a class leader in the Church Sunday School for over twenty years and as vice-president of the Methodist Waitsburg Academy Board.[70] However, his name was not listed among the Waitsburg pastors, although the family was known to be active Methodists.[71]

Emma married James W. "J.W." Morgan in 1877. He was born in Lancaster County, Pennsylvania in 1843 and came west to seek his fortune. He worked in the mines in Montana and drove a stagecoach. He arrived in Waitsburg in 1872, where he became active in business and civic affairs. He worked as a pharmacist and owned the brick building that housed his business. He also served in the territorial and state legislatures and as president of the First National Bank of Waitsburg.

Emma, like her parents, was active in the Methodist-Episcopal Church and served as a gracious hostess in her home. The couple had two daughters. Emma made many quilts and embellished bed linens later in her life. Compared to some of her other quilts, this one is the oldest and best executed, which might also indicate that someone else made it. After her husband died in 1928, Emma moved to Vancouver, Washington to live with her daughter and remained there until her death at the age of ninety-six.

My conclusion would be that Seven Stars is a more appropriate name for this quilt.

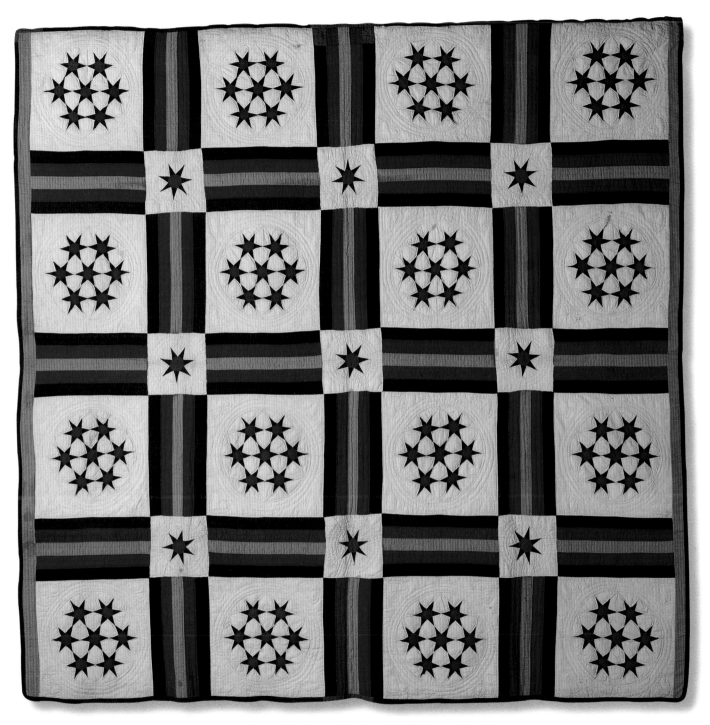

Seven Stars Quilt. *Collection of Charlotte Enfield, Bentonville, Arkansas*

PART IV
Those Who Wait

Rock Creek Station, painting by William Henry Jackson. *National Park Service/Scotts Bluff National Monument, Gering, Nebraska, SCBL21*

The Women and the Quilts

This book's main focus has been on the quilted treasures of the makers and families who actually experienced the Trail. During the search, an additional component became apparent: the quilts made in the "States" during the wait for someone who went West. Initially, this unexpected grouping was small, but as expected, when individual families reviewed their family history, additional "while waiting" treasures surfaced and several quilts from the first edition have been moved to this expanded section.

Now featured are five quilts made by Midwestern women, both young and old, who waited while loved ones went West to wander, to seek their fortune, and to establish themselves. For the young women living in Ohio and Indiana, the Overland Trail represented a significantly longer distance than from Missouri or Illinois. It was easier for all to let the young men venture west on their own and, hopefully, to return or call for the loved ones.

One of these quilts was a wedding gift for a brother and his bride (Quilt D-1); another was part of a personal hope chest (Quilt D-6); and a third was made while the maker and her young children stayed with her parents and waited to join her husband (Quilt D-2). The three older women in Illinois and Missouri waited until later to make the trip, until the railroad was constructed (Quilts D-4-5) or until the Overland Trail provided necessary services to make the journey easier and shorter (Quilt D-3). The quilts demonstrate the extensive amount of time and effort women were able to devote to their needlework while living with their supportive families. All express the romantic or emotional sentiment women of the period stitched into their quilts.

D-1

Quilt: Pine Tree
Category: Pieced
Size: 80" x 76"
Date: 1849
Maker: Catherine (1816-?) and Emmeline (1827-1899) Helman[1]
Where Made: Ashland County, Ohio
County Where Settled: Jackson County, Oregon

This Turkey red and white quilt is in the popular Pine Tree pattern. Trees have long been favorites among quiltmakers, and this variation of pieced triangles became popular in the mid-nineteenth century. The amount of effort to construct this quilt is substantial, with accurate, precise piecing needed to make the design work appropriately. At the time of migration, Americans were seeking stability and the pine tree represented the image of rootedness. The design gives an opportunity for the quilt owner to express a sense of connectedness with friends and family separated by miles.[2]

For one to view the trees with their strong roots upright in this set of blocks, the quilt should be studied from the side of the bed rather than the head or the foot.

The accession information indicates that the quilt was a wedding gift for Abel and Martha Kanagy Helman, married in 1849 in Ashland, Ohio, and made by the groom's sisters Catherine and Emmeline Helman.[3] The Turkey red fabric is an indication of the wealth of this family and the importance of the quilt to the makers. Turkey red was an expensively produced and imported fabric from the British Isles. In the 1840s, it was used sparingly in quilts.

Abel Helman was a man who wanted to investigate the West. His granddaughter, Almeda Coder, said: "There was that urge and that surge of traveling west. There were a great many people coming west at that time, so of course he was among those who wanted to come." Married less than one year, he left his wife in Ohio, expecting just to look the situation over, then return to his hometown. Instead, he met Eber Emery in the California mines and together they went north to southern Oregon, looking for a creek location to construct a flour mill and a sawmill. In 1852, they located a likely site and named it Ashland Creek, forming a settlement called Ashland Mills for his hometown in Ohio.[4]

In the meantime, communication between the couple was rare, and her family assumed he was not going to return. Two and one-half years later, he did return and discovered he had become a father.

In early 1853, the Helmans returned together to southern Oregon, shipping their household goods around the Horn from New York City while they booked a steamer to Nicaragua, shortening their trip by almost 1000 miles.[5]

The Helmans led active, community-oriented lives. Abel served as a contractor, a cabinetmaker, and the first postmaster of Ashland Mills starting in 1855. In the 1860 Census for Ashland, Martha is identified as the real estate owner valued at $1600 while Abel has a personal estate valued at $200.[6] In 1871, the town name was changed to Ashland.[7] Martha Helman had delivered eight children before she died in 1881 at the age of fifty-five. She was known locally for her skills in doctoring illnesses and extracting teeth.[8]

It is interesting to contrast the feelings of the two Ohio families about the lives of Abel and Martha K. Helman. Her family was sure he would not return, while his family made them a Pine Tree quilt to remind them of their roots and their connection to their Ohio home.

Abel and Martha Kanagy Helman with daughter Almeda. *Southern Oregon Historical Society, Medford, #403*

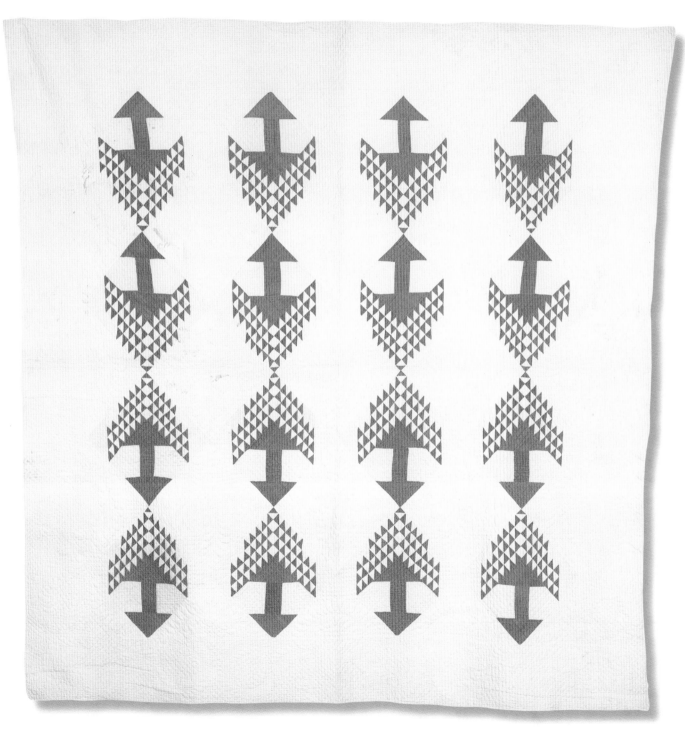

Pine Tree. *Collection of Southern Oregon Historical Society, Medford, #72.52.2*

D-2

Quilt: Star Quilt
Category: Pieced
Size: 88" x 90"
Date: circa 1850
Maker: Mary Ann Wilson Berry (1824-1910)
Where Made: Delphi, Carroll County, Indiana
County Where Settled: Jackson County, Oregon

Mary Ann Wilson Berry
(1824-1910)

Alexander Monroe Berry
(1817-1901)

This quilt is similar to many made in the Indiana and Ohio areas at the mid-nineteenth century. The large size and light weight indicate that it was probably meant for a defined use. It was known to be made for use on a particular carved wood bed.

The large size and light weight indicate that it was probably meant to cover other bedding that could have been stored on it during the daytime.

The quilt is entirely hand-pieced and hand-quilted with tiny stitches. The seventeen and a half inch star blocks are set on point. There are eight diamond segments in each star except for the ones in the upper and left corners. There the large diamonds are composed of many smaller ones, pieced together to make the number of blocks for the desired quilt size. There is a subtle variance in shade of the pink print fabric, depending on the placement of the diamond template on the fabric for cutting.

The extensive quilting is a gridwork pattern of squares three-quarters of an inch apart in the quilt's main body. The stars are quilted with parallel lines one-half inch apart. The large border contains hanging diamonds quilted in a defined repeat of three-quarter and seven-eighths inch spacing. There is a pieced triangle border on all four sides. The narrow binding is three-sixteenths of an inch wide.

Mary Ann Wilson was born in Hardy County, Virginia to Isaac and Rebecca Wilson in 1824. In 1829, the family moved from this Appalachian Mountains county to Delphi, Carroll County, Indiana. Mary Ann married Alexander Monroe Berry (1817-1901) in Delphi on June 18, 1850. Leaving his family

behind, Alexander went west in 1854 with a group of friends looking for opportunity. He eventually arrived in Jacksonville, in southern Oregon. On Christmas in 1854, he entertained the Helmans (Quilt D-1) and other Ashland Mills residents with his fiddle playing. Talented as a carpenter, he and a partner James Kerr were the contractors for nearby Jacksonville's St. Joseph's Catholic Church (1858) and the Masonic/Courthouse (1859).[9]

In 1857, Mary Ann took their two young children, Isaac and Sarah, plus household furnishings from Delphi to New York City by railroad train. Because regularly scheduled rail passenger and freight service was available across northern Indiana at this time, she chose this option over travel west by riverboat and wagon train.[10] In New York, they boarded a ship for the east coast of Panama. The young mother and children then crossed to Panama City on the west coast by train. There they boarded the double wheel steamer *Golden Age*, bound for San Francisco, where they transferred to the *Goliath*, a single wheel steamer bound for Crescent City in northern California. From there, over the Siskiyou Mountains to Jacksonville, they traveled by pack-mule train managed by John Bilger.[11]

The family resided in Jacksonville until 1868, when Alexander built a substantial home on their farm, a place known as the Berry Farm. Here, Mary Ann faced the tragic loss of her daughter to illness and her son in an accidental shooting while hunting.

After the death of Alexander in 1901, Mary Ann moved to the home of her daughter, Alice Kane, in Ashland, Oregon. In 1908, at the age of eighty-two, this woman, known for her energy, made the train trip alone back to Delphi, Indiana. Two years later, while again visiting her Indiana family, she passed away.

Star. *Collection of Nancy Walker Morgan, Keizer*

D-3

Quilt: Basket
Category: Pieced
Size: 74" x 68"
Date: circa 1860s
Maker: Nancy Callaway Nye (1810-1883)
Year Over Trail: 1865
Came: As an older woman but unsure who brought her
County Where Settled: Clark County, Washington Territory, Umatilla County, Oregon

This pieced quilt of empty baskets is made with a predominance of four fabrics, indicating the quantities available to the quilter. The backing fabric matches the solid block fabric on the front. This fabric has faded from gray to tan, although it may have started as a purple. It is unusual and perhaps an example of why gray fabric does not appear often in quilts of this period.[12]

A note reading "Grandma Nancy's quilt, brought from Missouri" was attached to the quilt when it was found among her granddaughter's personal belongings after her death.

Nancy Callaway Nye is typical of the women in the study who came west as widows, accompanying or joining their children. The idea of staying behind when one's children "took leave" was difficult to accept and often encouraged and inspired a widowed mother, a maiden aunt, or a cousin to join the migration.

Nancy was born in 1810 in Ashe County, North Carolina, the daughter of Thomas Callaway and Elizabeth Ray Callaway. In 1826, the family moved to Wythe County, Virginia, where Nancy married Dr. James Madison Nye on August 26, 1826. They had twelve children over twenty-two years, between 1826-1848. In 1840 or 1841, the family moved to Boone County in central Missouri, along the Missouri River.

In 1850, Dr. Nye and his son William started for the gold fields. Near Little Blue River, Nebraska, Dr. Nye died of cholera, trying to save the lives of others. William became ill but recovered enough to return home, where he died within a year.

Gradually, as the other children grew, they migrated to the West, so that by the end of the Civil War, the majority of them were living in Oregon country. In 1865, Nancy made the long trek over the Trail to Vancouver, Washington Territory, where she lived with her son John Wirt Nye. It is unknown who she came with, except that a number of emigrants were coming to Oregon from the area of Missouri where she lived. So, no doubt, there were friends and

Nancy Calloway Nye (1810-1883)

neighbors she could have accompanied. After John's early death at age thirty-five, she moved to eastern Oregon, closer to her son Adam, in Umatilla County, Oregon and her daughter Martha Jane Mays, in Columbia County, Washington. In the 1880 Census Nancy Nye was living as a boarder with Marion and Ella M. Walker in Greasewood, Umatilla County.[13] She died in 1883 at the home of her son Adam.[14]

Detail of fabric fading

Basket. *Collection of Michael Woodroofe, Ann Arbor, Michigan*

D-4

Quilt: Pieced Star
Category: Pieced
Size: 87" x 87"
Date: 1869
Maker: Mary Whitley Gilmour (1788-1877)
Year Over the Trail: 1870
Came: With her adult grandchildren by railroad train
County Where Settled: Linn County

In the first edition of this book, this quilt was included in Part Two (1851-1855), because it appeared the quiltmaker came over the Trail by wagon with her daughter and son. However, later research yielded new information, especially from a personal statement by her granddaughter Helen Crawford for the dedication of a DAR marker in the Sand Ridge Cemetery in 1931. From the new information, it became evident that Mary Whitley Gilmour had remained in Illinois until later, when the trip would be significantly shorter and easier.

This richly quilted, vividly-colored masterpiece quilt is part of the large collection at the Daughters of the American Revolution Museum in Washington, DC. It is a tribute to a pioneer woman who made the journey at age eighty-two, after her grandchildren, Georgiana Henderson and James B. Crawford, traveled back to Illinois to escort her by railroad train to San Francisco and then to the Willamette Valley. She is the oldest woman in this project. Her life spanned the period of the Kentucky frontier to the Oregon frontier.

The quilt is composed of nine hand-pieced twenty-four inch stars. The fabric colors are typical of the mid-nineteenth century: cheddar, blue, and green with a pink, a white, and a brown print.

Four large white blocks of twenty-four inches contain large quilted wreaths and leaves, while twelve small, white twelve-inch squares have a pineapple or flower sprig quilted in each. There are also grids of diagonal parallel lines.

The quilting thread is a six-ply cotton and the binding machine stitched. Both support the date of completion as 1869.[15]

Mary Whitley was born in 1788 to Colonel William and Esther Fuller Whitley in the first brick house in Kentucky. Little is known about Esther Whitley's family but William was the son of Irish immigrant Solomon Whitley, who married Elizabeth Barnett around 1745. Mary's birthplace, now a registered early Kentucky landmark, contains her portrait, painted in the later years of her life. Built by her father in 1786, the house is called "Sportsman Hill" because of

Mary Whitley Gilmour (1788-1877). *Kentucky Department of Parks, William Whitley State Historic Site, Stanford, Kentucky*

the horse racetrack. Earlier, it was called "Whitleys Station," a Kentucky reference to the homesteads, established near a fort. The practice was called "settling out." A cabin for the family would be built near a fort and ten acres of corn would be planted on the land claim, thus staking it for the family.[16] The house was the center of Kentucky political activity until the first legislature convened at Danville following Kentucky's separation from Virginia. Colonel Whitley, a Revolutionary War patriot, represented his county at the first convention. The large brick letters W. W. in black headers over the front doorway indicate this, while similar brick letters E. W. indicate Esther's role of supervising the domestic activities in the home.

Mary Whitley married Dr. James Gilmour (Gilmore) in 1814. By 1833, when they moved to Warren County, Illinois, she had given birth to ten babies. After his 1847 death, she continued to reside in Warren County with her daughter Jane Worman and her family until after the completion of the transcontinental railroad in 1869. This afforded her the opportunity to travel west with her grandchildren to Oakland, California by the Overland Train, arriving there on November 27, 1870.[17] They then traveled up the coast by steamer and into the Valley by stage coach. During her seven years in Linn County before her death, Mary was a popular person to visit for reminiscences of the early pioneer life in Kentucky and Illinois.[18] According to the documentation, Mrs. Gilmour was a skilled needle woman. A neighbor, Mrs. James McKnight, engaged her to piece several quilts for her. This quilt was given by Mrs. McKnight to her daughter Roma Jane McKnight.

Pieced Star Quilt. *Daughters of the American Revolution Museum, Washington, DC. Photo courtesy of the Oregon State Society of the Daughters of the American Revolution 90.45*

D-5

Quilt: Wild Goose Chase variation
Category: Pieced
Size: 84" x 61"
Date: circa 1865-1880
Maker: Sarah Moody Fuson (1813-1898)
Year Over Trail: Came by railroad train after 1884
Came: Alone on the railroad train
County Where Settled: Umatilla County, Oregon

This handmade quilt was made by Sarah Moody Fuson, mother of Margaret Lieuallen, while she was in the Midwest. It has the migration theme of movement and change in its strip piecing of triangles. The quilt shows some wear, particularly in the fading from pink to white of the triangles near the center of each block. The elbow/fan quilting is again reflective of the period of time and purpose, making bed covers within a reasonable length of time for regular usage. This quilting pattern was also often used at group quilting bees.

The borders are interesting to speculate about since there are brown ones on three sides varying in size. The treatment is similar to Quilt C-6 with no border on one long side. Perhaps it was for a bed against a wall; perhaps she used what fabric she had and ignored the fourth side. The second border matches the fabric of the backing.

There was a strong bond between mother and daughter. According to family history, Margaret Lieuallen was reluctant to leave her mother, Sarah Fuson, in Missouri at the time of her 1864 marriage and migration. Sarah's response was that she would never leave her parents, who had provided a home for her and the four children when they had needed it. Her husband, James Fuson, had died in Knox County, Kentucky prior to the move to Missouri. In the 1860 Missouri Census, the family was living near her parents James and Margaret Moody in Morgan Township of Mercer County, on the north central edge of Missouri.[19] By 1870, Sarah and her mother, Margaret Moody, were living with her son William and his family in DeKalb County, in northwestern Missouri.[20] In 1880, Sarah was living with another son James and his family in Falls City, Richardson County, Nebraska.[21]

A family history note indicates that sometime after 1880, Margaret Lieuallen asked to have her mother come live with them and William was preparing to go for Sarah when she was put on the railroad train and came alone.[22] Northeastern Oregon, the area near the Lieuallen farm, was connected to the transcontinental railroad in 1884.[23] So her journey would have been after that date. Considering the number of places that Sarah lived during her life, one might wonder whether she intentionally chose the Wild Goose Chase block for her quilt.

At her death in 1898, a special coffin had to be made because she was so stooped.[24]

Detail of fabric and quilting

Wild Goose Chase Variation Quilt. *Collection of Don and Gilberta Lieuallen, Adams, Oregon*

D-6

Quilt: Fruit and Flowers Quilt
Category: Appliqué
Size: 89" x 89"
Date: circa 1855
Maker: Mary Carpenter Pickering Bell (1831-1900)
Where Made: Belmont County, Ohio

This masterpiece quilt was made while Mary waited for the return of her friend John Bruce Bell, who had gone to Oregon from Belmont County, Ohio, in 1850. This was unusual, in that most young people married before crossing the Plains, in order to claim more land acreage.

The quilt was located during the author's search for quilts of the Oregon Trail after reading documentation submitted by the family when the quilt was donated to the Smithsonian Institution. The history provided by Dr. Robert Bell read:

> This quilt was made by Mary Carpenter Pickering in about 1850-1854 at St. Clairsville, Belmont County, Ohio. Her friend, John Bruce Bell (1829-1912), had left St. Clairsville in 1850 to accompany a wagon train to Oregon Territory. The nineteen-year-old Mary started the quilt after his leaving "to make the time go more quickly," but he did not return until eight years later. They were married on September 3, 1861. He was shortly to join the Union Army for service in the Civil War, and while he was gone, Mary made another quilt, a "crazy" quilt which would be subjected to use ... John and Mary started their family in Ohio but in 1864 moved to Keokuk County, Iowa ... The quilt won her a Blue Ribbon at the Ohio State Fair in the early 1850's.[25]

In addition, there is a letter in the appendix written from Oregon in 1855 by Bell to Mary Carpenter Pickering. This charming letter contains much of the feeling generally expressed by newcomers to the Oregon Territory. He also addresses the loneliness of being separated from friends back home.

The nine appliqué blocks contain the same basket and flowers motif stitched in Turkey red fabric. Each of the plain white blocks features a different quilted and stuffed fruit or flower design. The unbalanced placement of the baskets suggests a less precise eye than the intricately designed stuffwork. This leads to the supposition that the appliqué work was done earlier than the quilting and stuffwork. A family member confirmed this when she stated that her grandmother began the quilt at age thirteen.

The discrepancy on the start date of a quilt can happen when one acknowledges the

(Left to right) Seated: John Bruce Bell and Mary Carpenter Pickering Bell; standing: Bruce, Maggie, and Frank Bell

confusion about the time it takes to make and finish a quilt, especially a masterpiece. Mary Carpenter Pickering probably began the appliqué work as a young woman, at age thirteen. Then, judging from the amount of work and time required to complete an intricate quilt, it probably took her at least four years to finish it.

Mary Carpenter Pickering was from a well-to-do Quaker family in Wheeling Township, Belmont County, Ohio. Her parents were Samuel and Sarah Pickering, from New York and Pennsylvania respectively. Mary had a refined appreciation for fine linen, silver, and furniture.

Bell was a Scotch Presbyterian. A patriot loyal to the Union, he was a man of his times, eager to see the West and serve in the Civil War. In Oregon, his name has been found only in the public record as an affidavit to citizenship being awarded to a British immigrant Edward Robson on April 9, 1855.[26]

According to family records, Mary and John were married September 1861 M.C.D., meaning "married contrary to discipline," referring to their different religious backgrounds.[27] The couple moved to Jackson Township, Keokuk County, Iowa, where they raised their three children. Her mother Sarah, brother William, and sister Elizabeth later joined them and were living to Keokuk County by 1870.[28]

Detail of quilting and block with "Mary C. Pickering St. Clairsville, Ohio" embroidered

Fruit and Flowers Quilt. *Museum of American History Smithsonian Institution, Washington, DC #81-5766*

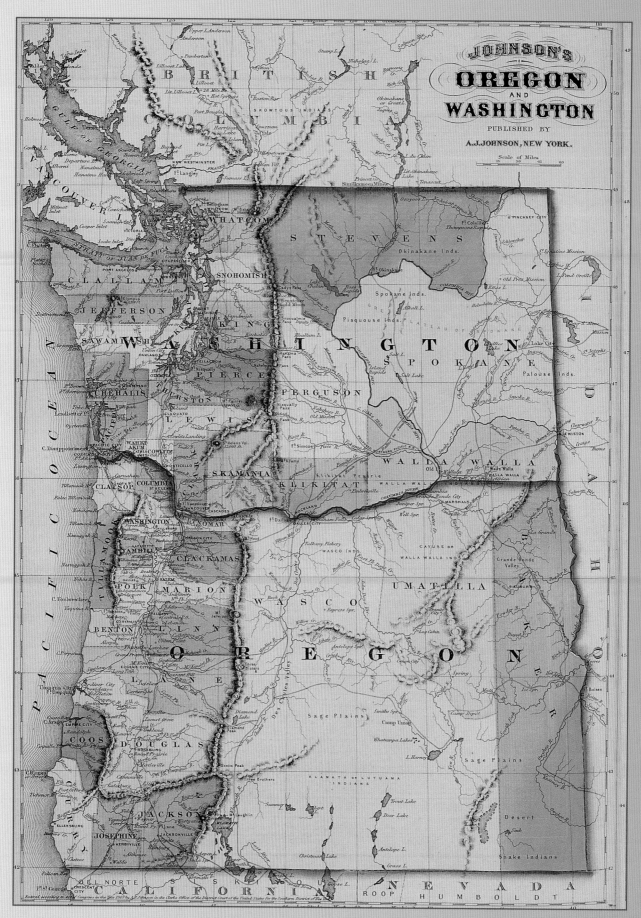

Counties in Oregon and Washington where Oregon Trail pioneers settled, circa 1865, *Collection of the author.*

Postscript

The Arrival

The challenging Trail experience, whether merely difficult or tragic, helped to ease the families and individuals into the frontier lifestyles they would be living once they reached Oregon. Having left the East in the spring, they would arrive in Oregon around December in the early years, or September in later years when travel was swifter. The average wagon train time "on the road" was four and one-half to five months.[1] The Reverend George H. Atkinson described the arrivals of early emigrants:

> An immigrant will come in during the Autumn, put himself up a log house with a mud & stick chimney, split boards and shingles, break eight or ten or twenty acres of prairie and sow it with wheat. You call upon him the next year & he will have a fine field ripe for the sickle. His large field will be well fenced with newly split fir rails. There will be a patch of corn, another of potatoes, & another of garden vegetables. Outside a large piece will be broken for the present year's sowing. His cattle & horse & hogs will be on the prairie, thriving and increasing without care. A few sheep may be around the house. He has a spring near. One of his children will be sent away 4 or 5 or 10 miles to a private school, taught by some young man or woman at $3 or 4 a term for each scholar. The farmer wears buckskin pants. His family are poorly clad. It is hard to get clothing. His wife has few cooking utensils, few chairs. No additions since they came into the Territory. The farmer takes his claim or buys it. He will only raise wheat & grain. He will make no improvements in his house until he knows whether Congress will allow his claim.[2]

First Stage of Frontier Development: Their Farms

Reflecting on the thirty-year period during which women and their families took the Trail to the Northwest, we can see that their lives mirror those of women found in other studies of the western frontier.[3] The first stage of establishing a home and farm took an average of two to five years. During this time, the skills developed while on the Trail served the women well, since they were living outdoors and sleeping in tents and wagon boxes. The first priority would be a place to winter over. The earliest period of Oregon Trail years (1840-1850) was difficult for the arriving emigrants since few people, houses, and services were in place. The Perkins family (Quilt A-4) noted the difficulty in finding housing during the hard winter of 1844. Elizabeth Currier Foster's family (Quilts A-8-11) was given shelter by a family in Rickreall during their first year of 1846. Tabitha Moffett Brown arrived on Christmas Day 1846 at a minister's home in Salem, at the end of her long journey.

This two- to five-year stage would be repeated by each group that arrived, but with differing degrees of services available, over the thirty-year span. Lansford W. Hastings wrote:

> A kindness and hospitality exist, among those pioneers of the west, which is almost unparalleled. Upon the arrival of emigrants, in the country,

immediate arrangements are made by the former settlers, to provide them with houses and provisions, and every aid is rendered them in making their selections of lands, and procuring houses for themselves … And I may add, that the Oregon emigrants are, as a general thing, of a superior order to those of our people, who usually emigrate to our frontier countries. They are not the indolent, dissolute, ignorant and vicious, but they are generally, the enterprising, orderly, intelligent and virtuous.[4]

During the second period (1851-1855), arrival and adjustment became easier for many who had either families or friends to receive them. During these years, between 30,000 and 35,000 people came into the Oregon Territory. Perhaps more than forty-five percent of Willamette Valley rural households had kinship and/or place of origin ties with at least one other household group in 1850.[5]

Before arrival, arrangements would have been made for a rental house or accommodations within family homes. By the end of their 1851 journey, the Robbins family (Quilt B-11) was ill and nearing starvation when they were rescued by their cousins William and Noah Herren and taken to a rented house in Salem for the winter. The Leonard family (Quilt B-2), of the Lost Wagon Train of 1853, were rescued by settlers of Lane County, the Harlows (Quilt A-17) being among the rescuers. The 1853 Bethel-Aurora scouts, including pregnant Emma Geisy (Quilt B-19), met with Captain U.S. Grant at Ft. Vancouver upon their arrival and followed his recommendation that they winter over at Ft. Steilacoom, a military outpost on the Puget Sound in Washington Territory where there was a cow available for possible milk supply. L. Jane Powell, pioneer of 1851, reminisced about their first winter in Oregon:

> We kept house over a year without a cookstove or fireplace irons or shovel … We commenced keeping house in December 1851 [after arriving September 16th, near the Santiam River in Linn County]. Our cooking utensils were: a teakettle, coffee pot, frying pan, stew kettle, two pans, and a deep skillet with a lid, to bake bread in. Grandpa bought wheat and had enough of it ground to do all of us through the winter. Pa and Uncle Steuben and Stephen worked to pay for it. William Earl had a large band of fat cattle to sell cheap for work. Pa and McFadden and Grandpa and Uncle Alfred would buy one, butcher and divide it, so we had plenty of good fat beef. Grandma and I did sewing and quilting for soap and potatoes. Dried apples was all the fruit we

had until wild strawberries and blackberries, which were plentiful and handy, were ripe … For several years wheat was used as legal tender, rated at one dollar a bushel. Wheat soon became very plentiful and was the main dependence for an income.[6]

Initially, early Oregon settlers hoped to recreate the kin-based, mixed subsistence-market agriculture they had known in the Midwest.[7] This changed with the discovery of gold in California in 1848. Many of the men, either before or after arriving in Oregon, left for the gold fields. Because of their close proximity to California (as compared to miners in the Midwest), these men generally were successful and returned with sufficient wealth, a total of some $5 million, to allow them to make improvements: better livestock, better buildings, and better equipment.

This led to expanding production and sales opportunities for their lumber, wheat, and beef. Merchants also profited with opportunities to pay off their existing debts. The later discoveries of gold in southern Oregon (1850) and eastern Oregon (1861) also sustained the economic boom and increased the population.[8] Since the medium of exchange was gold dust, even the Applegate women (Quilt A-2) profited. After a night of hosting returning miners, when they cleaned the east dorm room on the men's side of Charley Applegate's home, they would sift the gold dust from the dirt. Gleanings would be placed in Melinda Applegate's biggest blue sugar bowl and prominently displayed on the fireplace mantel, where its location caused others to contribute.[9]

For this period's first generation Oregonians, ownership of land was a primary motivating factor in coming West. Their plan was often to acquire property and maintain it for future generations to prosper and survive as farmers. The evidence for this was the small percentage in cultivation of their land claim. They cultivated twenty to thirty acres, only what was needed for their family to survive. Several of this era's men built their own racetracks and raced horses for competition and entertainment. These men included Harrison Wright (Quilt A-3), James Foster (Quilts A-8-11), Elias Buell (Quilt A-12), and William Vaughan (Quilt A-7).

Burial plots or family cemeteries on family land enabled a family to keep their loved ones close. This helped to keep the memory of significant loved ones and family members ever present in the minds of surviving family. The Applegate clan (Quilt A-2) had a cemetery on their Yoncalla land. The Dibble family (Quilts B 14-15) also had a family cemetery but allowed others in their community to be buried there, including Harrison Wright (Quilt A-3).

The placement on their acreage and style of their homes provided a sense of dignity for the family.[10] Often, they were placed on a knoll for a view or near a grove of trees. The homes were social centers for members who gathered

William Hatchette and Susan Mary Officer Vaughan House, Willamette Valley, circa 1895

to observe life passages, births, weddings, deaths, funerals, and community gatherings. Architectural styles were reminiscent of the New England salt boxes and colonial homes, with features that included symmetrically designed fronts, carved and turned window frames, a second story balcony, and quoins (wood blocks added to the corners). Through the years, those remaining have been identified as homes of the patriarchs of the family. Recently, with more awareness of the importance of women's domestic roles, the identifications are being changed to include her name as well.

The Foster house became the center for hospitality in the region. The house was built with space for a ballroom, which could be curtained off for dormitory sleeping. "Saturday night week ends," as they were called, were quite popular. Families would gather after the chores were done, about bedtime for the children, at a neighbor's home. Entertainment would be either a dance or a "gab fest" with embellished migration reminiscences always a favorite topic. The evening would close with singing. Sunday's activities would be games and amusements for the children, followed by a big dinner before everyone would start for home.[11]

During the first three years of the third period of migration (1856-1870), the numbers of people making the journey decreased to 5,000. In 1856-1857, this was partly due to the unsettled conditions between the Mormon settlement in the Salt Lake Basin and the federal authorities, increased hostilities with Native Americans along the Trail, and escalating tension in the States over issues related to slavery. The numbers increased over the next three years and then decreased again because of the Civil War.

Home of James and Elizabeth Foster, Summer Lake, Lake County, circa 1885.
Oregon State Society of the Daughters of the American Revolution Schminck Museum, Lakeview, Oregon

In this later period (1856-1870), arriving emigrants found established communities with full services available. The Simpson family, pioneers of 1853 (Quilt B-20), operated boardinghouses in Portland and later in Sterlingville in Jackson County. The four wagon trains arriving at the Aurora Colony in the 1860s found an established community ready to receive them.

> Aurora [was] like many other common villages of the period, with large houses lining the streets ... Each family appeared to have substantial food and clothing but there was no little ornamentation or luxury.
>
> There is evidently plenty of scrubbing indoors, plenty of plain cooking, plenty of everything that is absolutely necessary to support life ... and nothing superfluous.[12]

Although Aurora's communal society was a welcoming site, there was also dissension among the followers of Dr. William Keil, who, as a dynamic and forceful leader, defined the standards and regulated the activities. One was the practice of celibacy, with younger members discouraged from marrying and having children. Single men were housed at Keil's home and unmarried women remained at their family homes. This practice was considered less costly for the colony to support and inheritances were to revert to the colony upon death. Thus, there would be more money to operate the society.[13]

Emigrants arriving in the Valley by 1860 found most of the available land already claimed. About nine hundred thousand acres of land in the valley had been placed in production.[14] This encouraged many to end their overland journeys in eastern Oregon and southeastern Washington Territory. Many second-generation Willamette Valley pioneers also returned over the Trail for available land. Additional interest in this area was generated by the search for the lost Blue Bucket Mine of the 1845 migration. The mine was not found but the explorers, including Jacob Manley Currier (Quilts A-8-11) discovered the resources of gold, timber, and available rangelands.[15] Another reason for interest in the eastern Oregon area was resolution of the Indian Wars of 1855-56, in which the 9th Oregon Mounted Volunteers, including Plympton Kelly, secured the lands of the Columbia River Basin for Anglo settlement. (There is a ribbon on the Oregon Pioneer Ribbon quilt, C-1, recognizing the wife of an Indian War veteran, 1902-1903). These conflicts in the high plateau ended in the 1880s with the Indians' acceptance of dedicated reservations. The Lieuallen brothers (Quilts C-8-9) claimed their lands in northeastern Oregon. The Coyle family (Quilt A-6) moved from the Willamette Valley to the Walla Walla area of southeastern Washington. The families on the Wingville Quilt (Quilt C-2), including the Chandler, Osborn, Perkins, and Ison families, pioneers of 1862 and 1864, settled in the Baker Valley area of eastern Oregon.

Aurora women. *Oregon Historical Society, OrHi#770*

Second Stage of Frontier Development:
Their Communities

In general, studies of women on the frontier conclude that most women were desirous of returning to the nineteenth-century cultural norm of being a wife, mother, and housekeeper once they became securely established.

Several recent publications have studied the women's responses to their new Pacific Northwest environments. In his 1980 University of Oregon doctoral thesis, sociologist Christopher Carlson sought to understand rural Oregon women's cultural responses to the "sphere of domesticity." His research, which included some of this book's women, concluded:

> While they were familiar with the ideology of domesticity, rural women certainly did not view their role as lying there in the creation of private retreats. Instead, they viewed themselves as partners in the farm enterprise. It appears that rural women were struggling with this new ideology emanating from the east and the urban middle class and not exactly sure how it applied to their own lives. They accepted responsibility for the home and raising children but were unwilling to let go of their productive role in the family and the sense of importance it gave them. Therefore, while familiar with the ideology of domesticity, farmwomen expressed a view of the home as part of a work environment.[16]

Dean May concurred in his study of Sublimity in the Willamette Valley, *Three Frontiers: Family, Land, and Society in the American West 1850-1900.* Within the "kin/neighbor clusters" of farms and the individual family's efforts to establish their farm and maintain their land for future generations, women played an active role. Many of the important decision-making discussions took place within the social life centered in the family home, where the woman directed much of the social, spiritual, and economic activities. As the planner and administrator of the household economy, she determined the amounts to be planted, raised, and procured for her family to survive.[17] This early shared experience served many women well when they were widowed or their husbands became disabled. Jane Coyle (Quilt A-6), Elizabeth Wright (Quilt A-3), Jane Riggs (Quilt B-1), and Margaret Lieuallen (Quilts C-8-9) became the main decision makers in operating their farms.

Later, these farmwives were acknowledged as more independent than the city women because of the opportunity to earn pin money through selling eggs and butter, picking wild berries for jams and jellies to market, picking hops, and peeling bark from the American smoke trees for sale.[18] Among these quiltmakers, Susan Officer Vaughan (Quilt A-7) and Margaret Lieuallen (Quilts C-8-9) operated egg and butter sales routes; and Lucinda Cox Brown Allen Spencer (Quilt A-13) plaited straw bonnets and hats for income.

The second stage, community building, evolved from the first, or survival stage, as people began to establish social interaction through the need for resources such as educational and governmental units. Richard White comments in his 1991 *It's Your Misfortune and None of My Own: A New History of the American West* that this social interaction was based on recognizing members, bonding, and growing with one another. Although there is mutuality within community, there are also divisions based on gender and class divisions. Generally, while men remained in control, women maintained an informal social order through gossip, moral sanctions, and ability to bestow or withhold personal aid in times of need.[19]

Rozelle Applegate Putnam (1832-1861), a member of the Applegate clan (Quilt A-2), wrote to her husband Charles' family in Kentucky in 1852, describing their Yoncalla area in southern Oregon and expressing a hope that they would come to Oregon. In the letter, she responded to their question about neighbors and meetings:

...there is not a female beside in less than six miles—there are now four claims taken around us but the owners of them are all bachelors and likely to remain bachelors ... There is but one preacher in Umpqua, a Presbyterian who occasionally collects a few people, probably fifteen or twenty at a neighbors house, and holds prayers and addresses a few words of exhortation to them but these little gatherings are out of our reach & we only hear after they are over.★

With improvements on the farms and in the homes, women were freed to devote their time to other activities. As their social interactions increased and communities developed, several factors emerged that gave some of these female quiltmakers a sense of direction and purpose in their lives, which often included their quilting activities. First, there were Indians present when Anglos migrated to the West. Having overcome the much-publicized fear of Indians on the Trail, women who came into contact with them on their farms generally developed positive relationships with the Native Americans. The Riddle women (Quilts B-2-3) cared for their sick and negotiated agreements with the Rogue River area clans in the 1850s. Melinda and Cynthia Applegate (Quilt A-2) welcomed the two wives of the Yoncalla Chief Halo into their homes with their newborns. In exchange for their courtesy and assistance, the Indian wives, who gave birth to new babies as regularly as the Applegate women, gave their babies the same names.[20]

The second factor in the challenge to middle class families seeking a moral "quality of life" was the presence of the freewheeling, rootless men and women. These were the saloon crowd of wandering laborers and prostitutes. In the Oregon Territory, as elsewhere, an important aspect of community growth was the stability and respectability women provided to support the male investment of money, time, and energy. Women played an important part in community development because of their defined role as "moral reformers" by Victorian family standards. These institutions were considered extensions of women's roles as the keepers of purity and piety within their homes and families. The churches became the leading institution for shaping public morals. Their goals were to save souls, establish congregations, and reform society. Women left their homes and farms, taking their needles, thread, and quilting frames with them to their faith-based associations. Quilts like the Royal Presentation (Quilt B-13), the Oregon Pioneer Ribbon (Quilt C-1), and the Wingville Methodist Episcopal South (Quilt C-2) became concrete expressions of the members' shared values and worldviews. The Oregon Pioneer Ribbon Quilt has at least six badges for the W.F.M.S. (Woman's Foreign Missionary Society) of the Methodist Episcopal Church. Nationally, women created the Woman's Foreign Missionary Society in 1869 to address social needs in foreign lands. This was to compensate for being shut out of the all-male Methodist Episcopal Church General Conference meetings. Women wanted to make their contribution meaningful by creating their own organizations and retaining control over their activities. Through their annual meetings and regular publications, members across the country were made aware of efforts to solve the world's evils as they saw them.[21] In 1880, they formed the Women's Home's Missionary Society to address social issues within the states and territories.

Schools and churches were the first community buildings to be built, starting in the 1850s in the more settled areas. This spread across the state by the late 1860s and 1870s. Education offerings at all age levels became popular in Oregon's settlement. Schooling for children in the early years was offered by private academies sponsored by churches or by itinerant schoolmasters and 'marms. There were numerous quilt-related families involved in education: Mary Scoggin Chambers (Quilt A-5) provided housing for the schoolmistress in Washington County; Jesse Applegate (Quilt A-2) operated a school in his home; Abigail Scott Duniway (Quilt B-16) taught school in Eola and Lafayette; the Reverend J.H.B. Royal (Quilt B-13) taught at the Methodist Umpqua Academy in southern Oregon and established

Sunday Schools; David Roberts (Quilt C-11) was vice-president of the Waitsburg Academy; the Powell brothers (Quilt B-12) helped to establish Christian College; and Lucinda Leonard Worth (Quilt B-17) kept boarders attending that college in Monmouth.

As more settlers arrived with experiences in tax-supported schools, interest turned to the creation of public schools. Missionary Reverend George H. Atkinson' primary interest was education. He became known as the Father of Education in Oregon when he led the formulation and passage of the Oregon School Law in 1849. This replicated the New England and Iowa systems. Despite the early settlers' eagerness, it was not until 1872 that an effective public school program was established. Quilt owners continued to make contributions to education, however: Elizabeth Ann Kelly (Quilt C-1) taught in the Portland schools in the 1860s; Hester Hill (Quilt B-8) taught in the rural districts in Lincoln County for years; and George Mills (Quilt C-5) became the industrial instructor at the Chehalis Indian school in 1882.

For older children, generally male, settlers promoted lyceums, debating societies, literary clubs, and general discussion groups that provided the mental stimulation needed to balance physical labor. Later, women established similar organizations for ladies that focused on "culture." Churches often became the meeting places for the programs, providing not only the physical space but also often the lecturer. Libraries, either small private or semipublic, began to be established in towns and cities as early as 1850. They offered reading materials and a meeting place.[22]

The Chautauqua, a program of lectures and presentations by touring scholars, was "undoubtedly the greatest effort in organized adult education in the Pacific Northwest." Families would plan their vacation schedules around the dates of the programs and plan to stay the entire week or two. Early sites in the Northwest included LaGrande, Albany, The Dalles, Vashon Island on Puget Sound, and Gladstone Park near Portland, the third largest site in the country.[23]

For some, churches provided the only dependable, week-to-week entertainment for the community. Church functions were the only occasions that brought the entire community together; they became the only outlet for its social life, especially if dancing was considered sinful. In Wingville, the Methodist Church South had three weekly meetings: Sunday school, Sunday services, and Wednesday night prayer meeting. When revival meetings were held once or twice a year, almost everyone would attend, either to be annually "saved" or to be entertained.[24] After churches, the voluntary organizations were not far behind.

★The complete letter is in Triumph #3 in Appendix B.

These were often focused on self-interest and improvement: the grange associations, literary societies, and fraternal associations and their auxiliaries. Here, members could pursue their own goals more effectively. Founded as the Grange of the Patrons of Husbandry in 1866 in Boston, the Grange in Oregon became active in the early seventies and was more successful in Oregon than in other states. They were popular with women because the membership structure gave equal status to both men and women, reflecting the established partnerships on most farms. Meetings and activities were planned to draw the entire family into the social network. In addition, the Granges gave isolated farm women access to books, magazines, stereopticon views, correspondence lessons, and graphophone records through rural free mail delivery. They also hosted fairs and Chautauqua assemblies, and later, outings, and camps.[25] Making quilts, like the Oregon Pioneer Ribbon (Quilt C-1) and the Duniway (Quilt B-16), demonstrate avenues used to achieve those goals of self-interest and improvement. On the Pioneer Ribbon quilt, there are at least three badges for the Oregon State Grange. The Kellys helped to establish the Grange organization and played an important part in its Oregon history. There are also at least two ribbons from the Winslow Meade Circle #7 of the Ladies Grand Army of the Republic (G.A.R.) Portland, Oregon. This was an invitational social group with the mission of assisting Civil War veterans and their widows and orphans. Service in the war by a spouse was not a requirement for G.A.R. membership in Oregon. Neither Elizabeth Kelly's husband Plympton nor her son James Garfield Kelly served in the Union Army. The Duniway Quilt was made to donate to the First National Woman Suffrage Bazaar in 1899, but was purchased instead by the Portland Women's Club for the Oregon Historical Society.

Preserving the Experience

Pioneer Reunions

As the years passed it became evident there should be some means of preserving the past and saving it for the future. One means was through creation of the Oregon Pioneer Associations. They immediately became popular and their annual meetings were well attended. The program format included speeches and narratives of personal experiences, social interactions, and general reminiscences. These events were recorded and published in journals, including the *Oregon Pioneer Association Transactions*. Often group photos of old friends would be taken.

Oregon Pioneer Association flyer, 1876. *Oregon Historical Society, OrHi38005*

Reunion badges were often stitched onto show quilts to commemorate this group's activities and the individual pioneer's involvement. Several of these quilts are in collections across the country, including the Oregon Pioneer Ribbon (Quilt C-1) in the Museum of American Folk Art in New York and the Women's Relief Corp (WRC)/Oregon Pioneer Association Quilt in the Latimer Quilt and Textile Center in Tillamook, Oregon.

Oregon Pioneers, Champoeg Convention. (Left to right, back row): J.T. Hembree (1843), Cyrus T.Walker (1838), A.J. Haley (1843). (Left to right, front row): Edwin Eells (1841), Mrs. N.C. Bogart (1843), Wyman C. Hembree (1843), Mrs. Anne E. Hembree Cullen (1843), Vale N. Perry (1842). *Oregon Historical Society, OrHi53234*

Their Writings

Another avenue for preserving the past was through personal writings of memoirs and reminiscences, and publication of journals. Like many who experienced the major life change associated with migration, Grace Simpson Skeeters (Quilt B-20) recorded her experiences in a sixteen-page personal history. In addition to assisting her husband with his ministry, Emma Julia Cornell Royal, and later her daughter Emma (Quilt B-13), made the effort to collect family history and gather the many photographs important in documenting this significant family's contribution to settlement and church development in the Pacific Northwest. Even the men, like George Riddle (Quilts B-2-3) and W.B. Chandler (Quilt C-2), reminisced about and celebrated women's participation in migrating and in developing the culture of Oregon.

In 1932, Burt Brown Barker, grandson of Lucinda Cox Brown (Quilt A-13), commissioned *The Pioneer Mother* sculpture by Alex Proctor for the University of Oregon campus. The sculpture honors Barker's mother, Elvira Brown Barker, and all other pioneer mothers. Barker, as university vice-president, wrote the dedication:

The Pioneer Mother

"Others have perpetuated her struggles; I want to perpetuate the peace which followed her struggles. Others have perpetuated her adventure; I want to perpetuate the spirit which made the adventure possible. And the joy which crowned her declining years as she looked upon the fruits of her labor and caught but a faint glimpse of what it will mean for posterity.

I want to recall her as I recall my mother Elvira Brown Barker, a pioneer of 1847, in the sunset of her life after the hardships and the battles and the sorrows of pioneering were past and she sat in the afterglow of her twilight days resting from her labors. All her hardships and sorrows have softened in the telling in her later life. And her rugged endurance has mellowed with her fading memory but to us there lives that spirit of conquering peace which I wish posterity to remember."

May 11, 1932
Burt Brown Barker

The Pioneer Mother by Alex Proctor, 1932. *Oregon Historical Society, OrHi78952*

Their Needlework

The importance of needleskills in their lives was not forgotten. One pioneer of 1843, Bethina Owens-Adair, made a significant contribution in 1906 to the preservation of Oregon's early history by acknowledging the struggle women had to gain recognition and "make it respectable to earn her honest bread by the side of her brother, man." In her book, *Some of Her Life Experiences*, she included her mother Sarah Damron Owens' story and the loneliness she experienced:

> I think the most unhappy period of my life was the first year spent on Clatsop, simply for the want of something to do. I had no yarn to knit, nothing to sew, not even rags to make patches ... One day Mrs. Parrish gave me a sack full of rags and I never received a present before nor since that I so highly appreciated as I did those rags.[26]

Bethina Owens-Adair (1840-1926), along with her parents Thomas and Sarah Owens and her brother and sisters, came west in 1843 with the Applegate party (Quilt A-2). They lived on the Clatsop Plain until about 1853, during which time Mrs. Elizabeth Winn Parrish, wife of the Methodist missionary Rev. Josiah Parrish, was there as well. Bethina acknowledged her parents' contribution to textile resources on the Clatsop. On Good Friday in 1844, following the old custom, Sarah Owens planted the first flax in Oregon with seed she had brought from Kentucky. From the first crop's floss, she had enough to pad two quilts and spun shoe-thread to stitch her first pair of elk-skin shoes. From her later crops, she traded flax for salmon with the Native Americans. Her husband, Thomas, introduced the first sheep to the Clatsop Plain about 1847. He soon had a profitable business from the wool and the lambs.[27]

Recognized as one of the outstanding women in Oregon history, Bethina had a most successful life after an early marriage failed. One of her mentors was Jesse Applegate, whose advice was always an incentive. She went from being an illiterate young mother at age eighteen to becoming a successful doctor at age fifty. Her career history is fascinating and encouraging; she was a laundress, a teacher, a seamstress, and a millinery shop owner.[28]

Sewing machines and supplies were available fairly early in Oregon. Reference to them was made in publications like "The Darning Needle Story" about Grandma Drain (Quilt B-10), which is found in Triumph #8. Elizabeth Currier Foster's hand operated sewing machine at the Schminck Museum has a patent date of 1867 (Quilts A-8-11). The life story of Artenecia Riddle Merriman (Quilt B-3) notes her ownership of the first sewing machine, which she eagerly shared with her Rogue Valley neighbors. A clue to the distribution and sales of sewing machines appeared in the Talent, Oregon *News*, which noted when reporting the 1893 death of B.C. Goddard (Quilt C-6) that "He crawled to the house ... where about four hours later he was found lying on the porch by a sewing machine agent who at once went for assistance."[29]

Their Quiltings

Quilting and the quilts comprised another way of preserving the experience. Once settled in Oregon, women, especially older women, often returned to quiltmaking as a means of connecting with one another and of enjoying an experience previously rewarding and useful in their lives back East.

Two historic photos illustrate that return and the transition in community quiltmaking at the turn of the twentieth century. The first shows the family of Elizabeth Byers Stout, pioneer of 1853, taken on the North Santiam River circa 1900, when her adult married daughters returned for a visit from their Willamette Valley homes. It illustrates the continuing popularity of quilting among the older women, who are seated around the frame, while the younger women, standing behind, are not quilting. By this time, Oregon's economic growth and prosperity was such that many young women were freed from household labor and isolation, allowing them to pursue other goals. For example, many of the established Oregon woolen mills were making inexpensive blankets available.

Quilting Party at Mehama on the North Santiam River, circa 1900. *Oregon Historical Society, #889*

The second photo shows an Oregon quilting party at Mother Howlett's in the Eagle Point area of southern Oregon, taken in 1907 when her daughter's family visited. Mother Sarah Cooke Howlett played an important community role from 1901-1936 as the owner of the hotel, which served as the schoolroom, the infirmary, and public dining place. The number and age range of the women present indicates the value this woman had within her community.[30]

By 1890, railroads had been built through southern Oregon to the California border and through eastern Oregon to Idaho, making transportation easier and more comfortable than by stagecoach. By 1900, instead of Sunday afternoon drop-ins or family dinners among Willamette Valley pioneers, families would come to visit for longer periods of time—a week or more. People would spend time planning their visits and the activities associated with them. Quiltings were often one activity.[31]

As these women began to reflect publicly and privately on their Oregon Trail experience with the tools they had been taught to use—needles, pens, and books—they created treasures to share their lives. Their quilts and their written work are the records of their dreams and memories—disappointments and trials as well as accomplishments. Especially significant are the Harlow Album Quilt (Quilt A-17) and the Bonnett Crazy Quilt (Quilt B-21), in which the makers recorded their names and ages showing the importance of having survived their Oregon Trail experience and settlement. Grandma Harlow's quilt further shows the importance of her immediate community of family and hired help.

Through their treasured quilts, these women clearly demonstrated the conclusions of other studies of westering women by Butruille, Jeffrey, Myres, Riley, and Schlissel. While staying within the roles permitted by society, and overcoming the hazards of migration and settlement, these women showed their determination in making a successful transition. Once settled, they demonstrated the themes identified by Jean Ward and Elaine Maveety in *Pacific Northwest Women 1815-1925* as exhibited by other women. These included connecting with nature, coping with circumstances, caregiving to others, and communicating for self and others.[32] Their quilts, as visual records of their experiences that raised awareness of their names and stories, will continue to celebrate their contributions to Oregon's history.

Quilting Party at Mother Howlett, Eagle Point, September 1907. *Southern Oregon Historical Society, #216*

Analysis of these Treasures

Themes

Classifying the individual quilts into themes requires that one consider the options available and not available to mid-nineteenth century women. Each woman's life experience was unique. While many had a limited amount of formal education, most had extensive needlework skills. While most were occupied with producing bed linens and clothing needed in their home, many had time to create special quilts expressing passages of their lives. Although many women were isolated on the frontier, most eagerly shared their lives with one another whenever opportunities arose. While each person's preconceptions affected how they experienced the trip, all were exposed to the "shaping power" of the West on their environment. While quilts have generally been thought to have been made in one place and time, it is now known that many were begun in one location and carried to another for later completion.

The two themes most clearly identified with these quilts are those of celebration and migration. Celebration themes reflect significant events or honors in people's lives. They celebrate weddings, births, faithful service, accomplishments, and successes. The most important celebration found in this book is for having survived the wagon trip to Oregon and successfully established one's life and family in the new territory. The quilts with this theme serve as visual evidence of these women's desire to continue the feminine role of domesticity associated with nineteenth-century women back in the States, as well as to extend their role in their communities as active contributors. Several outstanding examples include the Harlow Album (A-17), the Royal Presentation Album (B-13), and the Bonnett Crazy (B-21) all with individuals' names; and the Oregon Pioneer (C-1) with its badges of pioneer associations. The Harlow Quilt was made by Frances Harlow in 1898 to celebrate her family with the names of all female family members, one grandson, and her housekeeper. Her block near the center carefully records the fact that she pieced the quilt at age eighty-three and proudly states her role as Grandma.

The Royal Presentation Quilt was made for The Reverend J.H.B. Royal in 1868 with the names of the daughters who lived along the Methodist Circuit Rider route he covered in southwest Washington Territory. This signifies the passing of the moral responsibility for caring for the church and their minister from the mothers to the daughters. It helps to clarify their future role in their communities.

The Crazy Quilt (B-21) bears the inscription "Mrs. Annis Bonnett Age 72 1894" proudly and boldly stitched across the ribbon on the quilt's front. This clearly states who she was and what she accomplished in 1894 at age seventy-two.

The Oregon Pioneer Ribbon Quilt (C-1) was assembled by Elizabeth A. Kelly and presented to her granddaughter as a visual record of her family's on-going celebration of their heritage and contribution to Oregon's growth.

Migration themes reflect nature or an outdoor experience, movement or change of location, friendship, and well being. They are expressed through interpreting objects connected to the pioneer era, such as an old fashioned flower or a log cabin. They can be graphically inscribed with actual words or symbols; they can be visually perceived through pattern and design; often, they can be a visual appeal of support from a higher power, an appeal for divine guidance through the harrowing experience the pioneers faced crossing the Plains.

Much of early life in America was spent outdoors—improving the land, planting and raising food and flowers, doing the tasks of washing, preparing food, preparing materials for cloth production, and making candles and soap. Using nature as a theme in quilt design was an established tradition. The quilts made before or brought over the Trail or made while waiting confirm this: Chambers (A-5), Currier Foster (A-9), Greer (B-6), Propst (B-12), Colver (C-6), Helman (D-1), and Pickering Bell (D-6).

This outdoor experience of the overland journey had a major effect on women's outlook toward nature. The unknown physical and emotional hazards and weather changes affected how they created a design from it. This is evident in the Glover Quilts (A-14-15) made while on the Trail, one with the reference to wind and the other with the reference to stars.

Quilts made after the Trail experience continued to use nature as a theme, but with a stronger expression and meaning. The Gilfrey Quilt (A-18) with its name of "Hovering Hawks and Peonies" is the most prominent example. The use of the adjective and noun to describe the triangular-shaped birds gives a sense of threat and power to the quilt's meaning. The peony has long been recognized as one of the hardest flowers to transplant, often taking three to four years before blooming again, thus adding an increased significance to the wish for recovery. This quilt was made about fifteen years after the migration of a young daughter traveling with her parents. A second quilt, the Weaver (B-9), which also uses triangles as birds and diamonds as peonies, carries the same message of movement and healing, subtle but encouraging images to someone traveling the Oregon Trail in the 1850s. It is interesting to note that the Weaver quilt was made in 1848, before the family's 1853 migration, by the aunt or grandmother who did not make the journey to Oregon but who had experienced a major migration in her own life, coming from Ireland to Ohio.

Quilt Patterns

These shapes and their designs have pattern names that are often easily identifiable. A word of caution is necessary at this point. Including quilt pattern names that are as universally known and widely used as Double Irish Chain and Drunkard's Path does not mean that *all* quilts using those patterns refer to migration or reflect a woman's Trail experience in the nineteenth century. Instead, if a quilt has these patterns and *all* the other clues point to the time frame of being made within the possible life span of someone who traveled the Trail, then it is probable that the maker wished to express a theme of migration in her quilt.

The easiest quilts to identify for these themes are those with actual documentation written on the quilt or in supporting notes that accompany them. Usually these have the name and date of someone directly connected to the quilt, and this information is traceable and accurate. This attention to detail by including this information confirms that the makers were using their needles and thread to convey themes meaningful to the events of their lives. The Robbins (B-11), known as the Oregon Rose Quilt, has the names and date of the family on it, along with scattered quilted initials, hearts, and wheels. It also is accompanied by extensive written documentation about who made the quilt and when.

Representational Designs

Birds, flowers, leaves, stars, and other objects found in nature have long been used as sources for design in both appliquéd and pieced quilts to express these themes. Quilt historian Elly Sienkiewicz compiled a lexicon of nineteenth-century flowers, birds, and fauna. The sentimental meanings identified for the objects appearing in these quilts are:

Dove: innocence, Holy Spirit, purity, peace – Chambers (A-5), Stone (B-18)
Grape: blood of Christ in the Eucharist – Chambers (A-5)
Hawk: divination – Gilfrey (A-18)
Honeysuckle: devotion, generous affection, mirth, love's bond, "we belong to one another" – Colver (C-6)
Peony: healing – Weaver (B-9), Gilfrey (A-18)
Pine Tree: fidelity, boldness, everlasting life, stability, venerability – Helman (D-1), Wingville (C-2)
Pineapple: hospitality – Gilmour (D-4)
Rose, full blown: "I love you" – Crawford (A-1), Robbins (B-11), Stone (B-18)
Rose of Sharon: romantic love, from Song of Solomon – Currier Foster (A-10)
Star: divine guidance – Chambers (A-5), Currier Foster (A-8), Riggs (B-1), Lieuallen (C-9), Berry (D-2), Gilmour (D-4)
Sunflower: homage, devotion – Stauffer (C-3)
Tulip: renown, fame, spring, dreaminess – Perkins (A-4), Vaughan (A-7), Propst (B-12),
Wheel: symbol of divine power – Glover (A-14-15)[1]

Geometric Shapes

Squares in pieced-pattern quilts give a visual sense of movement through the use of line, defined as the connection between two dots. Line has been an important design element in arts and crafts, for it serves to carry the eye across the design surface. This is especially true with diagonal lines. Nineteenth-century quilt makers knew this and they created line by piecing squares and triangles together. The Double Irish Chain is made by placing colored squares corner to corner as single units or units of nine to create lines or chains. The Double Nine Patch achieves the same affect through the use of color to make the line. There are a number of examples in the study, the Merriman (B-3) and Dibble Sawtell (B-15), as well as the Johnson Quilt at the Bowman Museum in Prineville, Oregon.

The same objects of birds, flowers, and stars stitched onto appliqué quilts are included in some of the book's thirty-eight pieced quilts. Here the design is more by implication through the use of geometric shapes than a representation.

Triangles are used to represent birds, mountains, and directional movement. Triangles pieced in clusters have been called Birds in Flight in Riddle (B-2) and Hovering Hawks and Peony Quilt in Gilfrey (A-18).

Triangles in a line appear as mountains in the Purdom/Leonard Delectable Mountains (B-17) and the Hargrave/Whiteaker Wandering Foot Quilt (B-7). They appear as the horizon in "Setting Sun" in Greer (B-6),

Triangles pieced in short lines give a sense of movement in the Drain quilt, Road to California (B-10). Other times the strips are used as radiating spokes and called Wild Goose Chase, as in Fuson (D-5), and Stars with Wild Geese, as in Lieuallen (C-9). Sometimes a long single line is called Flying Geese, as in Weaver (B-9). Other times, triangles pieced in a long line are popularly called Wild Goose Chase. The repeat pattern creates a sense of movement from one location to another. This imagery was also used in the writing of the period. John H. Clark wrote in 1852 about his trip to the California gold fields, "I was leaving all that was near and dear to me for a "wild goose chase."[2]

Triangles clustered together are used to create basket quilt patterns. Baskets were vitally important to the nineteenth-century person. They were used for many activities, from carrying to storing a wide range of household items including food, clothing, and other household items. The various sizes and styles matched the many needs. To a woman like Melinda Applegate (A-2), her sewing basket was one of her most important possessions, holding her notions and thread and keeping special treasures. Two of the basket quilts, Coyle (A-6) and Nye (D-3), contain empty baskets. Perhaps these signal an anticipation of future use and a sense of optimism, both important to a migrating woman. Three of the quilts have baskets containing flowers: Currier Foster (A-9,11), and Pickering Bell (D-6). These quilts reflect the trend of placing flowers in baskets that began in England in the 1820s and spread to America by mid-century. The later-made Vaughan Quilt (A-7) with its Tulip in Vase pattern also continued this popular interest of placing a few flowers in vases and incorporating the design on a quilt.[3]

Rectangles represent fish in Flashing Minnow in Cox (A-13). They represent movement in water and perhaps, the circumstances surrounding the death of the maker's young husband on the Trail.

Curved Pieces, as they appear in the Dibble quilt, Oregon Trail (B-14), are a variation of the popular pattern commonly referred to as Drunkard's Path because of its connection to a statement of physical condition and a sense of wandering in confusion. Brackman lists sixty-three names for the twenty-eight different arrangements of the blocks.[4] Here there is a direct connection to the Oregon Trail pioneer quiltmaker and the migration experience.

The Bryan quilt (C-10) was called Bachelor according to the family history. There is also a variation called Whirlwind connected to movement.

Diamonds as *Stars* have a long history of use in quilt pattern names, since most people were living in a world where astronomical elements influenced their daily routines. Here they have a migration theme with reference to divine guidance. Those traveling into the world of the unknown were placing their fate in God's hands, and they asked for help and guidance. An example of that faith would be the Pieced Star Quilt (D-2) made by Mary Ann Wilson Berry. She made the quilt while waiting for word from her husband, who had gone west leaving her with two small children in Indiana.

The Eight-Pointed Star (C-7) by Ersula Goddard Robison Dean, also called "Rolling Star," was noted as a diamond pattern.

The Wheel (A-15) is the name used by Sarah Koontz Glover. While more traditionally referred to as a star pattern, it deserves further exploration.

Wheel Patterns

As an element describing movement and rotation, the wheel is a strong migration theme. Beginning with the nineteenth-century meaning of the word as a symbol of divine power, it connects with the strong faith these people had in God as they began their journeys. Their diaries and letters contain many references to God and religion. One of the strongest examples was the prayer found in The Reverend J.H.B. Royal's papers. This prayer was in response to President William Henry Harrison's national request for ministers to pray for an end to the cholera epidemic.

The pioneers depended on wheels to carry them across the Plains, and they felt great despair when wheels were broken and a wagonload of precious objects had to be abandoned.

The wheel was important in people's lives to the degree that a wheelwright, the maker of wheels, was a respected occupation. Royal Hazelton, the father of Amanda Gilfrey (A-18), was a wheelwright. The family history notes the ease with which they joined a wagon train because of his profession.

Once a family was settled, wheels continued to be important in sheltering and feeding the family. Two of the first businesses to be established in the Oregon country were the sawmill and the gristmill, which used wheels to turn the saws and the mill stones. Elias Buell, husband of Sarah Hammond Buell (A-12), established the first mills in Polk County. Eli Perkins, husband of Sally Hull Perkins (A-4), set up the first mills in Yamhill County in the mid 1840s.

Further demonstration of the wheel's importance is the recognition that wagon wheels have long been kept as treasures and displayed at museums and private homes as symbols of success in the journey across the Plains.

In this project, wheels were pieced or appliquéd into the quilt tops and were also quilted into the design set or scattered over the surface of the quilts. The pieced quilts include the Wheel of Fortune (A-3) made by Lavina E. Frazier Wright after her 1843 journey; and the two Glover quilts, Pinwheel (A-14) and Wheel (A-15) pieced during Sarah Koontz Glover's journey westward in 1849. Another appliqué quilt studied for the project with a wheel motif was made by the mother of George W. Starr. He brought it to Oregon in 1876 (after the project's time line) when he was a young man of nineteen. It has red and green circles appliquéd along the border.

Wandering Foot Pattern

Another pattern name and design important in westward expansion and the Oregon Trail was called Wandering Foot. Today, the pattern is more commonly known as Turkey Tracks, whether it is pieced or appliquéd. In this project, it occurred three times in those brought to Oregon between 1850-1855, in the Hargrave/Whiteaker (B-7), Patterson (B-8), and the Morris (B-4).

Throughout American pioneer history, wanderlust, the desire to wander by men and boys to answer the call for exploration whether for gold, free land, or adventure. The desire to explore and settle the nation was a virtue to be celebrated in the days of building the country and strengthening the economy. Thus, making a quilt of this pattern was a way of sending a family member off to achieve his country's goals and/or find his fortune.

Exploration was a profession and travel a cultural exercise during the mid-nineteenth century. There were stories of families whose husbands and sons left for the West, not to be heard from for years or perhaps forever. An interesting discovery was made about this project's three Wandering Foot quilts, which were brought to Oregon in the years immediately following the Gold Rush and major migrations in the Midwest and Far West. The makers of these three quilts would have had the skill and time to devote to the accuracy required in the curved piecing and appliqué work. Two of the three quilts were made by relatives and sent west with the owner. The third was made while on the Trail by a married woman coming to join her parents. Another interesting factor about the Wandering Foot pattern is that it requires an advanced skill level in order to complete. This family connection reveals another difference with the quilts of my Mormon Migrations Quilt Project. There were no Wandering Foot quilts found in this latter study. Two possible explanations exist for this. Perhaps it was because they migrated with more complete family units—parents, children and grandchildren. Or, perhaps it was because if they left families behind, the separation was fostered by conflicts of religious beliefs and affiliations.

This pattern was also called Wandering Foot by an early twentieth-century quilt book author, Ruth Finley. She emphasized gathering the traditional pattern information from the makers in the area of Ohio and the East. Her goal was to make a definitive record of quilts as folk art and an interpretation of them within the time frame of their construction, the nineteenth century. She is now recognized as having gathered the facts but she romanticized them as myths and legends through her interpretation.[5] This pattern is a case in point.

Finley made the pattern mythical with the idea that sleeping under a Wandering Foot would encourage wanderlust and a tendency toward a discontented, unstable, and roving disposition. For a young girl, it was a bad influence. For a young boy, it could be fatal. "No bride with an ounce of good sense risked piecing a 'Wandering Foot' for her dower chest."[6] Over the years, though, as communication and transportation methods improved, the name was changed to Turkey Tracks in an effort to dispel the curse and save the quilt pattern.[7]

My supposition is that the name change occurred in the late 1800s as people began to settle down on one piece of property for a longer time, when, through westward migration, they had acquired large enough farms to be able to divide the property among sons and daughters and thus keep them connected to one location. At the same time, job opportunities in new towns were being created, eliminating the need to explore or travel or venture out to make a living. This is supported by Dean May's evidence that early settlers to the Willamette Valley sought to claim land that was to support and sustain their families for generations. They claimed large acreage but farmed just enough to provide what they needed with plans to save the land for future generations.[8]

The focus of the quilter could turn from the worry and sadness brought on by the departure of family members migrating to the challenges of operating a homestead and farm. The tasks of tending the chickens, milking the cows, and caring for the geese and turkeys became women's work, as men tended to work in the fields or off the farm. The on-going task of keeping track of wandering turkeys could now be expressed humorously in a quilt pattern. The vision of four turkeys fleeing four directions at one time is clear in the pattern's design.

While a number of quilts with the name Turkey Tracks are found in collections today, some likely were contributed without a name or were given one that was contemporary to the cataloger's or donor's life rather than the maker's. Some of the cotton quilts with the name Turkey Tracks on the inventory cards are actually Wandering Foot, made in the period when exploration and wanderlust were considered something important a boy had to accomplish to become a man.

Log Cabin Pattern

The pieced quilt pattern group called Log Cabin has long been a symbol of new land and settlement. This was especially true in the Pacific Northwest, where large enough trees were readily available on most property claims. To make the quilt, strips of fabrics or "logs" are stitched around a center square built one upon another until the block size is complete. There are two wool quilts in the project. One was made by Grace Simpson Skeeters (B-20) years after her 1853 migration. The other, not included in the book, is a brown and blue one made by Margaret Bailey (1830-1907) in the 1860s prior to her move from Illinois to Oregon. It is part of the Junction City Historical Museum collection at Junction City.

Fabric Colors

There were eighteen red and green appliqué quilts made throughout the entire Trail time span. This color combination,

with added touches of pink, orange, and blue, and the construction dates between 1840-1865 corresponds with the general popularity of these quilts with women of the mid-nineteenth century. This style of quilt has been classified as the classic floral pattern by quilt historian Ricky Clark. She identified the characteristics as: "predominantly red and green color scheme on a white ground, repeated blocks surrounded by a related border, and a red or green binding, and conventionalized botanical motifs that are simplified, flat, and two-dimensional."[9] Ten of these quilts were made before the women came over the Trail, with several being created while they prepared to leave. The Robbins Oregon Rose (B-11) and the Powell Propst Tulip (B-12) were known to be made by relatives and friends as the families prepared to leave. In contrast to the quilts in my Mormon Migrations Quilt Project, these indicate that relatives and neighbors had time to create these labor-intensive quilts as gifts for their leave-taking friends and kin. The Mormons had only one red and green quilt of this style among their Trail heirlooms. That one was completed while the women and children waited at Winter Quarters in the winter of 1846-1847.[10] For their migrations, they were forced to flee and/or limited in the amount they could carry.

Some of the quilts contain the prized Turkey red print fabrics imported from the British Isles in the mid-nineteenth century. This was a colorfast dye used to create prints reminiscent of the fabrics from Turkey. These expensive fabrics were not produced in America because production involved a time-consuming and labor-intensive process of thirteen to twenty steps in a very long timeframe. Because of the cost, dressmakers and seamstresses usually limited the amount and use of the fabric to very special projects. The quilts that contain Turkey red were of that category. They include Currier Foster (A-9-11), Riggs (B-1), Weaver (B-9), Helman (D-1), and Pickering Bell (D-6).

The eleven indigo-blue and white quilts found in this study support Brackman's conclusion that the high quality fabrics available to mid-nineteenth century quilts were more expensive than other fabrics because of the colorfastness. Quilters here demonstrate their ability to plan and adjust the amount of indigo fabric required in their designs. Cecelia Hargrave (B-7) used the indigo fabric as the ground, requiring more of it. Jane Riggs (B-1) used indigo fabric only in the diamond point of each star, thus requiring significantly less. The maker of Coyle (A-6) required larger indigo triangles for the basket pattern, while Artie Riddle Merriman (B-3) and Eliza Dibble (B-15) used small one-and-a-half inch squares to create their nine patch blocks. Nancy Drain (B-10) and Catherine Purdom (B-17) used a medium amount of indigo blue, with the Drain quilt having one print and the Purdom/Leonard having fifteen different prints. Maximillia Riddle placed the seven triangular indigo pieces in the very center of her fabric, the place of most importance to many quilters.

Quilting Designs

The stitched lines used to hold the layers of the quilt together often carry meaning in their designs and symbols. Among these quilts, the following arrangement of quilting designs exist.

Scattered. This term refers to random placement over the quilt's surface. This was a format often used with appliqué quilts of the mid-nineteenth century. Hearts, wheels, stems of flowers, and leaves, as well as initials and dates, are there, often to be discovered by the curious eye. These are the clues within the quilt regarding date, people, and meanings. Often there is more than one of these motifs in a quilt. For example, there are wheels in five quilts: Buell (A-12), Robbins (B-11), Stauffer (C-3), Mills (C-5), Colver (C-6), and Morgan (C-11).

Block by block. In the period 1840-1870, quilt designs moved away from the whole cloth, central medallion, or large appliqué blocks to the smaller format of pieced blocks. The appearance of the quilting designs changed with the advent of a block-by-block repeat of a quilting design. This design is often a wreath or sunflower. Quilts with this format include: Crawford (A-1), Merriman (B-3), Dibble Sawtell (B-15), Women of Aurora (C-4) and Gilmour (D-4).

The Weaver (B-9) and the Pickering Bell (D-6) quilts have the additional feature of stuffwork. As the quilting was completed, the petals of the wreaths and the pieces of fruit were stuffed with cotton to give extra height and visual appeal. Women who had the extra time to devote to quilt-making made both quilts in Ohio, where doing stuffwork was popular.

All-over. Quilting styles began to change from elaborate close quilting and stuffing to simpler forms, as demands on women's time increased and as they grew older. They began to use faster ways of drawing patterns and designs easier to mark and quilt. All-over patterns of straight lines and grid work placed equal distance apart were drawn and quilted. The Coyle (A-6), Cox (A-13), Lieuallen (C-8) and Berry (D-2) quilts are examples.

The curved lines of elbow/fan quilting were also easy to place for quilting. A series of marks were spaced equidistant along a board. As the lines were needed, the elbow, as the pivot point, was placed on the appropriate mark and the line drawn as the arm swung the curve across the quilt. This process was repeated until all the lines were marked within a given distance. It is usually easy to identify the quilt corner where the marking was begun. A number of the quilts have this style, including: Wright (A-3), Morris (B-4), Giesy (B-19), and Fuson (D-5).

The third style where the quilting line echoes the line of the pieced pattern is called echo. Additional lines fill in the space, either repeating the pattern of the first or establishing a gridwork. Quilts with this format include Currier Foster (A-11) and Morgan (C-11).

Using these data and conclusions as a guide, clues are now available to study other migration-related quilts. Owners and families are encouraged to compare their treasures with those found in trunks of families, museums, and historical societies, lovingly preserved and interpreted for an interested and caring public. Educators are encouraged to include the meaning of the different pattern designs in their units on western migration and settlement.

Quilt List

Maker/Family	Year	Quilt Name	Nbr	Page
Crawford	1842	Seth Thomas	A-1	18
Applegate	1843	"Wedding Dress"	A-2	20
Frazier Wright	1843	Wheel of Fortune	A-3	22
Perkins	1844	Red and Green Tulip	A-4	24
Chambers	1845	White on White	A-5	26
Coyle	1845	Basket	A-6	28
Officer Vaughan	1845	Tulip in Vase	A-7	30
Currier Foster	1846	Star	A-8	32
Currier Foster	1846	Poke Stalk	A-9	34
Currier Foster	1846	Rose of Sharon	A-10	36
Currier Foster	1846	Mexican Lily	A-11	38
Buell	1847	Lily	A-12	40
Cox	1847	Flashing Minnow	A-13	42
Glover	1849	Pin Wheel	A-14	44
Glover	1849	Wheel Pattern	A-15	46
Medley	1850	Hexagon Quilt Blocks	A-16	48
Harlow	1850	Harlow Album Quilt	A-17	50
Gilfrey	1850	Hovering Hawks/Peonies	A-18	52
Riggs	1851	Star	B-1	58
Riddle	1851	Birds in Flight	B-2	60
Merriman	1851	Single Irish Chain	B-3	62
Morris	1851	Wandering Foot	B-4	64
Morris	1851	Floral	B-5	66
Greer	1852	Setting Sun	B-6	68
Hargrave/Whiteaker	1852	Wandering Foot	B-7	70
Patterson	1852	Wandering Foot	B-8	72
Weaver	1852	Peony with Flying Geese	B-9	74
Drain	1852	Road to California	B-10	76
Robbins	1852	Oregon Rose	B-11	78
Powell Propst	1852	Tulip	B-12	80
Royal	1852	Royal Presentation	B-13	82
Dibble	1852	Oregon Trail	B-14	84
Dibble Sawtell	1852	Double Nine Patch	B-15	86
Duniway	1852	Hexagon	B-16	88
Purdom/Leonard	1853	Delectable Mountain	B-17	90
Stone	1853	Rose variation	B-18	92
Geisy	1853	Running Squares	B-19	94
Skeeters	1853	Log Cabin	B-20	96
Bonnett	1854	Crazy Quilt	B-21	98
Kelly	1860	Oregon Pioneer Ribbon	C-1	106
Wingville	1862-64	Tree of Life Signature	C-2	108
Stauffer	1863	Sunflower	C-3	110
Women of Aurora	1863	Pink and Green	C-4	112
Mills	1863	White on White	C-5	114
Colver	1864	Honeysuckle	C-6	116
Dean	1864	Eight-Pointed Star	C-7	118
Lieuallen	1864	Princess Feather	C-8	120
Lieuallen	1864	Stars with Wild Geese	C-9	122
Bryan	1864	Bachelor	C-10	124
Morgan	pre 1870	Seven Sisters	C-11	126
Those Who Wait				
Helman	1853	Pine Tree	D-1	130
Berry	1857	Star	D-2	132
Nye	1865	Basket	D-3	134
Gilmour	1870	Star	D-4	136
Fuson	Unkwn	Wild Goose Chase	D-5	138
Pickering Bell		Fruit and Flowers	D-6	140

Triumphs and Tragedies: Letters and Narrations of the Oregon Trail Experience

The following letters and narrations are ones collected during this research that enrich the understanding of the experience in terms of women and their quilts. They are arranged chronologically, with brief explanations.

Triumph #1

THE 1846 JOURNEY AND OREGON EXPERIENCE OF TABITHA MOFFETT BROWN

One of the most famous women in Oregon history who used her needlework skills to establish herself and achieve her goal was Tabitha Moffett Brown, now recognized by the state as the Mother Symbol of Oregon, representative of the distinctive pioneer heritage and the charitable and compassionate nature of Oregon's people.

Tabitha Moffett Brown (1780-1857). *Pacific University Museum, Forest Grove, Oregon*

Born in Brimfield, Massachusetts on May 1, 1780, she married The Reverend Clark Brown about 1799. After he died in Maryland in 1817, leaving her with two sons and one daughter, she moved to Missouri where she organized and successfully ran a school. At the age of sixty-six, she crossed the Plains in 1846 with her son, Orus Brown, and his wife and eight children; her daughter, Pherne Brown Pringle, and her husband and five children, her brother-in-law, seventy-seven year old Captain John Brown, for whom she kept house after her husband had died thirty years earlier. Completing the long and difficult journey of nine months with Jesse Applegate's first wagon train over the Applegate Trail, she arrived in the Willamette Valley. Part of the difficulty was a leg paralysis requiring the use of cane.

In a letter she wrote to her brother and sister in August 1854, Tabitha Brown reviewed her journey West and told of the school she started:

> On Christmas day at 2 P.M. I entered the house of a Methodist minister, the first house I had set my feet in for nine months. For two or three weeks of my journey down the Willamette I had felt something in the end of my glove finger which I supposed to be a button. On examination at my new home in Salem, I found it to be a six and a quarter cent piece. This was the whole of my cash capital to commence business with in Oregon. With it I purchased three needles. I traded off some of my old clothes to the squaws for buck skins, worked them into gloves for the Oregon ladies and gentlemen, which cleared me upwards of thirty dollars.
>
> Later I accepted the invitation of Mr. and Mrs. Clark of Tualatin Plains to spend the winter with them. I said to Mr. Clark one day, "Why has Providence frowned on me and left me poor in this world? Had He blessed me with riches as He has many others, I know right well what I would do." "What would you?" "I would establish myself in a comfortable house and receive all poor children and be a mother to them." He fixed his keen eyes upon me to see if I were in earnest. "Yes, I am," said I. "If so, I will try," said he "to help you." He proposed to take an agency and get assistance to establish a school in the plain. I should go into the old log meeting house, and receive all the children, rich and poor. Those parents who were able were to pay one dollar a week for board, tuition, washing and all. I agreed to labor one year for nothing, while Mr. Clark and others were to assist as far as they were able in furnishing

provisions. The time fixed upon to begin was March, 1848, when I found everything prepared for me to go into the old meeting house and cluck up my chickens. The neighbors had collected what broken knives and forks, tin pans and dishes they could part with, for the Oregon pioneer to commence housekeeping with. I had a well educated lady from the East, a missionary's wife for a teacher and my family increased rapidly. In the summer they put me up a boarding house. I now had thirty boarders, of both sexes and of all ages, from four years old to twenty-one. I managed then and did all my work except washing. That was done by the scholars.

In the spring of '49, we called for trustees. Had eight appointed. They voted me the whole charge of the boarding house free of rent and I was to provide for myself. The price of board was established at two dollars per week. Whatever I made over my expenses was my own. In '51 I had forty in my family at two dollars and fifty cents per week; mixed with my own hands 3,423 pounds of flour in less than five months. Mr. Clark made over to the trustees a quarter section of land for a town plat. A large and handsome building is on the site that we selected at the first starting. It has been under town incorporation for two years and at the last session of the legislature a charter was granted for a university, to be called Pacific University, with a limitation of $50,000. The president and professor are already here from Vermont. The teacher and his lady for the academy are from New York.

I have endeavored to give general outlines of what I have done. You must be judges, whether I have been doing good or evil. I have labored for myself and the rising generation, But I have not quit hard work and live at my ease, independent as to worldly concerns. I own a nicely finished white frame louse, on a lot in town, within a short distance of the public buildings. That I rent for $100 per year. I have eight other town lots without buildings worth $150 each. I have eight cows and a number of young cattle. The cows I rent out for their milk and one-half of their increase. I have rising $1,100 cash due me. $4000 of it I have donated to the university, besides $100 I gave to the academy three years ago. This much I have been able to accumulate by my own industry, independent of my children, since I drew six and a quarter scents [sic] from the finger of my glove.[1]

Tragedy and Triumph #2
THE 1847 JOURNEY AND OREGON EXPERIENCE OF ELIZABETH GEER

Her life was one of terrible tragedy and delightful triumph, as reflected in her diary and letters. For Elizabeth Geer, the arrival in Oregon City was bleak with a sick husband, seven children, and a bed:

November 30. Raining. This morning I ran about trying to get a house to get into with my sick husband. At last I found a small, leaky concern with two families already in it … you could have stirred us with a stick … My children and I carried up a bed. The distance was nearly a quarter of a mile. Made it down on the floor in the mud. I got some men to carry my husband up through the rain and lay him on it

and he was never out of that shed until he was carried out in his coffin. Here lay five of us bedfast at one time and we had no money and what few things we had left that would bring money I had to sell. I had to give ten cents a pound for fresh pork, seventy-five cents a bushel for potatoes and four cents a pound for fish. Thee are so many of us sick that I can not write any more …

January 15, 1848. My husband is still alive, but very sick. There is no medicine here except at Fort Vancouver, and the people there will not sell one bit—not even a bottle of wine.

January 31. Rain all day. If I could tell you how we suffer you would not believe it. Our house, or rather a shed joined to a house, leaks all over. The roof descends in such a manner that the rain runs right down into the fire. I have dipped as much as six pails of water off our dirt hearth in one night. Here I sit up night after night with my poor sick husband, all alone, and expecting him every day to die … I have not undressed to lie down for six weeks. Besides our sickness I had a cross little babe to care of. Indeed, I cannot tell you half.

February 1. Rain all day. This day my dear husband, my last remaining friend, died.

February 2. Today we buried my earthly companion. Now I know what none but widows know: that is, how comfortless is a widow's life; especially when left in a strange land without money or friends, and the care of seven children.[2]

Butteville, Oregon Ty., Yamhill County, Sept. 2, 1850.

Dear and Estimable Friends,
Mrs. Paulina Foster and Mrs. Cynthia Ames:

I promised when I saw you last to write to you when I got to Oregon, and I done it faithfully, but as I never have received an answer, I do not know whether you got my letter and diary or not, consequently I do not know what to write now. I wrote four sheets full and sent it to you, but now I have not time to write. I write now to know whether you got my letter; and I will try to state a few things again. My husband was taken sick before we got to any settlement, and never was able to walk afterwards. He died at Portland, on the Willamette River, after an illness of two months. I will not attempt to describe my troubles since I saw you. Suffice it to say that I was left a widow with the care of seven children in a foreign land without one solitary friend, as one might say, in the land of the living; but this time I will only endeavor to hold up the bright side of the picture. I lived a widow one year and four months. My three boys started for the gold mines, and it was doubtful to me whether I ever saw them again. Perhaps you will think it strange that I let such young boys go; but I was willing and helped them off in as good style as I could. They packed through by land. Russell Welch went by water. The boys never saw Russell in the mines. Well after the boys were gone, it is true I had plenty of cows and hogs and plenty of wheat to feed them on and to make my bread, Indeed, I was well off if I had only known it; but I lived in a remote place where my strength was of little use to me. I could get nothing to do, and you know I could not live without work. I employed myself in teaching my children; yet that did not fully occupy my mind. I became as poor as a snake, yet I was in good health, and never was so nimble since I was a child. I could run a half a mile without stopping to breathe. Well, I thought perhaps I had better try my fortune again, so on the 24th of June, 1849, I was married to a Mr. Joseph Geer, a man 14 years older than myself, though young enough for me. He is the father of ten children. They are all married, but two boys and two girls. He is a Yankee from Connecticut and he is a Yankee in every sense of the word, as I told you he would be if it ever proved my lot to marry again. I did not marry rich, but my husband is very industrious, and is as kind to me as I can ask. Indeed, he sometimes provokes me for trying to humor me so much. He is a stout, healthy man for one of his age.

The boys made out poorly at the mines. They started in April and returned in September, I think. They were sick part of the time and happened to be in poor diggings all the while. They only got home with two hundred dollars apiece. They suffered very much while they were gone. When they came home they had less than when they started. Perley did not get there. He started with a man in partnership. The man was to provide for and bring him back, and he was to give the man half he dug; but when they got as far as the Umpqua River, they heard it was so very sickly there that the man turned back; but Perley would not come back. There were two white men keeping ferry on the Umpqua, so Perley stayed with them all summer and in the fall he rigged out on his own hook and started again; but on his way he met his brothers coming home, and they advised him for his life not to go, and so he came back with them.

At this time we are all well but Perley. I cannot answer for him; he has gone to the Umpqua for some money due him. The other two are working for four dollars a day. The two oldest boys have got three town lots in quite a stirring place called Lafayette in Yamhill County. Perley has four horses. A good Indian horse is worth one hundred dollars. A good American cow is worth sixty dollars. My boys live about 25 miles from me, so that I cannot act in the capacity of a mother to them; so you will guess it is not all sunshine with me, you know my boys are not old enough to do without a mother. Russell Welch done very well in the mines. He made about twenty hundred dollars. He lives 30 miles below me in a little town called Portland on the Willamette River. Sarah has got her third son. It has been one year since I saw her. Adam Polk's two youngest boys live about wherever they see fit. The oldest, if he is alive, is in California. There is some ague in this country this season, but neither I nor my children, except those that went to California, have had a day's sickness since we came to Oregon.

I believe I will say no more until I hear from you. Write as soon as possible and tell me everything. My husband will close this epistle.

—Elizabeth Geer.

Butteville, Sept. 9, 1850.

Dear Ladies:

As Mrs. Geer has introduced me to you, as her old Yankee husband, I will say a few words, in the hope of becoming more acquainted hereafter. She so often speaks of you, that you seem like old neighbors. She has neglected to tell you that she was once the wife of Cornelius Smith. She has told you how poor she became while a widow, but has not said one word about how fat she has become since she has been living with her Yankee husband. This is probably reserved for the next epistle, so I will say nothing about it.

Of her I will only say she makes me a firstrate wife, industrious, and kind almost to a fault to me, a fault, however, that I can cheerfully overlook, you know.

We are not rich, but independent, and live agreeably together, which is enough. We are located on the west bank of the Willamette River, about 20 miles above Oregon City, about 40 yards from the water—a very pleasant situation. Intend putting out a large orchard as soon as I can prepare the ground; have about ten thousand apple trees, and about 200 pear trees on hand. Trees for sale of the best kinds of fruit. Apple trees worth one dollar, and pears $1.50 apiece. I have not room to give you a description of this, the best country in the world, so I will not attempt it; but if you will answer this I will give you a more particular account next time. I will give a brief account of myself. I left my native home, Windham, Conn., Sept. 10, 1818, for Ohio; lived in Ohio till Sept. 9, 1840, when I left for Illinois. Left Illinois April 4, 1847, for Oregon; arrived here Oct. 18, 1847. Buried my first wife Dec. 6, 1847.

Now I wish you or some of your folks to write to us and let us know all about the neighbors, as Mrs. Geer is very anxious to hear from you all.

Direct to Joseph C. Geer, Sen., Butteville, Marion County, Oregon Territory.

My best respects to Mr. Ames, and if there is a good Universalist preacher there, tell him he would meet with a cordial welcome here, as there is not one in this Territory.

I must close for want of room. Yours respectfully,

Joseph C. Geer, Sen.
Mrs. P. Foster, and Mrs. C. Ames.

Triumph #3
THE 1852 EXPERIENCE OF ROZELLE APPLEGATE PUTNAM

Rozelle Putnam was the niece of Melinda (Quilt A-2) and the eldest daughter of Jesse and Cynthia Applegate, born in 1832. At the age of sixteen, she married Charles Putnam, a young printer from Lexington, Kentucky. Rozelle was a student in the school her father maintained in their home. Her letters, written to Charles' parents and sister answering their questions and encouraging them to join the couple in southern Oregon, offer insight into their southern Oregon world. Rozelle was the first woman to set type in Oregon country, helping Charles to edit a small newspaper, *The Oregon American and Evangelical Unionist*. She died at twenty-nine after giving birth to eight children.

Yoncalla, Umpqua, Jan. 25ᵗʰ, 1852

Mrs. S. Putnam, Kentucky

Dear Father and Mother

… In the old settled parts of the Willamette there are plenty of excelent peaches & apples—but in the Umpqua there are but three bearing apple trees & one peach tree—these are at an old Hudson's Bay Fort—there are all maner of dried & preserved fruits for sale in the stores—which are cheap enough when we consider the price of home production—for instance I can get five pounds of dried peaches or apples for one pound of butter. You see I am still remembering more questions to answer—another is about neighbors and meetings … there is not a female beside in less than six miles—there are now four claims taken around us but the owners of them are all bachelors and likely to remain bachelors. I think they are mostly of a class of transitory settlers very numerous in this country who take claims with the expectation of making a little something by a future sale. The nearest house is about a half mile from ours and can be seen from the door…There is but one preacher in Umpqua, a Presbyterian who occasionally collects a few people, probably fifteen or twenty at a neighbors house, and holds prayers and adresses a few words of exortation to them but these little gatherings are out of our reach & we only hear of them after they are over.

We have plenty of reading to pass off the evenings and Sundays. Chas. takes an Oregon paper the New York Tribune & Harpers Monthly Magazine published in New York. Though we live a very quiet retired life it is a very pleasant one & any other kind would make us very uneasy for a while—for it is all habit. When Charles is away from home I have some of my brothers to stay with me—sometimes father sends an old man that lives with him to stay with me—he is quite a treasure in a family—he allways brings a sac of tools with him & spend his time in arranging conveniences about the house—he made our door and table a few chairs a small work table or rather candle stand with a single drawer—cupboard book case mantle board clothes shelf & in short he has made our little quite a comfortable little place.[3]

—Rozelle Putnam

Triumph #4
THE JOURNEY AND 1850 OREGON EXPERIENCE OF E.E. PARRISH AND WIFE SERAPATHIA

This letter was written to relatives back East, telling of their accomplishments in Oregon and their solutions to the challenges of the journey. As such, it is a personal statement on their dreams and the measure of their success. The letter is from the collection of Wanita Propst Haugen, owner of Quilt B-12.

Near Syracuse Marion County, Oregon Territory

Nov. 15th, 1850

Hugh & Sarepta Nickerson der Children

By this you may see that we still live, it is by the mercy of a kinde & indulgent Heavenly father that we are thus favored. Seven long years have hastened away since we took the parting hand with our friends upon the old walks of Ohio, to go, we then knew not where, but our kind guide conducted us safely to this good land, and now may we not inquire, what shall we render to God for all his benefeits. Oh, what cause of thankfulness have we, seeing that we all live, and enjoy life, and the bounties of a good providence. While we are continually hearing of the doings of the monster Death, and, notwithstanding, we feelingly condole with our friends in their losses and bereavments, yet, we all have cause to thank God that it is no worse; for when we mornc, not as those do, who have no hope, we find in the cup of sorrow, a mixture of joy which nothing but the religion of Jesus can inspire. O, then let us lean on the Saviour for support, and all will be well—As for my own family, we have nothing to complain of except our own unworthyncss, and not much to desire that we have not, except it is religion and the means of grace, we have long looked and desired to see the day when some of our good preachers would come to our releaf. And we are now cheered with prospect and are beginning to sing. There is a better day a coming—we are pleased to here that our friends arc waking up to a sence of their own intrust in view of coming to this country, the best we honestly believe on this side of Heaven. When we try to discribe it, we fall short about half way, yet the people of the States think it is romance.

Business is now verry lively in this territory. Markets arc pretty good. Jackson and his mother has just returned from Oregon Ct. with the team. They sold 23 bushels of onions at seven dollars per bushel, 126 pounds of butter at one dollar per pound, 24 hed of cabages at fifty cents per hed, 14 bushels of oats at two dollars per bushel—Beets were worth four dollars per bushel but they took none with them—They bought good calico at 12-1/2 cents per yd by the bolt. Bleached muslin at 18 cents pr yd by the bolt. Brown muslin at the same. Sugar at 18 cts. per pound, salt 4 cents per pound. We sold our peaches this year at six dollars pr bushel and from .25 to .50 pr doz. In this way we took in some 300 dollars. Potatoes are worth three dollars at the Citty, but we have sold them at home this year for one dollar, and as low as fifty cts, they arc plenty here now, for all the prices are so high, yet provisions of all kinds are exceding by plenty for every boddy, hereabouts. I wish to say to you, and threw you to all my relations and old acquaintances that we arc prepairing to supply you with provisions, on the cheepest terms, we have already planted considerable many potatoes, and but for the school, we should be at it today, as the weather is fine. While I am writing I look out at the window upon the prairies and fields and they remind me of your middle of May. The emigrants have bin coming in, more or less for two months, their stock is poor, but all they have to do is to let them loos and look after them a little and they soon come out of the kinks. A large portion of this years Emigration started for California, but on hearing of the grass being burned of on that road they turned for Oregon, but being so verry late in the season, fall raines came on, then snow caught them in the Cascade Mountains. Much of their stock died, they had to leav Waggons and all behind, and be carried out on hors back. O, take warning of this, start early on Brother

Clancics plan, and when you start, press on, be fourmost if possible. You may be here by the tenth of August at farthest, then you may bring in your stock in good condition, weather dry and pleasant—bring your beads and clothing with plenty of provision. Feather beds are harder to come at then anything els, if I was Hugh & Mc. I would bring a small box of small tools, such as match plains and the like with plain bits, as timber is plenty in Oregon. Broad axes, addzes, augers and the like are plenty and of good quality. I wish Hugh and _____ and the friends to help McClure to a deacent outfit so that he may bring his familly along with the rest of the friends as comfortably and as independantly as the rest, having his own Wagon and team, and I will take it as a faivour, and will refund the money on your arrival at my place. The proppcr way will be to take his note or receit and present it to me, as I cannot bare the idea of having him left—I want to say a word on a dilicate subject. It is this—it sometimes comes to pass that we are admonished that before we can posably get threw this long journey that we must have an increas of family, and of cours we cannot go this season, now for the information of all such, we can inform you that we had a great many such ocuranccs in our Emigration and are prepaircd to say that we a whole, we never knew Mothers and infants to do better, our frolicks mostly came on in the nite, and when the signs of the times indicated a storm it was easy to select a suitable place in the incampment and we were always ready to role out in the morning with the company—I want to say a word about the journey, that it is long and tiresom, is a matter none of ya need doubt, but if you can keep health, the continual occurance of knew objects will make the time pass along more agreeably—how to preserve health, in ordinary seasons you will not be likely to git sick if you conduct with prudence untill you reach the great Plat River. This river is like no other River, perhaps in the world, it is made by the streams of the Rocky Mountains, water pure at first, but it flows down with a courant bold and majestic, its bed is sand and that continually, conciquently, the water is muddy, looks like it is not fit for man or beast to drink. To avoid this dificulty, our Emigration resorted to well diging with a spade. You can dig a well two or three feet deep in a few minutes when clean water imediately comes in plenty, this practice became general, and the conciqucnce was we soon had sickness plenty, the River water is the best by far, and you should avoid those stink holes as you would avoid poison. Now friends I wish you to take this advise, provide buckets or other vesels sufficient to hold water nough to do you threw the night and some to put in your water bag in the morning, by standing threw the night it settles with the sand at the bottom—but if you put a little sweet milk in the water, it settles in a few minits reddy for use, take this cours and plenty of good Cayanne and Labeliei with the blessing of God and industry and you may get threw in good time and perhaps better health than when you started—One word more for McClure, we wish him and his family to take courage. I think he will get money before you get this, as James R. Robb (a good fellow) has written to his partner at New York to send him money, but if he should not git it in that way, let the friends who can, advance it for him doubting not

Robb, Gamaliel and myself all stand readdy and pledged to refund the cash on sight, my wish is that you take pains to let this paper have a circulation among all the friends—my opinyan is that prices will be a little reduced by the time you arive, but if prices should keep up, all the better, as it will soon be your turn to sell to others—This is the easiest place to make a living, to make property, or even cash if you pleas that you ever saw—My sheet is now full, I must bid you fairwell for a while, be sure, write when you start from Misoury and tel us know who is coming.

— E.E. Parrish & Wife

to Hugh & Sarepta Nickerson

Tragedy and Triumph #5
THE 1851 JOURNEY AND EXPERIENCE OF ESTHER MCMILLAN HANNA

One journal that graphically describes the end of the journey for a young, energetic eighteen-year-old woman is that of Esther McMillan Hanna. She mentions using a quilt and later staying in a cabin where the dying man is the husband of Lucinda Powell Propst (Quilt B-12). She and her husband, The Reverend Joseph A. Hanna, left Pittsburgh, Pennsylvania within an hour of their wedding ceremony for the trip across the country to establish the second Presbyterian Church in Oregon at Marysville, now called Corvallis. After six months, Esther is exhausted and frail when the following entry picks up. They have come down Laurel Hill on the west slope of Mt. Hood and are headed to "Foster's place."

Wednesday, 15th. Last night it commenced raining about midnight. We were lying out with a quilt and two blankets. We got up, put our sack containing a few personal things under Mr. H.'s gum coat. We then hoisted our umbrella over our heads, lay down again and slept! This morning our quilt was wet through and all our clothing damp. We had a hard bed as the ground was very uneven, with nothing but a blanket under us. I felt very sore and my limbs were stiff from the effects of walking so far yesterday and the damp of last night. ... I burst into a flood of tears. It seemed that trouble and trials came thick and fast upon us, and at a time when we could least bear it. Mr. H tried to comfort me although he was so much agitated as to be hardly able to speak. We started on again with troubled hearts and weary feet.

Thursday, 16th. We all slept comfortably and arose this morning in fine spirits, as we hope to reach the valley today. ... Part of our road this day was good and part very bad, having some steep ascents and descents to make. Got along fairly well and about four o'clock we came in sight of houses and gardens, fields and fences! My heart arose in gratitude to God that we had been spared to reach this land! Six long months have elapsed since we left our native land, and now after having passed through dangers seen and unseen, sickness, trial and difficulty, toil and fatigue, we are safely landed on the Pacific shores! Thus far the Lord has led us on. "Hitherto He has helped us. What shall we render unto His name for his goodness unto us?"

Saturday, 18th … have become quite domesticated in our little cabin. Have been baking and cooking all afternoon! The sick man in the other room is in a dying state. He has been insensible since yesterday. No friends near him but his oldest, a lad of 14. The rest of his children, 4 in number, having been sent on up the valley, 30 miles to an uncle. He was a man of property in Illinois, but owing to the persuasion of his wife, who wished to come here to her brother, at her solicitation, he sold all and came West. She died of fever on the Umatilla river, and he is dying here alone among strangers, lying on a pallet of straw with no kind friend to smooth his pillow! His brother-in-law has not yet arrived. There is a great deal of sickness and distress in the mountains. Every team here lost more or less of their cattle. Some have even lost all and have been obliged to leave their wagons and all. Some are entirely out of provisions and a great number are sick—almost every wagon that comes in have sick in it!

Sabbath, 19th. The poor emigrant in the next room died at 3 this morning. His brother-in-law came last evening with a carriage expecting to take him home, little thinking that he was so near his long home. Persons in the states would think it awful to see the near relations of the deceased lay out the corpse, clothe it, dig the grave and assist in filling it up again. But I witnessed that sad sight today! … The coffin was of plain boards, unpainted and unlined. The corpse was shroudless with but a checked shirt and drawers. Before lifting the corpse, Mr. H attended to singing and prayer, making a few appropriate remarks, We then attended the remains to their resting place. It was a heart-breaking time for all of us![4]

Tragedy #6

THE LOST WAGON TRAIN OF 1853 EXPERIENCE OF LUCINDA ANN LEONARD WORTH'S FAMILY

The Lost Wagon Train of 1853 involved two of the quilts in this study, the Purdom/Leonard (Quilt B-17) and Harlow (Quilt A-17). Over 1,500 emigrants chose to follow the suggestion of Elijah Elliott to cut miles off the journey by heading into the southern end of the Willamette Valley, a journey taken as great risk. Because of the number of unknowns, many became lost in the rugged Cascades for up to two months. The personal accounts of families who took this route indicate the eagerness to get to their destination before the weather changed and the supplies ran out.

Many Oregonians of today can trace their family's involvement in this experience as either victims or rescuers. There are several others quilts in this project that connect with families who were a part of this fateful trip. "The Joseph Leonards were with the Millers, and the McClures nearby."[5] The young couple, Alan and Rachel Bond, who brought only what they could carry, including the bundle of fabrics, were with the McClure party.

Francis Burris Tandy Harlow, maker of the autograph quilt with the names of her daughters and granddaughters, was one of the rescuers organizing her family and neighbors to pack a wagon full of supplies, food, and clothing.[6]

The story of this particular train's experience reflects the desperation many people faced after having been as long as five months on the Trail, always seeking water and food for livestock, fresh supplies for themselves, and respite from the long journey's toll of boredom, dust, illness, and death. It also illustrates the risks they took at following new leads to better supplies and shorter travel times. Information was passed on by word of mouth, often without personal knowledge by the speaker.

Elijah Elliott, the leader of the train, had come West in 1852, traveling with the largest wagon-carried migration movement ever to cross the Trail. He left his wife and family in Illinois, with the plan being to stake his claim in Oregon and then to fetch them the following year. Settling in Lane County, near Eugene, he saw the new town being planned and heard talk of the new road being charted over the Cascades to lead people to the area. He was assured by the planners that the road would be blazed by autumn. He also had heard that Stephen Meek had come across this way in 1845; but he did not know the degree of difficulty that Meek had encountered, wandering for weeks to find a way across the mountains. Going to meet his family at Ft. Boise, he experienced an area of central and eastern Oregon's mountains, flats, alkali lakes, and deserts where he had never been. He was perplexed by the experience and recommended the group go north around the lakes. There was disagreement among the other leaders and Elliott was overruled. He led the group south through the marshes and deserts, taking up to three weeks to travel a distance of a few dozen miles.[7]

Catherine Leonard Jones, the granddaughter of Katherine Purdom, who made Quilt B-17, recorded the experience of the Leonard family in a letter:

Marquam, Oregon, November 12, 1903

All went nicely until we came to Malheur River about eighteen miles this side of Snake River. There we met a man that came to meet his family, his wife and his two lovely children who were traveling with us. He had been in Oregon two years and told us of a road that was two hundred miles nearer and we could get good feed for our poor worn out teams. This was the first of September. Well, father thought if Mr. Elliott was willing to risk his family that he must be telling the truth, so we consented to go with him. We gathered three large trains of forty wagons in each and we started into the Blue Mountains. We kept on old Meek's road that was traveled in 1845 or 46 until we crossed the Blue Mountains, then we came to chalk and glass mountains or hills. When we came in sight of the lake which I suppose is Harney Lake, Mr. Elliott said we must go south, so we left the road and went to the south of the lake. You may be sure that we had a hard time traveling without a road through in Indian country. …

We went around the lake and then struck out on a barren desert, nothing but sagebrush and sometimes a spot of wild onions. Plenty of water in the winter, I suppose, but in October when we came through, it was dry as ashes. We traveled on this desert all day and night long and in the morning when our teams gave out we loosened them from the wagons and the men took kegs on their backs and followed the cattle about ten miles and found water. We had to stay there six days for the teams to get so they could come back to the wagons. The men went every day and brought water to drink. When we started from there we went by the little stream and stopped all night and then went on across another desert, but were more cautious about filling our canteens.

At the first desert I saw a lot of men draw up two wagons and tie the end of the tongues together, they said they were going to hang Mr. Elliott for leading us through that road. Father, Mother and several of the men begged them to spare his life. He admitted he did not know anything about the road but thought it was all right and claimed that the people in the upper end of the valley said they would pay him five hundred dollars to pilot the emigrants through that way. He offered all his cattle to be killed for food for the starving people for we were without flour or anything to eat. Everyone that was sick died ... After we crossed the second desert, we could see three snow peaks in the distance which were the Three Sisters and came to an old Indian trail to Fall River or Deschutes ...

Here we stayed six days hunting a road: finally we started up the river, traveled about forty miles, then forded it. Now here was a place that we out-fitted those two younger men to go for assistance. It was then in November. People threw in and bought an old mare, than gave them dried meat and bedclothes and they started not knowing what was before them. Here the snow fell; we went through six inches of snow, it was terribly cold and wet; we crossed the summit. Oh! such a road, here we found a grindstone that showed someone had been here. The road was cut in some places; they had bridged over logs four feet through rather than cut them out; the suffering was intense as we came down the Willamette, the stream was narrow and swift and we could ford it every little while; every time it was a little deeper until the last time Father said we could not make it.

We were near it, sitting down eating boiled beef straight when two men came riding up to us, threw us down some flour and potatoes, never was morsel more gladly received. The boys had taken in word of starving people. ... That night the citizens of that place made up five hundred dollars of provisions for the emigrants. And plenty of men and pack animals loaded with provisions went out after us. Every man, when his pack was unloaded, would take some of the emigrants on their horses to the valley.[8]

Treasure #7
THE 1855 OREGON EXPERIENCE OF JOHN BRUCE BELL

This treasure found among the family items of Mary Carpenter Pickering (Quilt D-6) was a letter written by John Bruce Bell from Oregon in 1855. The letter is charming and shows much of the sentiment and feeling expressed about the Oregon Territory in the mid-1850s, and what separation from friends meant.

Plum Valley, Polk County, O.T. May 21st, 1855
Friend Mary
It has been a long time since I received your letter, and I really feel ashamed to think that I have so long neglected to answer. I have no excuse but think not Mary that you

were forgotten. I can never cease to remember all the friends so linked together when fond memory brings the light of the other days around me. Though far separated and in a strange land with none of the friends of my youth around, to cheer or with whom I can talk over the merry times when were boys together, how can I then forget. No, while I have a heart to feel, and memory carries me back to the scenes of old Belmont you shall be ever cherished as one worthy and bright spot in my memory. I sometimes wish myself back once more, when I think of the friends I left behind and the many hallowed associations which made them dear to me, of the many pleasures, and of all and everything which were once so familiar to me. I almost wish I had never left and often long to return.

We had a very mild pretty winter. There was no cold weather of any consequence. Spring with all her charms, is now upon us, and all Oregon is now clothed in her richest robes. At no time does this country look prettier. The prairies are covered with flowers. It is still showery, and the grass is much better this spring than I have ever seen it. I am in hopes that we will have dry weather all the time before long. We will soon have plenty of fruit. Peaches do not do well here. I think it is rather too cool during the summer for them, but I think this will be a great country for apples. There is but a few orchards of grafted fruit bearing yet, but you will scarcely find a farm, which has not a large orchard planted, and it will not be long until we shall have plenty of fruit. I have not had two dozen apples since I left the states. There is none about here and when they are, they sell at from ten to fifteen dollars per bushel. We have no wild fruit, except berries, and I do not know how many kinds of berries there are here but I know there are some which I never saw in the states. Strawberries are ripe now and are very plenty. I was out with the women this forenoon. They promised to give me a strawberry dinner if I would go out and help them gather. Well I went, but it was a great sacrifice for me to put any in a vessel when they look so tempting and seemed to say eat me. I thought when I was out, that if it had been yourself and Sister Marth, instead of two O. women I would have seen more pleasure. I wish there was a band of the Buckeye girls here, I would like to take a romp over these hills and have them for company. It is well enough however to please the old women occasionally, and get a little into their good graces by minding the little Oregonians and other little chores, and then a person can ask little favors such as sewing on a button and such like little things with a better face. I believe I have told you something about the girls here. Well I have not fallen in love with any of them yet. There are but very few that have come to years of accountability and they act as though they never saw anything in their lives but their parents. I do not know from experience but fellows who have tried visiting them, say the only place they can be found is behind the door, whither they flee to avoid the sight of man. Well I will make allowance for them. They have been raised up in a new country have had no opportunities for education and are not accustomed to society and have had a poor chance. But still I think they should have sense enough not to marry so soon. If they would only wait till they were eighteen or twenty they would be of some account. Well there is no danger of me robbing any of the cradles here while I keep my senses. I suppose that of the girls of my acquaintance have married and I did expect to hear that you had gone and done likewise and I know not but that you are gone or going. Well I hope there will be some left until I return and I will not let many years roll round until I bid welcome to my native hills once more. Young men are plenty here and a great many have about the same opinion of the girls as I have, and intent to go back. I like the people here better now than at first. They are mostly Missourians, and have not time to describe one to you, but they have been raised among slaves, and you can guess what they are like. What Buckeyes that are here are the best citizens we have, and if Oregon was settled with them it would be the best place in the world. Oregon is very healthy but very little ague and that only in some places. I had a letter from Marth lately I would like to see her so much, she is always so kind and good humored. I have no heard from Nancy lately. I think she must have a notion of getting married. Well I must go home and see all the folks before long or I will forget how they all looked. I could spend a few months in Ohio now with pleasure. But is no use to regret. I am here and I can't help it now, only by going back when I can. Give my love and respects to all, and may I ask you to write soon, and to not do as I have done. And now I must bid you good bye, asking to be remembered by you, and with wishes for your welfare and happiness hoping that nothing will mar the smooth current of your life, I still remain your friend in Oregon.

Mary C. Pickering   Good Bye   J.B. Bell of Belmont[9]

Triumph #8
THE STORY OF THE DARNING NEEDLE OWNED BY NANCY GATES ENSLEY DRAIN (QUILT B-10)

The triumphant story about the darning needle is part of Oregon folklore. It was told and retold and eventually recorded in *With Her Own Wings*, a collection of sketches about pioneer women compiled by Portland's Federation of Women's Organizations.

Part of the successful outcome is related to the role of Aaron Meier, founder of Oregon's Meier and Frank Department Store.

The Darning Needle Story

This is an example of pioneer folklore, a story told and retold by oldtimers. Most of the story was told by Mary Drain Albro of Portland. Howard M. Corning has verified enough of the facts to convince us that the incident could have occurred in 1852 or 1853.

Grandmother Drain had a darning needle, and it was the only darning needle among the settlers in Pass Creek Canyon.

The folks who lived in Pass Creek Canyon had come across the plains by wagon train. By the time they got to the top of the Cascades, they were so eager to end their journey they settled at the first likely spots as they went down the west slopes. Every natural clearing close to water was the site of a land claim. Pass Creek Canyon was quite thickly settled, at least there were ten or fifteen families living within a few miles of each other, and

they neighbored back and forth, sharing what they had. In those days families had to get along with each other. No one knew when he might need help.

Grandmother Drain's darning needle was one of the most cared-for-possessions in the community, because it was the only one, and clothes had to be patched and mended until new ones could be secured, and who knew when that would be? The women learned to make pins out of slivers of dogwood, but for mending nothing was so handy to use as the darning needle.

Women in the lower canyon shared the needle for a day or two, then women up farther would take turns catching up on the family mending.

All went well until the day Mrs. Chitwood sent the needle back to Grandmother Drain's by Jimmy.

Jimmy was eight years old, and he was a responsible boy—boys had to be responsible and do their share of the work.

Mrs. Chitwood put a long red raveling through the eye of the needle and knotted it, then she put the needle into a potato so that Jimmy could carry it safely to the Drain cabin.

Jimmy walked through the canyon trail in the spring morning sunshine which filtered through the tall firs. He paid no attention to rabbits and squirrels that crossed the path in front of him. He scarcely looked up when blue jays scolded. He stopped for a moment when a doe raced a few yards down the trail as though being chased, but he did not leave the trail. He was on an errand with the only darning needle in Pass Creek Canyon.

But when a mother bear with two cubs came into sight, he jumped from the trail and hid behind a serviceberry bush to watch them. He was not afraid, he said to himself because bears didn't harm, but of course a mother bear was different when she had cubs. No, he was not afraid, but it was best to hide just the same. He stood behind the bush, then stooped down. It would be nice, he thought, if Father were here to see the bears, too. He was not afraid, but he wished the bears would hurry along on their way. And after a bit they did.

Jimmy stood up again and went back onto the trail. He walked a little, thinking of the bears and wishing that sometime he might have a cub all his own, without a mother bear.

Then he remembered the darning needle! He looked down at his hand. The potato and the needle were gone!

Oh, I lost it in the bushes, he thought. I'll have to go find it. He went back as fast as he could, but he could not find the serviceberry bush. Here are those bracken, and here was where I came out to the trail again, but where is the bush? What shall I do?

He ran down the trail as fast as he could and told his mother. Mrs. Chitwood was alarmed.

"Oh, Jimmy!" she exclaimed. "To think it had to be lost when we had it. Well, we'll just have to find it. Go tell your father."

Jimmy ran to the edge of the clearing where his father and some other men were trimming logs. When Jimmy told what he had done, the men stuck their axes into the logs and went with Jimmy. "We'll have to help, too," they said.

The men and Jimmy went to the cabin. Mrs. Chitwood had sent word to the other neighbors, and they all went up onto the trail where Jimmy thought he had seen the bears.

They looked for bear tracks and found one or two, but the earth was dry. They all looked for the serviceberry bush Jimmy had hidden under, but there were many serviceberry bushes, and where was that one?

Everyone was worried, but no one scolded Jimmy except his sister. She was ten, and she said, "You won't be a good woodsman if you can't even remember landmarks. Don't you know you should always have landmarks?"

Jimmy was white and tearful, but he tried to show his mother exactly where he had been. After a while, he said, "I know there was a stump under the bush. A funny stump."

All the men and women, and children, too, began looking for a red raveling near a stump under a serviceberry bush.

Suddenly Jimmy left the others. He said nothing but walked through a bramble of bracken. When he came out, he went straight to his mother and handed her the potato with the red raveling hanging from it.

"It was by the stump," he said.

"Why, Jimmy," replied his mother, "you are a woodsman, and a reliable boy, to find what you lost. Give it to Grandmother Drain. Quick! Before you lose it again."

Everyone, and that was about twentyfive people, came together to share the joy of finding the needle. Then the men went back to trimming logs, the women went home to get their suppers, and the children went back to their play.

The darning needle was found, and it was kept all that summer and into the fall, but one day when Grandmother Drain was sewing, the head of the needle broke off, and all the women had to make neat piles of clothing to be mended, hoping that before long, someone would come from Fort Vancouver or the East with a needle. Each time women were together they talked of their sewing and hoped that another needle would soon be provided.

One day, about Thanksgiving time, a peddler with a mule came over the pass and down through the canyon. The children playing school on some logs saw him and ran to tell their mothers a visitor was coming.

The mothers, one by one, hurried to see the goods the peddler had brought and to hear news of people to the east. Several hurried to buy combs. One bought a china doll's head. Two women enthusiastically bought dress goods before they thought of needles and thread to sew it with.

Then one of the mothers said, "Oh, do you have any needles? We'll have to have a needle."

"Oh," said Mrs. Chitwood, "how could we forget when it is the one thing we need most—a good needle with a large eye! We need one at least, now that Grandmother Drain's needle is broken." Mrs. Chitwood told the story of the lost darning needle, glancing occasionally at Jimmy who was stroking the mule's neck and pretending not to notice.

Those standing around talked, too, and the peddler listened. Then he reached into his inside pocket.

"My people do not celebrate Christmas," he said, "but I suppose you good people will soon be having a holiday with presents. Are you going to give any presents, sonny?" asked the peddler.

Jimmy looked up quickly. "Oh, yes, sir, that is, I guess I will."

"Well," said the kindfaced man, "suppose you and I give the ladies of Pass Creek Canyon each a Christmas present right now, shall we?"

Jimmy looked puzzled. The peddler opened the thin package he had taken from his pocket. "Here are some darning needles, all I have, but I believe there will be enough for every family in the canyon to have one."

No one said anything for a moment, then there was a gasp of astonishment. The women smiled to each other, "He's a good man."

The peddler and Jimmy passed out the needles to those gathered around, and the next day Jimmy delivered the rest of the needles up and down the canyon.

The peddler left, and no one saw him again for many months, but that was just the first of many kindnesses shown the women in Pass Creek Canyon by Aaron Meier who later founded the store of Meier and Frank in Portland.

The peddler Aaron Meier, born in Germany in 1831, came to America at age twenty-four to work in the store belonging to his two older brothers in the California gold fields. Part of his job was to make the long trips peddling their wares through the Oregon Territory as far north as the Columbia River. He carried his pack on his back as he walked the difficult terrain of the Cascade Mountains.

After two years of this exhausting work, he decided to open his own store in Portland in 1857. Over the years, working with his wife Jeannette Hirsch and son-in-law Sigmund Frank, they developed Meier and Frank Company into one of America's great family-owned department stores.

Meier and Frank advertisement, *Oregonian*, January 1, 1967. *Collection of Joanne Nelson*

Meier and Frank has used the darning needle story in at least one full-page ad in *The Oregonian*, the state's main newspaper, on January 1, 1967. The headline read "Have you ever heard the story of "The Potato and the Darning Needle?" At the end of the story was an invitation to all to come into Meier and Frank's Fabric Center to receive a complimentary needle.[10]

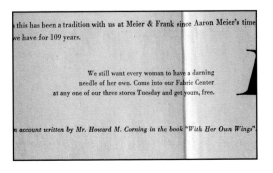

Meier and Frank advertisement. *Collection of Joanne Nelson.*

Connecting the Treasures
to Their Communities

The majority of these quilts are housed in museums and historical societies throughout the country. Without the dedication and interest of the staff and volunteers, this book would not have been possible.

In the past, the role of these public and private institutions has been defined in three ways. They were to collect and preserve artifacts of the past; to interpret these in exhibits and activities; and to provide an educational outreach to the community. Through these roles, they played an important part in preserving and interpreting our nation's heritage.

Recently, a new goal has been added to their agenda. They are responsible for explaining their area's heritage to their communities and facilitating conversations through public presentations.

We, as area residents, can assist them with their mission because they are deserving of our support and interest. Because they shared their resources, I was able to provide them with information about their quilt collection. The Oregon Council for the Humanities, through the Latimer Quilt and Textile Center, provided funds for me to revisit the places I had studied quilts and report to them what I learned about their nineteenth-century quilts and makers.

It is important for would-be donors and those interested in preserving the heritage of the past to understand how these organizations work. To collect and preserve the artifacts of the past, a society usually works within a clearly defined territory of time and place, seeking to identify and gather the materials that reflect the heritage of its location. In the past, museums have been inclined to take any and all objects brought to their door. In this day of limited financial resources, narrowly defined categories within the mission statement determine exactly which artifacts it should have in its collection.

Once the materials are collected, it is important to inventory and register each of the collection's objects to be able to access them when needed and to know what is available. In the case of quilts, this means carefully recording the physical description by noting such things as size, date, fabric content, construction technique, and condition. The computer has helped with this initial recording because digital images of the quilt can be included in the online record. This helps researchers and staff because it eliminates the need to access and unroll the quilts.

With quilts, it is becoming increasingly important to provide information about the maker, who she was, when and where she lived, and any other important information that would enhance the quilt's interpretation, as has been done in this study.

A further dimension of this gathering of resources is to provide proper storage space for the objects. A wide range of solutions is possible, depending on financial resources, and can include a sophisticated, climate controlled environment or simply shelves out of direct sunlight and free of dust.

For someone considering the donation of a quilt, it is appropriate to ask questions about each of these matters and to provide as much information as possible about the artifact.

In interpreting the artifacts in exhibits and providing activities to enrich the community's understanding, the focus is usually on an activity or a place or time relevant to the object. For instance, at a quilting demonstration, people are invited to add stitches to a new quilt being made. A quilt exhibition can focus on a certain theme, as the traveling show accompanying this book did.

If a privately-owned quilt would complement an exhibition, it is considered generous to make it available for loan. Several of the quilts of this project are privately owned. All add additional information to the themes and they greatly enrich the project. This is especially true in this new edition. The leads provided by the eight additional quilts enrich awareness of the Oregon Trail experience.

The educational outreach of the museum or historical society can be achieved through programs, lectures, or publications geared to the community's different age groups. These may be the work of staff personnel or other educators interested in teaching the public about its past history and using a museum's collection of census records, public and personal histories, maps, photographs, and newspapers. The extensive collections of the Oregon Historical Society in both artifacts and supporting research materials that are available for research add interesting dimensions to the understanding of Oregon's history. The Internet with its wide range of historical and genealogical resources also makes accessing family history much easier than before.

Some quilts can assist historical organizations in explaining their communities' heritage and facilitating discussion in public presentations. This is especially true of presentation and commemorative quilts made by local churches, fraternal organizations, veterans associations, and professional affiliations. Often they contain the names of members and dates that help to identify the specific time and place. Sadly, too often there has been a disconnect between the organization and the quilt's owner. Another style of quilt that can often help enrich an area's cultural heritage is a crazy quilt or show quilt bearing many ribbons, badges, or commemorations. These often make excellent research projects for interested volunteers or students working on local history projects.

As demonstrated by this quilt project, the more complete material found, the more interesting and valuable the quilt became. It is vitally important, then, to provide as much documentation as possible when making a donation to a museum. The basic information should include who, what, when, where, why, and how. Then any additional materials in the forms of letters, pictures, quilt construction materials, and sewing items that would lend additional value to the quilt's interpretation should be included. In addition, it would be helpful to include a bibliography of sources, a list of family descendants, or other notations. When an item is donated, it receives a number and an accession sheet that is used to record all this information, and sometimes a file folder to hold the extra materials.

In deciding to make a donation of a family treasure, there are several important guidelines. One is to choose the best possible location for the object. After gathering as much information as possible about the quilt, consider various museums where it might be placed in order to determine the most appropriate disposition. Knowing when and where a quilt was made or used, plus learning the museum's mission statement about its territory, its goals, and its existing quilt collection can help the potential donor make a comfortable decision. If a museum already has a number of quilts of a particular kind or era, it may not be interested in receiving another. If a museum's focus is elsewhere rather than textiles, it is not an appropriate choice. By being patient and carefully evaluating the options, eventually the right museum will be found.

Even if a donation is not being considered, it is a good idea to organize information about the quilt at home so other family members will be able to learn and appreciate more of their own history. It also helps them if a suggestion is made regarding a future permanent location for a quilt or other artifacts.

As these public and private institutions have shared so generously with me, I hope you will visit them in person or online to support their work. A list of locations follows:

Oregon Historical Societies and Museums

Old Aurora Colony Museum
Second and Liberty Streets
PO Box 202
Aurora, OR 97002
503.678-5754
www.auroracolonymuseum.com

Benton County Historical Museum
1101 Main St.
PO Box 35
Philomath, OR 97370
541.929.6230
www.bentoncountymuseum.org

Coos Country Historical Society Museum
1220 Sherman Ave.
North Bend, OR 97459
541.756-6320
www.cooshistory.org

Crook County Historical Society
Bowman Museum
246 N. Main St.
Prineville, OR 97754
541.447-3715
www.bowmanmuseum.org

Douglas County Museum of History
123 Museum Drive
Roseburg, OR 97470
541.957-7007
www.co.douglas.or.us/museum/

The High Desert Museum
59800 S Highway 97
Bend, OR 97702-4754
541.382-4754
www.highdesertmuseum.org

Lane County Historical Museum
740 W. 13 St.
Eugene, OR 97402
541.682-4242
www.lchmuseum.org

Latimer Quilt and Textile Center
2105 Wilson River Loop Rd.
Tillamook, OR 97141
503.842.8622
www.oregoncoast.com/latimertextile

Lee House Museum
Junction City Historical Museum
655 Holly St.
Junction City, OR 97448
541.998-6154
www.junctioncity.com/history

Klamath County Museum
1451 Main St.
Klamath Falls, OR 97601
541.883-4208
www.co.klamath.or.us

Molalla Area Historical Society
Dibble House
c/o Isabelle Williams
616 S. Molalla Ave.
Molalla, OR 97038
503.829-5521

Museum of the Oregon Territory
Clackamas County Family History Society
211 Tumwater Drive
Oregon City, OR 97068
503.655-5574
www.orcity.com/museum

Oregon Coast History Center
545 SW 9th St.
Newport, OR 97365
541.265-7509
www.oregoncoast.history.museum/

Oregon Historical Society
1200 SW Park Ave.
Portland, OR 97205
503.222-1741
www.ohs.org

Philip Foster Farm
29912 SE Highway 211
Estacada, OR 97023
503.637-6324
www.philipfosterfarm.com

Pioneer Mother's Memorial Cabin Museum
Champoeg State Park
St. Paul, OR 97137
503.633-2237
www.oregonstateparks.org/park_113.php

Sherman County Historical Museum
200 Dewey St.
Moro, OR 97039
541.938-4636
www.shermanmuseum.org

Schminck Memorial DAR Museum
128 South E St.
Lakeview, OR 97630
541.947-3134
www.lakecountyoregon.com/schminck.htm

Southern Oregon Historical Society
106 N. Central Ave.
Medford, OR 97501
541.773-6536
www.sohs.org

Washington County Museum
17677 NW Springville Rd.
Portland, OR 97229
503.645-5353
www.washingtoncountymuseum.org

Heritage Station: The Umatilla County Museum
1205 SW Court Ave.
Pendleton, OR 97801
541.276-0012
www.umatillahistory.org

Yamhill County Historical Museum
605 Market Street
Lafayette, OR 97127
503.864-2308
www.sites.onlinemac.com/history/YCHShome.htm

Other Museums and Historical Societies

DAR Museum
1776 D St.
Washington, D.C. 20006
202.628-1776
www.dar.org

National Museum of American History
Smithsonian Institution
Washington, D.C. 20560
202.633-3794
www.americanhistory.si.edu

Northwest Museum of Arts and Culture
2316 W. First Ave.
Spokane, Washington 99122
509.363-5308
www.northwestmuseum.org

National Historic Trails Centers

End of the Oregon Trail Interpretive Center
1726 Washington St.
Oregon City, OR 97045
503.657-9336
www.endoftheoregontrail.org

National Historic Oregon Trail Interpretive Center
22267 Highway 86 Flagstaff Hill
Baker City, OR 97814
541.523-1843
www.blm.gov/or/oregontrail/

Columbia Gorge Discovery Center
The Dalles, OR
541.296-8600
www.gorgediscovery.org

Tamastslikt Cultural Institute
Pendleton, OR
www.tamastslikt.com

Applegate Trail Interpretive Center
Sunny Valley, OR
www.rogueweb.com/interpretive/

National Oregon/California Trail Center
Montpelier, Idaho
www.oregontrailcenter.org

National Historical Trails Interpretive Center
Casper, Wyoming
http://www.wy.blm.gov/nhtic/

Oregon-California Trails Association
524 South Osage St.
PO Box 1019
Independence, Missouri 64051
888-811-6282
www.octa-trails.org

Scotts Bluff National Monument
P.O. Box 27
Gering, Nebraska 69341
www.nps.gov/scbl

Websites for General Information

Oregon National Historic Trail
www.nps.gov/oreg

The Oregon Territory and Its Pioneers
www.oregonpioneers.com

Quilt History
www.womenfolk.com/historyofquilts/
www.quiltindex.org

H-Quilts@H-NET.MSU.edu

American Quilt Study Group
www.h-net.org/~aqsg/

Research Data

Trail Years 1840-1850

TRAIL CONDITIONS

Primitive, isolated, no printed guides, few experienced leaders, few services available, hazardous river crossings.

Length of travel time usually seven to eight months, starting April and lasting until December.

Numbers of people going fairly small, plenty of food and water, Indians relatively peaceful.

People were upwardly mobile, looking for free land and coming from free land.

QUILTS

Of the project's eighteen:
    Four were quilted when came.
    Ten were quilted after.
    Two pieced while on Trail.
    One not quilted.
    One unknown.
Span of time represented by quilts: circa 1825-1915.
Number by year (family):

1842:	1 (1)	1847:	2 (2)
1843:	2 (2)	1848:	0
1844:	1 (1)	1849:	2 (1)
1845:	3 (3)	1850:	3 (3)
1846:	4 (1)		

Categories of quilts:
    Whole cloth: One
    Appliquéd: Seven
    Pieced: Ten
Themes:
    Migration: Seven
    Celebration: Four
    Unknown: Seven

QUILT MAKERS

Of the project's fourteen:
    Age range from 14 to 51.
    Eight came with extended families.
    Three with husbands.
    One with parents.
    One with mother.
    One with brother and sister.
    Six making first migration.
    Five making second migration.
    Two making third migration.
    One unknown.
    One woman died at the end of the Trail.

Reasons for coming:
    Fourteen came for economic and business opportunities.
    Three came for land.
    One against slavery.
    One came because of religious affiliation.
Husbands who went to the gold fields:
    None went before bringing family.
    Three went after.
Thirteen settled in the northern Willamette Valley:
    Four in Clackamas County.
    Two in Marion County.
    Three in Yamhill County.
    One each in Benton, Linn, Polk, and Washington Counties.
One settled in the southern Willamette Valley in Lane County.
Moved again after arriving in Oregon:
    Two to Umpqua County (Douglas County) in southern Oregon.
    Two to Lane County in southern Willamette Valley.
    One to Benton County.
    One to Washington Territory.
    One to Lake County in southeastern Oregon.
Role achieved in Oregon:
    Thirteen worked to establish farm and family.
    One founded a church.
    One used her needle skills to establish in business.
    Four were caregivers.
    One took in boarders.

QUILTING ACTIVITY (as determined by dates of the quilts)

Before:
    Four quilted between zero and five years before going on Trail.
    One quilted between five and fifteen years.
    One between fifteen and twenty-five years.
After:
    None quilted after getting here between zero and five years.
    Four quilted between five and fifteen years.
    One between twenty-five and thirty-five years.
    Seven quilted after more than thirty-five years.
    Elizabeth Currier Foster made one after being in Oregon sixty-four years and another after sixty-nine years.
    Frances Tandy Harlow quilted one after being here forty-eight years.
    Mary Officer Vaughan made her quilt after being here forty-five years.

Trail Years 1851-1855

TRAIL CONDITIONS

Beginning of commercialism with Indians and trappers operating ferries, bridges, and supply stations, guidebooks available.

Experienced guides or husbands who knew Trail and western climate conditions.

Federal government established army posts, mounted riflemen travel the length of the Trail

Travel time shortened by one month.

More extended families going or there to receive arriving families.

Wagon trains larger, bringing more supplies and animals.

Food and water supplies often very limited.

Illnesses and disease become major problems.

QUILTS

Of the project's twenty-one quilts:
>   Twelve were quilted when came.
>   Eight quilted after.
>   One pieced while on Trail.

Span of time represented by quilts: 1830-1900

Number of quilts by year (family):
>   1851:   5 (4)
>   1852:   11(10)
>   1853:   4 (4)
>   1854:   1 (1)
>   1855:   0

Categories of quilts:
>   Appliquéd: Six
>   Pieced: Fifteen
>   Crazy: One

Themes:
>   Migration: Thirteen
>   Celebration: Five
>   Unknown: Three

QUILT MAKERS

Of the project's twenty-one:
>   Age range from 6 to 44.
>   Five came with extended families.
>   Twelve came with husbands.
>   Five came with parents.
>   One came with party of scouts to locate land.
>   Nine making first migration.
>   Eleven making second migration.
>   One making fourth migration.
>   One died on the Trail.

Reasons for coming:
>   Twelve for economic and business opportunities.
>   Eleven for land.
>   Two for religious opportunities.
>   Two to join family.
>   One against slavery.
>   One to remain with family.

Husbands who went to the gold fields:
>   Five went before bringing family.
>   One went after bringing family.

Fifteen settled in the northern Willamette Valley:
>   Three in Clackamas County.
>   Two each in Benton, Linn, Polk, Marion, and Yamhill County.
>   One in Multnomah and Washington County.

One settled in the southern Willamette Valley in Lane County.

Four settled in southern Oregon:
>   Three in Douglas County.
>   One in Jackson County.

One settled in Washington Territory

Moved again after arriving in Oregon:
>   One to Clackamas, Linn, Lincoln, Marion, Multnomah (Portland), Umatilla County in eastern Oregon and Washington Territory.
>   Two to Jackson and Polk County.

Role achieved in Oregon:
>   Twenty worked to establish farm and family.
>   One worked to relocate communal society.
>   Two organized a church.
>   Two served as liaisons with Indians.
>   Two were caregivers.
>   One took in boarders.
>   One established a town and operated a hotel.
>   One was a school teacher, set up a millinery shop, printed a newspaper, worked for woman's suffrage and was first woman to vote in Oregon.

QUILTING ACTIVITY (as determined by dates of the quilts)

Before:
>   Six quilted between zero and five years.
>   Four quilted between five and fifteen years.
>   Two quilted between fifteen and twenty-five years.

After:
>   One quilted between two and five years of arriving.
>   One quilted between five and fifteen years.
>   Two between fifteen and twenty-five years.
>   One between twenty-five and thirty -five years.
>   Four over thirty-five years.
>   Annis Bonnett made her Crazy Quilt forty years later.
>   Abigail Scott Duniway finished her Hexagon Quilt forty-eight years later.
>   Susannah Good Morris quilted throughout her elder years.
>   Zeralda Bones Stone made quilts sixty years later.

Trail Years 1856-1870

TRAIL CONDITIONS

Becomes commercialized and populated with trading posts, stagecoach stops, road houses, telegraph lines, army posts—no longer empty horizons and sense of loneliness as route becomes more secure.

Indians become a real challenge because of increased deaths, changes in buffalo herds, and threat to native lands.

Use of experienced guides increases.

Major problem was fear and disrespect shown the Indians by the emigrants.

Numbers going increase significantly with supplies of food and water decreasing and disease increasing.

Travel time shortened by another month.

Emigration declined during the Civil War.

QUILTS

Of the project's eleven quilts:
Three were quilted when came.
Seven were quilted after.
One appliquéd on the Trail.

Span of time represented by quilts: circa 1850-1925

Number by year (family)

1856	0	
1857	0	
1858	0	
1859	0	
1860	1	(1)
1861	0	
1862	1	(1)
1863	3	(3)
1864	5	(5)
1865	0	
1866	0	
1867	0	
1868	0	
1869	0	
pre1870	1	(1)

Categories of quilts:
Appliquéd: Four
Pieced: Eight

Themes
Migration: Four
Celebration: Four
Unknown: Three

QUILT MAKERS

Of the project's eight individual and two group:
Age range from 9 to 38 (?).
Four came with husbands.
Three came with parents.
Two came with extended communities of people.
One came with extended family.
One unknown.

Three making first migration.
Four making second migration.
One making third migration.
Two unknown.
None died on the Trail.

Reasons for coming:
Three came for economic and business opportunities.
Three came for religious opportunities.
Two came for land.
Three came because against slavery.
One came to improve living conditions.
One came for adventure to be a school teacher.

Husbands going to the gold fields:
Two went before coming to Oregon.

Six settled in the Willamette Valley:
Two in Yamhill County.
One each in Lane, Multnomah, Marion, Washington County.

Two settled in eastern Oregon:
One in Umatilla County.
One in Baker County.

Two in Jackson County in southern Oregon.
One in Washington Territory.

Moved again after arriving in Oregon:
Two to Washington Territory.
One to Lake County.
One died.

Role achieved in Oregon:
Seven worked to establish homes and families.
Two participated in communal society work.
Two worked to establish churches.
One was a school teacher.
One was a caregiver.

QUILTING ACTIVITY (as determined by the dates of these quilts)

Before:
Five quilted between zero and five years of coming.
One quilted between five and fifteen years.
Five unknown

After:
One quilted between zero and five years of arriving.
Four quilted between five and fifteen years.
The Wingville Quilt was made about thirty years after the women arrived.
Elizabeth A. Kelly made her Pioneer Ribbon Quilt about sixty-five years after she arrived.

Those Who Wait

REASON FOR WAITING:
> Two waited until husbands established.
> Three waited until families established.
> One waited until the man returned to Midwest.

QUILTS
Of the project's six:
> Four were quilted before coming.
> One was quilted after arriving.
> One never came to Oregon.

Span of time represented by quilts: 1849-1880
Year brought to Oregon:
> 1853:   1
> 1857:   1
> 1865:   1
> 1870:   1
> Unkwn: 1
> Never: 1

Categories of quilts:
> Appliquéd: One
> Pieced: Five

Themes:
> Migration: Three
> Celebration: One
> Unknown: Two

QUILT MAKERS
Of the project's six:
> Age range from 26 to 82 with one unknown.
> One came with husband by ship.
> One came by herself with two young children by ship.
> One came with grandchildren by rail.
> One came over the Trail but unknown who she traveled with.
> One came by herself by rail.
> One didn't travel to Oregon.
> One making first migration.
> One making second migration.
> Three making third migration.

Reasons for coming:
> Two for economic and business opportunities.
> Three to be with adult children and family.
> Two settled in Jackson County.
> One settled in Linn County.
> One settled in Clark County, Washington Territory.
> One settled in Umatilla County.

Endnotes

Introduction

1. Lillian Schlissel, *Women's Diaries of the Westward Journey* (New York: Schocken Books, 1982), 10.

2. Schlissel, *Women's Diaries*, 155.

3. Rachel Maines, "Textiles as Hisory," *American Quilts, A Handmade Legacy*, edited by Thomas Frye (Oakland, California: Oakland Museum of Art, 1981), 41.

Preface

1. Leonore Gale Barette, "Christmas in Oregon Territory in 1853," In Glenn Mason, *A Piece of the Old Tent of 1853* (Eugene, Oregon, Lane County Historical Museum, 1976,) 27.

2. Gaston, Joseph, *The Centennial History of Oregon, 1811-1912* (Chicago: S.J. Clarke Publishing, 1912), volume 4, 412-22. In Stephen Dow Beckham, *Land of the Umpqua: A History of Douglas County, Oregon* (Roseburg, Oregon: Douglas County Commissioners, 1986), 70.

3. Harvey J. McKay, *St. Paul, Oregon 1830-1890* (Portland, Oregon: Binford and Mort, 1980), 26.

4. John Wesley Lieuallen, Letter to Josiah Lieuallen, 1864, Collection of Gilberta Lieuallen.

5. Lydia Louisa Whittemore Hutchins, Sampler, 1824, Collection of Harriet Fowler, Nicholasville, Kentucky.

6. Elaine Hedges, "The 19th-Century Diarist and Her Quilts." In Frye, *American Quilts*, 60.

7. McCormick's advertisement: *Democratic Standard* (Portland), October 18, 1855. In Sidney Warren, *Farthest Frontier: The Pacific Northwest* (New York: Macmillan Company, 1949), 236.

8. Anne Hyde, "The Significance of Perception and Interpretation in the History of the American West," Paper presented at the National Endowment for the Humanities Research Conference, Utah State University, Logan, Utah, July 1992.

9. Julie Roy Jeffrey, *Frontier Women: The Trans-Mississippi West 1840-1880* (New York: Hill and Wang, 1979), 87.

PART I

1. Joseph Ware, *The Emigrant's Guide to California*. Quoted in *The Emigrant's Guide to New Mexico, California, and Oregon Giving the Different Overland and Sea Routes Compiled from Reliable Authorities*, with a map (New York: J. Disturnell, 1849).

2. Redpath and Hinton, *Hand-book to Kansas Territory* 145; Rudolph B. Marcy, *The Prairie Traveler: A Handbook for Overland Expeditions* (New York: Harper and Brothers, 1859), 40; O. Allen, *Allen's Guide Book and Map to the Gold Fields of Kansas and Nebraska and Great Salt Lake City* (Washington, D.C.: R.A. Walters, 1859), 5-6. Quoted in Barbara Brackman, "Quilts on the Kansas Frontier," *Kansas History, a Journal of the Central Plains*, volume 13, number 1 (Spring 1990), 19.

3. Dorothy Johansen, *Empire of the Columbia* (New York: Harper and Row, 1967), 191.

4. John Clark, 1852. In Merle Mattes, *The Great Platte River Road* (Nebraska State Historical Society, 1969), Vol. 25, 61: "The elephant was the popular symbol of the Great Adventure, all the wonder and the glory and the shivering thrill of the plunge into the ocean of prairie and plains…It was the poetic imagery of all the deadly perils that threatened a westering emigrant."

5. Catherine Haun, *A Woman's Trip Across the Plains in 1849*. In Jeffrey, *Frontier Women*, 41.

6. Charlotte Stearns Pengra, *Diary*, 1853. In Schlissel, *Women's Diaries*, 81.

7. Pete Peterson, *Our Wagon Train is Lost* (Eugene, Oregon: New American Gothic, 1975), 20.

8. Jeffrey, *Frontier Women*, 45.

9. Winifred McKenzie, "Noah Franklin Lieuallen 1839-1876," Lieuallen Family Papers, Collection of Gilberta Lieuallen, Adams, Oregon.

10. Violet Mumford, *The Royal Way West*, volume 2 (Baltimore: Gateway Press, 1988), 21.

11. Caroline Dodds, *Men of Champoeg* (Portland, Oregon: Metropolitan Press, 1932), 156.

12. Lonny W. Fendall, "Medorem Crawford in Old Oregon," History Thesis (University of Oregon, March 1969), 131.

13. Fendall, "Medorem Crawford," 131.

14. Gaston, Joseph, *The Centennial History of Oregon, 1811-1912* (Chicago: S.J. Clarke Publishing, 1912), volume 4, 412-22. In Stephen Dow Beckham, *Land of the Umpqua*, 70.

15. Shannon Applegate, *Skookum: An Oregon Pioneer Family's History and Lore* (New York: William Morrow, 1988), 120.

16. Dean L. May, *Three Frontiers: Family, Land, and Society in the American West, 1850-1900* (Cambridge: Cambridge University Press, 1994), 181.

17. Gail McCormick, "Area's First Settler Struck Down by Smallpox," *Everything's Fine-o in Mulino!* (Mulino, Oregon: Self-published), volume 2, number 4.

18. Brackman, *Clues in the Calico* (EPM Publications, 1989), 69.

19. Brackman, "The Quilt Detective: Clues in the Needlework," digital newsletter, bbrackman@sunflower.com, May 22, 2005, 1.

20. Perkins Family Papers, Yamhill County Historical Museum, Lafayette, Oregon.

21. Amelia Peck, *American Quilts and Coverlets in the Metropolitan Museum of Art* (New York: Metropolitan Museum of Art, 1990), 180-181.

22. Brackman, telephone conversation with the author, June 1992.

23. Rachel Maines, "Paradigms of Scarcity and Abundance: The Quilt as an Artifact of the Industrial Revolution." In *Heart of Pennsylvania Symposium Papers* (Lewisburg, PA: Oral Traditions Project, 1986), 86.

24. Virginia Churchill Bath, *Needlework in America* (New York: Viking Press, 1979), 135-147.

25. Fred Scoggin, letter to author, June 1992.

26. Barbara Bowerman, correspondence with the author, December 2005.

27. Ruby Lacy, *Oregon Territory 1850 Census* (Self-published, 1984), 73.

28. U.S. Census, 1860, Oregon, Washington County, Forest Grove, 1226.

29. U.S. Census, 1870, Oregon, Wasco, east of Deschutes River, 59.

30. U.S. Census, 1870, Oregon, Washington County, 483.

31. Documentation File #848, Lane County Historical Museum, Eugene, Oregon.

32. Dena Katzenburg, *Blue Traditions: Indigo Dyed Textiles and Related Cobalt Glazed Ceramics From the 17th through the 19th Century* (Baltimore: Baltimore Museum of Art, 1973), 70.

33. Eileen Trestain, *Dating Fabrics: A Color Guide 1800-1900* (Paducah, KY: American Quilter's Society, 1998), 42.

34. "Historic Sodaville Spring Park Notes 90th Birthday," *Albany Democrat Herald* (Albany, Oregon, August 7, 1961).

35. Barbara Brackman, *An Encyclopedia of Pieced Quilt Patterns* (Lawrence, Kansas: Prairie Flower Publishing, 1984), number 740.

36. May, *Three Frontiers*, 181.

37. H.K. Hines, *An Illustrated History of the State of Oregon* (Chicago: The Lewis Publishing Co, 1893), 1242-1243.

38. Philip Joseph Currier, Currier Family Records of U.S.A. and Canada, vol. 2 (Concord, NH: Capital Offset Company, 1984), and vol. 5 (West Rutland, Vermont: Daamen, Inc., 2002).

39. www.applegatetrail.com.

40. Rita Adrosko, *Natural Dyes and Home Dyeing* (New York: Dover Publications, 1971), 30.

41. Schminck Scrapbook Number 17 (Lakeview, Oregon: Schminck Memorial Museum), 13.

42. Elias Buell, "This is a True Copy of the Genealogical Account of the Buells, Which was Written by Elias Buell in 1870." In Mary Fletcher, *History of Polk County* (Dallas, Oregon: Polk County Historical Society, 1987), 70.

43. JoAnn L. Wiss, letter to author, August 3, 1992.

44. Benton County Cemetery Records (Corvallis, Oregon, Mid-Valley Genealogical Society, 1987-1989), volumes 3, 8.

45. Lenice Bacon, *American Patchwork Quilts* (New York: Bonanza Books, 1973), 16.

46. "Mrs. Lucinda Spencer," *Transactions of the Fifteenth Annual Reunion of the Oregon Pioneer Association for 1887* (Portland, Oregon: Press of George H. Himes, 1887), 74-78.

47. Sidney Warren, *Farthest Frontier*, 83-84.

48. Nettie Spencer, "Lucinda Cox," *With Her Own Wings*, ed. by Helen Krebs Smith (Portland, Oregon: Fine Arts Department of Portland, Oregon Federation of Women's Organizations, 1948), 106-108.

49. Mabel Glover Root, *Family History of the Oregon Pioneer Families of Philip Glover and John H. Palmer*, unpublished manuscript, Collection of Louise Godfrey, Portland, Oregon, 54.

50. Glover-Palmer genealogy chart, Collection of Louise Godfrey.

51. Root, *Family History*, 54.

52. Brackman, *An Encyclopedia of Pieced Quilt Patterns*, number 3772.

53. U.S. Census 1870 Calapooia Precinct, Douglas County, Oregon, 104.

54. U.S. Census 1880, Oregon, Lane County, Springfield Precinct.

55. Harlow-Tandy family reunion notes, Collection of Rosalie Willet, Thibodaux, Louisiana.

56. Hazelton Family Papers, Lane County Historical Museum Archives, Eugene, Oregon.

57. U.S. Census 1900, Oregon, Lane, South Eugene Precinct 2, 121.

58. Accession File #63-96, Lane County Historical Museum, Eugene, Oregon.

PART II

1. Gloria Lathrop, "Introduction." In Laury, *Ho for California* (New York: E.P. Dutton, 1990), 15.

2. "Dr. T., 1849." In Ingvard Eide, *Oregon Trail* (Chicago: Rand McNally, 1972), 112-113.

3. Percival G. Lowe, *Five Years a Dragoon and Other Adventures on the Great Plains*, edited by Don Russell. In John Unruh, *The Plains Across* (Urbana, Illinois: University of Illinois Press, 1993), 210.

4. Unruh, *The Plains Across*, 201-243.

5. Charles Martin, "Report of Captain Medorem Crawford," *Overland Journal*, Summer and Fall, 1984, volumes 3 and 4.

6. Peter D. Olch, MD., "Trailing the Elephant's Tail," *Overland Journal*, volume 6, number 1, Spring 1988, 25-31.

7. James Madison Powell, *Powell Family History* (Portland, Oregon: Design Printing, 1977), 35-36.

8. Dan Stebbins, wheelwright and historian at Wyoming Territorial Prison, conversation with author, August 1992.

9. Rosemary G. Palmer, "The Sabbath According to Female Diarists on the Trail," *Overland Journal*, volume 22, number 4, Winter 2004/2005, 160-169.

10. Jeffrey, *Frontier Women*, 43.

11. James H.B. Royal, "Journal of James H.B. Royal While Crossing the Plains in 1853." University of Oregon Archives, Eugene, Oregon, 9.

12. Violet Mumford, *The Royal Way West*, volume 2, 128-135.

13. Lois Riggs, "The Zadoc S. Riggs Family," *Polk County Pioneer Sketches* (Dallas: Sarah Childress DAR Polk Chapter #6, 1927).

14. Starr-Riggs family papers, Manuscript file #2637, Oregon Historical Society Research Library.

15. Accession #62.3.6.1 Southern Oregon Historical Society, Medford, Oregon.

16. George W. Riddle, *History of Early Days in Oregon*. (Riddle, Oregon: The Riddle Enterprise, 1920), 41.

17. Riddle, *Early Days*, 63.

18. Riddle, *Early Days*, 17.

19. U.S. Census 1870, Oregon, Jackson County, 40.

20. William Alley, "Gracie's Visit to the Rogue River Valley," *Oregon Historical Quarterly* (Portland, Oregon: Oregon Historical Society, volume 106, number 2, Summer 2005), 295-306.

21. Henry E. Morris, "Eliam Morris Family History 1811-1958," *Champoeg Pioneer*, volume 2, number 30, July 1958, 2.

22. W.B. Chandler, "I Was a Third Generation Pioneer," *Oregon Historical Quarterly*, volume LXVI, number 3, September 1965, 210.

23. www.ancestry.com – Susannah Louisiana Good.

24. George H. Greer, "The James Greer Family," Polk County Pioneer Sketches (Dallas, Oregon: *Polk County Observer*, 1927), 34-35.

25. *Portrait and Biographical Record of the Willamette Valley, Oregon* (Chicago: Chapman Publishing Co., 1903), 381-382.

26. Barbara Brackman, *The Quilt Detective: Clues in Style*, Number 1, April 2, 2006, 2.

27. Accession file #705, Lane County Historical Museum, Eugene, Oregon.

28. Joseph Gaston, *The Centennial History of Oregon 1811-1912*, volume 2 (Chicago: S.J. Clarke Publishing, 1911), 249.

29. U.S. Census 1870, Oregon, Lane County, Pleasant Hill Township, 508.

30. Elly Sienkiewicz, *Spoken Without a Word* (Washington, DC: Self-published, 1983), 45.

31. A.C. Seely Papers, Douglas County Museum of History and Natural History, Roseburg, Oregon.

32. Beckham, *Land of the Umpqua*, 131.

33. Joseph Gaston, Centennial History of Oregon 1811-1912, volume 3, 281.

34. Brackman, *Encyclopedia*, number 1963.

35. Beckham, *Land of the Umpqua*, 127.

36. *Historic Douglas County, Oregon* (Roseburg: Douglas County Historical Society, 1982), 120-121.

37. "Hon. Charles Drain," *History of Southern Oregon* (Portland, Oregon: A. G. Walling, 1884), 526-527.

38. Steven Grafe, "Walking in Strange Gardens: Early Floral Design In the Columbia River Plateau." In *Painters, Patrons, and Identity: Essay in Native American Art to Honor J.J. Brody*, edited by Joyce Szabo (Albuquerque, New Mexico: University of New Mexico Press, 2001), 263-278.

39. Kevin Mittge, *The Robbins and Herren Families of the Pacific Northwest* (Kirkland, Washington: Self-published, 1988), 12.

40. Mittge, 61.

41. Mittge, 83.

42. Wanita Propst Haugen, interview with author, Albany, Oregon, May 1992.

43. Sienkiewicz, *Spoken Without a Word*, 49.

44. Powell, *Powell History*, 310.

45. Wanita Propst Haugen, *Quilt Documentation*, 1992.

46. Emma E. Royal O'Sullivan, letter to Alan, October 9, 1947, United Methodist Archives-Oregon, Salem, Oregon.

47. Ruth Stoller, letter to author, July 1992.

48. Richard White, *It's Your Misfortune and None of My Own: A New History of the American west* (Norman, Oklahoma: University of Oklahoma Press, 1991), 307-316.

49. Erle Howell, *Methodism in the Northwest* (Nashville: Parthenon Press, 1966), 209.

50. Emma Royal O'Sullivan, "Mrs. James Henry Bascom Royal (1850-1940)." In Smith, *With Her Own Wings*, 91-93.

51. Brackman, *Encyclopedia*, number 1462.

52. Brackman, *Clues*, 91-92.

53. "The Dibbles and the Dibble House 1856-1859," Collection of Gena Cline, Molalla Historical Society, Molalla, Oregon.

54. Pat Ferrero, Elaine Hedges, Julie Silber, *Hearts and Hands: The Influence of Women and Quilts on American Society* (San Francisco: Quilt Digest Press, 1987), 18.

55. "The Dibbles and the Dibble House 1856-1859."

56. "Teasels: Wool Industry," Scrapbook 38, Oregon Historical Society Research Library, 77.

57. Alfred L. Lomax, *Later Woolen Mills in Oregon* (Portland, Oregon: Binford and Mort, 1974), 183.

58. Quilt number 1721, Oregon Historical Society, Portland, Oregon.

59. Abigail Scott Duniway, "Editorial Correspondence," *New Northwest*, July 15, 1880. In Ruth Barnes Moynihan, *Rebel for Rights, Abigail Scott Duniway*. (New Haven, Connecticut: Yale University Press, 1983), 153.

60. www.ancestry.com – John Tucker Scott.

61. Letter from Aunt Etty (Harriet) to Clyde Duniway, March 24, 1925, Duniway Papers. In Moynihan, *Rebel for Rights*, 31.

62. Abigail Scott Duniway, *From the West to the West: Across the Plains to Oregon* (Chicago: A.C. McClurg, 1905), 147. In Moynihan, *Rebel for Rights*, xiii.

63. John Bunyan, *Pilgrim's Progress*. In Myron and Patsy Orlofsky, *Quilts in America* (New York: McGraw-Hill, 1974), 265.

64. U.S. Census 1860 Oregon, Polk, Monmouth, B.

65. www.rootsweb.com/~carpenter/index.html.

66. U.S. Census 1850 Missouri, Cass County, Sixteenth District, 95.

67. *Genealogical Material in Oregon Donation Land Claims* (Portland, Oregon: Genealogical Forum, 1957, volume II), 58.

68. Charles Nordhoff, *The Communistic Societies of the United States* (New York: Dover Publications, 1996), 311.

69. Clark Moor Will, "Colony Mothers help write Colony History," Collection of the Aurora Colony Historical Society. Aurora, Oregon.

70. "1985 Aurora Colony Quilt Show," Collection of the Aurora Colony Historical Society.

71. U.S. Census 1870 Oregon, Marion County, Aurora, 74.

72. Grace Jane Simpson Skeeters, "The Life of Mrs. Grace Jane Skeeters," Southern Oregon Historical Society Archives, Medford, Oregon.

73. Penny McMorris, *Crazy Quilts* (New York: E. P. Dutton, 1986), 12.

74. U.S. Census 1870, Oregon, Lane County, Springfield township, 52.

PART III

1. Larry Carten, "Pioneers Found Blue Mountains Main Obstacle on Oregon Trail," *Oregon Journal*, February 12, 1956.

2. L. Jane Powell, "Incidents of Journey Across the Plains of Captain John A. Powell and Company," *Powell History* (Portland, Oregon: Design Printing, 1977), 37.

3. Charles Hoffman, *The Search for Oregon's Lost Blue Bucket Mine* (Medford, Oregon: Webb Research Group, 1992), 89.

4. Mrs. Elizabeth Currier Foster, interview in 1914, Collection of the Schminck Museum, Lakeview, Oregon.

5. Riddle, *Early Days*, 29.

6. www.applegatetrail.com.

7. Carten, "Pioneers...," 10.

8. Powell, *Powell History*, 38.

9. Powell, *Powell History*, 38

10. William Denison Lyman, *Old Walla Walla County* (Chicago: S.J. Clarke Publishing Co., 1918), 609-610.

11. Brackman, "Quilts on the Kansas Frontier," *Kansas History*, volume 13, number 1 (Spring 1990), 19.

12. "Diary of Nathaniel Myer." In Edward Ham, "Journey into Southern Oregon: Diary of a Pennsylvania Dutchman," *Oregon Historical Quarterly* (September 1959), 385-386.

13. Andrew S. McClure, "Journal, 1853" In Peterson, *Our Wagon Train is Lost*, 21.

14. Pengra, "Diary, 1853." In Schlissel, *Women's Diaries*, 99.

15. John Boardman, "The Journal of John Boardman: An Overland Journey from Kansas to Oregon in 1843." In Ingvard Eide, *Oregon Trail*, 191.

16. E.L. Meyers, *Barlow Toll Road 1846-1919: The Story of Two Men from Fort Deposit* (Portland, Oregon: Genealogical Forum, 1972), 5.

17. Kelly, Plympton, Miscellaneous Family Papers, MSS 871, Oregon Historical Society Research Library, Portland, Oregon.

18. U.S. Census 1860, Oregon, Multnomah County, Portland, 25.

19. "Address of Mrs. Plympton Kelly before the Public School at Lents on Friday, May 12, 1903," MSS 871, Oregon Historical Society Research Library.

20. "The Midwinter Fair," *Morning Oregonian*, December 5, 1893, 10.

21. www.ancestry.com – Euda Aletha Kelly.

22. Michael family history, Collection of Cydney Bush, Portland, Oregon.

23. Yarnes, Thomas, *A History of Oregon Methodism* (Parthenon Press, n.d.), 193.

24. *Illustrated History of Baker, Grant, Malheur and Harney Counties*, n.p., 1902.

25. Helen Rand, *Gold, Jade, and Elegance* (Baker, Oregon: self-published, 1974), 27.

26. Chandler, *Oregon Historical Quarterly*, 208.

27. Dean L. May, *Three Frontiers*, 78.

28. Suzzy Chalfant Payne and Susan Aylsworth Murwin, *Creative American Quilting Inspired by the Bible* (Old Tappan, New Jersey: Fleming H. Revell, 1983), 23.

29. Rosemary Makhan, *Biblical Blocks: Inspired Designs for Quilters* (Woodinville, Washington: Martingale, 1993), 24.

30. *Settlement Records 1878*, Aurora Colony Historical Society, Aurora, Oregon, 49.

31. Clark Moor Will, "1863 Water Trip of the Knight's and Genger's Families," Unpublished manuscript, Aurora Colony Museum.

32. Mildred Baker Burcham, *Our Knight Heritage*, Aurora Colony Historical Society.

33. U.S. Census 1870, Oregon, Clackamas County, Canimah Precinct, 9 and Marion County Aurora Precinct, 150.

34. U.S. Census 1880, Oregon, Marion County, 30.

35. John E. Simon, "Wilhelm Keil, Founder of Aurora," M.A. Thesis, University of Oregon, 1935, 78.

36. *Settlement Records 1878*, 2.

37. Stauffer Family Papers, *Collection of Vera Yoder*, Woodburn, Oregon.

38. Nordhoff, *The Communistic Societies*, 312.

39. Clark Will, *The Story of Old Aurora in Picture and Prose 1856-1883* (Self-published, 1972), 24.

40. Nordhoff, *Communistic Societies*, 316.

41. Patrick Harris, interview with author, July 1992.

42. Martin, *Overland Journal*, Fall, 1984, 27.

43. Mrs. George Blankenship, *Early History of Thurston County, Washington Together with Biographies and Reminiscences of Those Identified with Pioneer Days* (Olympia, Washington: no publisher, 1914), 214.

44. Blankenship, *Early History of Thurston County*, 212-218.

45. Sienkiewicz, *Spoken without a Word*, 39.

46. Goddard and Robison Family History, Collection of Bonnie Furry, Medford, Oregon; Lida Childers, telephone conversation with author, August 1992.

47. Ruth Finley, *Old Patchwork Quilts and the Women Who Made Them* (Newton Center, Massachusetts: Charles Branford, 1957), 93.

48. U.S. Census 1880, Oregon, Jackson, Eden Precinct, 133.

49. Goddard and Robison Family History.

50. Mabel Lieuallen Wagner, *Water From the Spring*, unpublished manuscript, Collection of Don and Gilberta Lieuallen.

51. Sally Lieuallen, "Diligent Search Gains Century Farm Award," *Pioneer Trails* (Pendleton, Oregon: Umatilla County Historical Society, June 1980), volume 4, number 3.

52. Dorothy Lieuallen, *Peyton and Jemima Lieuallen*, manuscript, Collection of Don and Gilberta Lieuallen, Adams, Oregon.

53. Brackman, *Clues*, 66-67.

54. Betina Havig, *Missouri Heritage Quilts*. (Padacuh, KY: American Quilter's Society, 1986), 62-63.

55. Brackman, *Encyclopedia*, number 3842.

56. U.S. Census 1880 and 1900 Oregon, Umatilla County, Weston Precinct.

57. Lena Lieuallen and Mabel Lieuallen Wagner, *Memories of Grandpa and Grandma Lieuallen*, unpublished manuscript, Collection of Don and Gilberta Lieuallen.

58. Bryan Family History. In Joyce Gross, *Quilts of the West* (Exhibition Catalog, Mill Valley, California, 1976), 9.

59. Brackman, *Encyclopedia*, number 3536.

60. Hazel Spraker, *The Boone Family: A Genealogical History of the Descendants of George and Mary Boone who Came to America in 1717* (Baltimore, Maryland: Genealogical Publishing Co., 1922), 505.

61. U.S. Census 1870 Oregon Yamhill County, Sheridan Precinct, 544.

62. U.S. Census 1900 Oregon Lake County, Crooked Creek Precinct, 188.

63. U.S. Census 1910 Oregon Lake County, Crooked Creek Precinct, 18.

64. Tedde Pruett, *Way Down Yonder: Quilts of the Deep South*, American Quilt Study Group Seminar Study Center, Denver, Colorado, 2005.

65. Brackman, *Encyclopedia*, number 241.

66. Gaye Ingram, telephone conversation with the author, March 2006.

67. M.H. Pope, "Seven, Seventh, Seventy," *Interpreter's Dictionary of the Bible*, edited by Keith R. Crim and George A. Buttrick (Nashville, Tennessee: Abingdon Press, 1992), volume 4, 295.

68. Charlotte Enfield, telephone conversation with the author, February 25, 2006.

69. U.S. Census 1870 Oregon, Washington County, Forest Grove, 4.

70. Adda Roberts, *The David Roberts-Jane Anderson Family*, Collection of Janice Roberts Zuger, Waitsburg, Washington.

71. Laura Jean Hevel, e-mail to author, February 13, 2006.

PART IV

1. Robin Helman, e-mail to author, December 4, 2005.

2. Suellen Meyer, "Pine Tree Quilts," *The Quilt Digest* (San Francisco:

The Quilt Digest Press, 1986), 14.

3. Helman, e-mail.

4. Bippi Soukey, "Ashland's Original Granddaughter," *Ashland Plaza*, May 1978.

5. Kay Atwood, *Mill Creek Journal Ashland Oregon 1850-1860* (Ashland, Oregon: Self-published, 1987), 31.

6. U.S. Census 1860 Oregon, Jackson, Ashland, 95.

7. Lewis McArthur, *Oregon Geographic Names* (Portland: Oregon Historical Society, 1992).

8. Soukey, *Ashland Plaza*.

9. Atwood, *Mill Creek Journal*, 188.

10. Loren Horton, telephone conversation with author, Iowa City, Iowa, December 13, 2005.

11. Don McKinstry, "Overland to the West," unpublished manuscript, September 7, 2000, Collection of Nancy Walker Morgan

12. Brackman, letter to author, July 15, 1992.

13. U.S. Census 1880 Oregon, Umatilla County, Greasewood, 104.

14. Helen Barrett Woodroofe, "Quilt Recalls a Strong, Good Woman," *The Callaway Journal*, volume 8, 1983, 62.

15. Nancy Tuckhorn, Associate Curator, DAR Museum, letter to the author, July 1992.

16. *William Whitley House Historic Site*, Kentucky Department of Parks, 1992.

17. Louis Rasmussen, *Railway Passenger Lists of Overland Trains to San Francisco and the West*, San Francisco Historic Records, volume I, 73.

18. Helen Crawford, *Life of Mary Whitley Gilmour, 1931*, Collection of Georgiana Gilbert, Eugene, Oregon.

19. U.S. Census 1860 Missouri, Mercer County, Morgan Township, 141.

20. U.S. Census 1870 Missouri, DeKalb County, Polk Township, 503.

21. U.S. Census 1880 Nebraska, Richardson County, Falls City, 427.

22. Charles Carey, *History of Oregon* (Chicago: Pioneer Historical Publishing, 1922), 40.

23. William Robbins, *Landscapes of Promise* (Seattle: University of Washington Press, 1997), 171.

24. Lena Lieuallen, family history note, Gilberta Lieuallen, Adams, Oregon

25. Note attached to quilt by Robert S. Bell, M.D.

26. Genealogical Material in Oregon Donation Land Claim, Genealogical Forum, 1957, volume II, number 5022.

27. Telephone interview with Frances Bell Metzger, Scottsdale, Arizona, May 1992.

28. U.S. Census, 1870, Iowa, Keokuk County, 353.

Postscript

1. Greg Franzwa, "Folio: Newsletter of Patrice Press" (Tucson, Arizona: Patrice Press, May 1996).

2. George Atkinson, "Diary of Rev. George Atkinson 1847-1858," ed. E. Ruth Rockwood, *Oregon Historical Quarterly*, 1939, volume XL, 348-349.

3. Jeffrey, *Frontier Women*, xv.

4. Lansford W. Hastings, *The Emigrants' Guide to Oregon and California*, original edition 1845 (Princeton, New Jersey: Princeton University Press, 1932), 58.

5. White, *It's Your Misfortunate and None of My Own: A New History of the American West* (Norman, Oklahoma: University of Oklahoma Press, 1991), 299.

6. Powell, "Pioneer Days," *Powell Family History*, 39-40.

7. David Alan Johnson, *Founding the Far West: California, Oregon, and Nevada, 1840-1890* (Berkeley: University of California Press, 1992), 41. In David Peterson del Mar, *Oregon's Promise: An Interpretive History* (Corvallis, Oregon: Oregon State University Press, 2003), 77.

8. Dorothy Johansen, *Empire of the Columbia*, 264-265.

9. Shannon Applegate, *Skookum*, 126.

10. Dean May, *Three Frontiers*, 178-181.

11. Sidney Warren, *Farthest Frontier: The Pacific Northwest* (New York: Macmillan Company, 1949), 83.

12. Charles Nordhoff, *The Communistic Societies*, 305-320.

13. Simon, "Wilhelm Keil, Founder of Aurora," 78.

14. Peterson del Mar, *Oregon's Promise*, 104.

15. Hoffman, *Search for Oregon's Lost Blue Bucket Mine*, 89.

16. Christopher Carlson, "The Rural Family in the 19th Century: A Case Study in Oregon's Willamette Valley," Ph.D. Dissertation, University of Oregon, 1980, 186-193.

17. May, *Three Frontiers*, 130-135.

18. Clara Humason Waldo, "The Woman on the Farm," 169. In Mary Osborn Douthit, *The Souvenir of Western Women* (Portland: Anderson and Duniway, 1905), 170.

19. Richard White, *It's Your Misfortunate and None of My Own*, 298-299.

20. Beatrice Brewer, "Cynthia and Melinda Applegate." In *With Her Own Wings*, 105.

21. Rosemary Skinner Keller, "Creating A Sphere for Women." In *Women in New Worlds*, Hilah F. Thomas and Rosemary Skinner Keller, eds. (Nashville: Abingdon, 1981), 250-251.

22. Warren, *Farthest Frontier*, 221-222.

23. Warren, *Ibid.*, 235.

24. Chandler, *Oregon Historical Quarterly*, 215.

25. Waldo, *The Souvenir of Western Women*, 169.

26. Bethina Owens-Adair, *Some of Her Life Experiences* (Portland: Mann and Beach, 1906), 151-152.

27. Owens-Adair, *Some of Her Life Experiences*, 157-158.

28. "Mrs. Dr. Owens-Adair," *History of the Pacific Northwest: Oregon and Washington* (Portland, Oregon: North Pacific History Company, n.d.), 502-506.

29. "B.C. Goddard," *Talent News*, volume 2, number 14, Talent, Oregon, August 15, 1893.

30. Carol Barrett, *Women's Roots in Southern Oregon and Northern California* (Medford, Oregon: Self-published, 1993), 38-39.

31. Carlson, "The Rural Family in the 19th Century," 186-193.

32. Jean M. Ward and Elaine A. Maveety, *Pacific Northwest Women 1815-1925* (Corvallis, Oregon: Oregon State University Press, 1995), 7.

Appendix A

1. Sienkiewicz, *Spoken without a Word*, 31-49.

2. John H. Clark, "Overland to the Gold Fields of California in 1852," Louise Berry, ed., *Kansas Historical Quarterly*, 11, August 1942, 229. In Sandra Myres, *Westering Women and the Frontier Experience 1800-1915* (University of New Mexico Press, 1982), 101.

3. Susan Curtis, "Blessed Be God for Flowers: Nineteenth-Century Quilt Designs," Patricia Cox Crews, editor, *Flowering of Quilts* (Lincoln, Nebraska: University of Nebraska Press, 2001), 18.

4. Brackman, *Encyclopedia*, 170-172.

5. Virginia Gunn, "Romance and Reality: A Century in Quilt Scholarship 1890-1990." Paper presented as part of panel, Directions in Quilt Scholarship, Bibliography Conference, Louisville, Kentucky, February 6-8, 1992.

6. Ruth Finley, *Old Patchwork Quilts and the Women Who Made Them* (Newton Centre, Massachusetts: Charles Branford, 1929), 130.

7. Finley, *Old Patchwork Quilts*, 130-131; Carrie Hall and Rosa Kretzinger, *The Romance of the Patchwork Quilt in America* (New York: Bonanza Books, 1935), 74.

8. May, *Three Frontiers*, 146.

9. Ricky Clark, *Quilted Gardens: Floral Quilts of the Nineteenth Century* (Nashville, Tennessee: Rutledge Hill Press, 1994), 3, 21.

10. Mary Bywater Cross, *Quilts and Women of the Mormon Migrations* (Nashville, Tennessee: Rutledge Hill Press, 1996), 50-51.

Appendix B

1. Tabitha Brown, letter to brother and sister, August, 1854. In *Pacific University Bulletin*, volume 32, number 6, December 1936.

2. Elizabeth Geer, journal. In Ingvard Eide, *Oregon Trail*, 219-220.

3. Sheba Hargreaves, "The Letters of Rozelle Putnam, 1849-1852," *Oregon Historical Quarterly*, volume 29, 256-257.

4. Eleanor Allen, *Canvas Caravans* (Portland: Binford and Mort, 1946), 116-123.

5. Leah Collins Menefee and Lowell Tiller, "Cutoff Fever," *Oregon Historical Quarterly*, volume 78, number 3 September 1977, 213.

6. Pete Peterson, *Our Wagon Train is Lost*, 15.

7. *Ibid*, 28-29.

8. Catherine Leonard Jones, letter to Mrs. C.H. Dye, November 12, 1900. Collection of Patricia Erlandson, Medford, Oregon.

9. John Bruce Bell, letter to friend Mary, May 21st, 1855. In the collection of Mrs. Robert S. Bell.

10. Lois Ann Stewart, letter to the author, June 1992.

Glossary

1. Virginia Bath, *Needlework in America* (New York: Viking Press, 1979), 144-145.

Glossary

Appliqué: a category of quilts constructed by laying one fabric on top of another and stitching the two together.

Bed Rug: a twentieth-century term used to define the rug used on a bed in the seventeenth and eighteenth centuries when it was referred to as a rug. It was a heavily embroidered or hooked wool-based covering. Surface designs from these were used as whole cloth quilt designs.

Binding: the finish to the raw edge of the quilt, usually a strip of straight or bias fabric

Block: the unit or section of the quilt made by joining fabric pieces or appliquéing them together. It is often the unit of design of the quilt pattern.

Border: the band of fabric stitched to the edge of the top to give the extra needed width or length.

Cholera: a rapidly fatal disease that could strike and kill within hours of the first symptoms, usually diarrhea, followed by sore throat, abdominal pains, leg cramps, chills, fever and ending with vomiting, the worst and final symptom. If a dose of medicine such as laudanum were available early enough, recovery was possible.

Crazy Quilt: a style of quilt made in the last half of the nineteenth century where irregular shapes of fabric are stitched together and embellished with embroidery stitches, beads, ribbons, paintings, and stamped designs.

Design: the overall organization of the quilt, or a specific pattern.

Drawnwork: embroidery done on an area where the threads have been withdrawn in one direction.

Elbow or fan quilting: the style of quilting lines made using the elbow as a fulcrum for marking the lines on the quilt top. A series of marks are made evenly spaced on a surface. Then, the elbow is placed on a mark and an arc is made marking the line for quilting by swinging the hand in an arc. This was a very effective and fast method of marking quilt lines if one was not quilting a separate motif in each block or outlining each design.

Indigo-blue: a color produced by a multi-process. First, a vat process of fermentation to get the dye liquid from the Indigofera plant. Then, a process of oxidation to color the fabric by soaking up the liquid and exposing it to air followed.

Indigo-blue and white fabric: colorfast textiles featuring interesting design elements, mass produced and readily available to quilt makers in the States with the development of the textile industry in America, including improved dying and printing processes.

Medallion: a quilt with a large central motif on the top surrounded by additional designs and/or borders.

Mourning Prints: the fine black lines and figures printed close enough on a white background fabric to appear gray. They were called this in the mail-order catalogs of the late nineteenth century.

Nooning: the break taken at mid-day during the journey for food and rest for people and animals.

On point: the arrangement of quilt blocks with the corners touching the baseline and one another.

Pieced: the category of quilts constructed by joining the edges of fabrics together to make the top, usually in a geometric pattern.

Quilt: two layers of fabric placed with a batting between stitched or tied together, a textile sandwich.

Rainbow print: the fabric produced by varying the shades of color on the printing press roller to produce a rainbow of colors or different intensities of the same color. The use in quilts was popular between 1820 and 1860.

Roller print fabric: a revolutionary step in textile production in the late 1700s where the flat plate was wrapped around a roller on the printing press, allowing the continuous printing of fabric. The effect was immediate, producing significantly more and better quality printed fabrics by the 1830s.

Set: the arrangement of the quilt blocks or squares

Template: the pattern piece followed in cutting the fabric for a design.

Tufted Candlewicking: the process of using a thick thread of several strands of wicking to make the loops of the running stitch. Using a stick or wire as gauge, these stitches are left about one quarter of inch in height above the surface of the cloth instead of drawing the thread down to the surface. These loops are cut to create a tuft or pile. More often there is a combination of embroidery, uncut candlewicking, and tufted pile. The uncut candlewicking gives greater clarity to the design while the tufted pile gives a greater richness.[1]

Turkey red: the most popular fabric of the 1840s, made of the colorfast dye, Turkey red, used to create the expensive prints imported from England. They were not produced in America because it was time-consuming process of thirteen to twenty steps in a very long timeframe. They were considered quite expensive to purchase as an imported fabric.

White work: a quilt top of all white fabric with white embroidery or quilting.

Whole Cloth: a quilt top made of one fabric, either a solid piece or several stitched together.

Bibliography

Quilts and Quilt History

Many excellent quilt books are available today for research and study of quiltmakers and their art. This bibliography, however, limits itself to those that made a direct contribution to the research for this volume on the quilts and quiltmakers of the Oregon Trail.

Adrosko, Rita. *Natural Dyes and Home Dyeing.* New York: Dover Publications, 1971.

Bacon, Lenice. *American Patchwork Quilts.* New York: Bonanza Books, 1973.

Bath, Virginia Churchill. *Needlework in America.* New York: Viking Press, 1979.

Better Homes and Gardens. *American Heritage Quilts.* Des Moines, Iowa: Meredith Corporation, 1991.

Bowman, Doris. *The Smithsonian Treasury American Quilts.* Washington, D.C.: Smithsonian Institution, 1991.

Brackman, Barbara. *An Encyclopedia of Pieced Quilt Patterns.* Lawrence, Kansas: Prairie Flower Publishing, 1984.

——. *Clues in the Calico: A Guide to Identifying and Dating Antique Quilts.* McLean, Virginia: EPM Publications, 1989.

——. *The Quilt Detective: Clues in the Needlework,* 2005, digital newsletter.

Bresenhan, Karoline Patterson, and Nancy O'Bryant Puentes. *Lone Stars: A Legacy of Texas Quilts, 1836-1936.* Austin, Texas: University of Texas, 1986.

Clark, Ricky. *Quilted Gardens: Floral Quilts of the Nineteenth Century.* Nashville, Tennessee: Rutledge Hill Press, 1994.

Clark, Ricky, George Knepper, and Ellice Ronsheim. *Quilts in Community, Ohio's Traditions.* Nashville, Tennessee: Rutledge Hill Press, 1991.

Cross, Mary Bywater. *Quilts and Women of the Mormon Migrations.* Nashville, Tennessee: Rutledge Hill Press, 1996.

Dewhurst, C. Kurt, Betty MacDowell, and Marsha MacDowell. *Artists in Aprons: Folk Art by American Women.* New York: E.P. Dutton, 1979.

Ferrero, Pat, Elaine Hedges, and Julie Silber. *Hearts and Hands: The Influence of Women and Quilts on American Society.* San Francisco, California: Quilt Digest Press, 1987.

Frye, Thomas, ed. *American Quilts, A Handmade Legacy.* Oakland, California: Museum of Art, 1981.

Finley, Ruth. *Old Patchwork Quilts and the Women Who Made Them.* Newton Center, Massachusetts: Charles Branford, 1929.

Gross, Joyce. *Quilts of the West.* Mill Valley, California: Self-published, 1976.

Hall, Carrie, and Rose Kretsinger. *The Romance of the Patchwork Quilt in America.* New York: Bonanza Books, 1935.

Havig, Betina. *Missouri Heritage Quilts.* Paducah, Kentucky: American Quilter's Society, 1986.

Jenkins, Susan, and Linda Seward. *The American Quilt Story.* Emmaus, Pennsylvania: Rodale Press, 1991.

Katzenburg, Dena. *Blue Traditions: Indigo Dyed Textiles and Related Cobalt Glazed Ceramics from the 17th through the 19th Century.* Baltimore: Baltimore Museum of Art, 1973.

Kimball, Jeana. *Red and Green: An Appliqué Tradition.* Bothell, Washington: A Patchwork Place, 1990.

Lasansky, Jeannette. *In the Heart of Pennsylvania: 19th & 20th Century Quiltmaking Traditions.* Lewisburg, Pennsylvania: Oral Traditions Project, 1985.

Laury, Jean Ray and California Heritage Quilt Project. *Ho for California.* New York: E.P. Dutton, 1990.

Makhan, Rosemary. *Biblical Blocks: Inspired Designs for Quilters.* Woodinville, Washington: Martingale, 1993.

McMorris, Penny. *Crazy Quilts.* New York: E.P. Dutton, 1986.

Orlofsky, Myron and Patsy. *Quilts in America.* New York: McGraw-Hill, 1974.

Payne, Suzzy Chalfant, and Susan Aylsworth Murwin. *Creative American Quilting Inspired by the Bible.* Old Tappan, New Jersey: Fleming H. Revell, 1983.

Peck, Amelia. *American Quilts and Coverlets in The Metropolitan Museum of Art.* New York: Dutton Studio Books, 1991.

Robertson, Elizabeth. *American Quilts.* New York: Studio Publications, 1948.

Sienkiewicz, Elly. *Spoken Without a Word.* Washington, D.C.: Self-published, 1983.

Stowe, Harriet Beecher. *Minister's Wooing.* New York: Hurst and Company, n.d.

Swan, Susan. *Plain and Fancy: American Women and Their Needlework, 1700-1850.* New York: Holt, Rinehart, and Winston, 1977.

Trestain, Eileen. *Dating Fabrics: A Color Guide 1800-1900.* Paducah, Kentucky: American Quilter's Society, 1998.

Twelker, Nancyann J. *Women and Their Quilts: A Washington State Centennial Tribute.* Bothell, Washington: That Patchwork Place, 1988.

Warren, Elizabeth V., and Sharon L. Eisenstat. *Glorious American Quilts: The Quilt Collection of the Museum of American Folk Art.* New York: Penguin Studio Books, 1996.

Webster, Marie. *Quilts: Their Story and How to Make Them.* New York: Tudor, 1915.

Historical Background

Books

Allen, Eleanor. *Canvas Caravans.* Portland, Oregon: Binford and Mort, 1946.

Applegate, Shannon. *Skookum: An Oregon Pioneer Family's History and Lore.* New York: William Morrow, 1988.

——. *Living Among Headstones: Life in a Country Cemetery.* New York: Avalon Publishing Group, 2005.

Atwood, Kay. *Mill Creek Journal, Ashland Oregon 1850-1860.* Ashland, Oregon: Self-published, 1987.

Beckham, Stephen Dow. *Land of the Umpqua: A History of Douglas County, Oregon.* Roseburg, Oregon: Douglas County Commissioners, 1986.

Blankenship, Mrs. George. *Early History of Thurston County, Washington with Biographies and Reminiscences of Those Identified with Pioneer Days.* Olympia, Washington: no publisher, 1914.

Blair, Karen. *Northwest Women: An Annotated Bibliography of Sources on the History of Oregon and Washington, 1787-1970.* Pullman, Washington: Washington State University Press, 1997.

Butruille, Susan. *Women's Voices from the Western Frontier.* Boise, Idaho: Tamarack Books, 1995.

Carey, Charles. *History of Oregon.* Chicago: Pioneer Historical Publishing, 1922.

Carlson, Christopher. *The Rural Family in the 19th Century: A Case Study in Oregon's Willamette Valley.* Eugene, Oregon: University of Oregon, 1980.

Dodds, Caroline. *Men of Champoeg.* Portland, Oregon: Metropolitan Press, 1932.

Douthit, Mary Osborn. *The Souvenir of Western Women.* Portland: Anderson and Duniway, 1905.

Eide, Ingvard. *Oregon Trail.* Chicago: Rand McNally, 1972.

Fendall, Lonny W. *Medorem Crawford in Old Oregon.* History Thesis, University of Oregon, March 1969.

Fletcher, Mary. *History of Polk County.* Dallas, Oregon: Polk County Historical Society, 1987.

Gaston, Joseph. *The Centennial History of Oregon 1811-1912, Volume II.* Chicago: S.J. Clarke Publishing, 1911.

Genealogical Material in Oregon Donation Land Claims, Volume II. Portland, Oregon: Genealogical Forum, 1957.

Hastings, Lansford W. *The Emigrants' Guide to Oregon and California,* original edition 1845. Princeton, New Jersey: Princeton University Press, 1932.

Hines, H.K. *An Illustrated History of the State of Oregon.* Chicago: The Lewis Publishing Company, 1893.

History of Southern Oregon. Portland, Oregon: A.G. Walling, 1884.

Hoffman, Charles. *The Search for Oregon's Lost Blue Bucket Mine*. Medford, Oregon: Webb Research Group, 1992.

Howell, Erle. *Methodism in the Northwest*. Nashville, Tennessee: The Parthenon Press, 1966.

Hyde, Anne. *An American Vision: Far Western Landscape and National Culture, 1820-1920*. New York: New York University Press, 1990.

Jeffrey, Julie Roy. *Frontier Women: The Trans-Mississippi West 1840-1880*. New York: Hill and Wang, 1979.

Johansen, Dorothy. *Empire of the Columbia*. New York: Harper and Row, 1967.

Kirkpatrick, Jane. *A Clearing in the Wild*. New York: WaterBrook Press, 2006.

Lacy, Ruby. *Oregon Territory 1850 Census*. Self-published, 1984.

Lomax, Alfred. *Later Woolen Mills in Oregon*. Portland, Oregon: Binford and Mort, 1974.

Lyman, William Denison. *Old Walla Walla County*. Chicago: S.J. Clarke Publishing Co., 1918.

Mason, Glenn. *A Piece of the Old Tent of 1853*. Eugene, Oregon, Lane County Historical Museum, 1976.

Mattes, Merrill. *The Great Platte River Road*. Lincoln, Nebraska: University of Nebraska Press, 1969.

May, Dean L. *Three Frontiers: Family, Land, and Society in the American West, 1850-1900*. Cambridge: Cambridge University Press, 1994.

Mittge, Kevin. *The Robbins and Herren Families of the Pacific Northwest*. Kirkland, Washington: Self-published, 1988.

Moynihan, Ruth Barnes. *Rebel for Rights, Abigail Scott Duniway*. New Haven, Connecticut: Yale University Press, 1983.

Mumford, Violet Coe. *The Royal Way West Volume II, Crossing the Plains, 1853*. Baltimore, Maryland: Gateway Press, 1988.

Myres, Sandra. *Westering Women and the Frontier Experience 1800-1915*. Albuquerque, New Mexico: University of New Mexico Press, 1982.

Nordhoff, Charles. *The Communistic Societies of the United States*. New York: Dover Publications, 1966.

Palmer, Rosemary Gudmundson. *Children's Voices from the Trail: Narratives of the Platte River Road*. Spokane, Washington: Arthur H. Clark, 2002.

Peterson del Mar, David. *Oregon's Promise, An Interpretive History*. Corvallis, Oregon: Oregon State University Press, 2003.

Peterson, Pete. *Our Wagon Train is Lost*. Eugene, Oregon: New American Gothic, 1975.

Polk County Oregon Marriage Records 1849-1879, no publisher.

Pope, M.H. "Seven, Seventh, Seventy." *Interpreter's Dictionary of the Bible*, edited by Keith R. Crim and George A. Buttrick. Nashville, Tennessee: Abingdon Press, 1992.

Portrait and Biographical Record of the Willamette Valley, Oregon. Chicago: Chapman Publishing Co., 1903.

Powell, James Madison. *Powell History*. Portland, Oregon: Design Printing, 1977.

Rasmussen, Louis J. *Railway Passenger Lists of Overland Trains to San Francisco and the West*. Colma, California: San Francisco Historic Records, 1966.

Riddle, George W. *History of Early Days in Oregon*. Riddle, Oregon: The Riddle Enterprise, 1920.

Riley, Glenda. *Women and Indians on the Frontier, 1825-1915*. Albuquerque: University of New Mexico Press, 1984.

——. *A Place to Grow: Women in the American West*. Arlington Heights, Illinois: Harlan Davidson, 1992.

Robbins, William. *Landscapes of Promise: The Oregon Story, 1800-1940*. Seattle: University of Washington Press, 1997.

Schlissel, Lillian, Bryd Gibbens, and Elizabeth Hampsten. *Far from Home, Families of the Westward Journey*. New York: Schocken, 1989.

Schlissel, Lillian. *Women's Diaries of the Westward Journey*. New York: Schocken Books, 1982.

Simon, John E. *Wilhelm Keil, Founder of Aurora*. Masters Thesis, Eugene, Oregon: University of Oregon, 1935.

Smith, Helen Krebs, editor, *With Her Own Wings*. Portland, Oregon: Oregon Federation of Women's Organizations, 1948.

Unruh, John. *The Plains Across*. Urbana, Illinois: University of Illinois Press, 1993.

Warren, Sidney. *Farthest Frontier: The Pacific Northwest*. New York: Macmillan Company, 1949.

White, Richard. *It's Your Misfortunate and None of My Own: A New History of the American West*. Norman, Oklahoma: University of Oklahoma Press, 1991.

Will, Clark. *The Story of Old Aurora in Picture and Prose 1856-1883*. Self-published, 1972.

White, Virgil D. *Index to Indian Wars Pension Files 1892-1926 Volume I: A-K*. Waynesboro, Tennessee: National Historical Publishing Company, 1987.

World Atlas. Chicago: Rand McNally, 1968.

Yarnes, Thomas. *A History of Oregon Methodism*. Oregon Methodist Conference Historical Society, n.d.

Articles, Family Histories, Letters, Magazines, Pamphlets, Papers

Albro, Mary Drain. "The Darning Needle Story." Gerry Frank, Salem, Oregon.

Alley, William. "Gracie's Visit to the Rogue River Valley." *Oregon Historical Quarterly*. Portland, Oregon: Oregon Historical Society, Volume 106, Number 2, Summer 2005.

Atkinson, Reverend George. "Diary of Reverend George Atkinson 1847-1858." Edited by E. Ruth Rockwood. *Oregon Historical Quarterly*, Volume XL, 1939.

Bell Family Papers, National Museum of American History, Smithsonian Institution, Washington, D.C.

Bell, John Bruce. "Letter to Friend Mary, May 21st, 1855." Mrs. Robert S. Bell, Burlington, Iowa.

Brackman, Barbara. "A Chronological Index to Pieced Quilt Patterns 1775-1825." *Uncoverings: The Journal of the American Quilt Study Group*. Edited by Sally Garoutte, 1983.

——. "Quilts on the Kansas Frontier." *Kansas History*, Volume 13, Number 1, Spring 1990.

Brown, Tabitha. "Letter to Brother and Sister, August, 1854." *Pacific University Bulletin*. Volume 32, Number 6, December 1936.

Burcham, Mildred Baker. "Our Knight Heritage." Aurora Colony Historical Society, Aurora, Oregon, no date.

Carten, Larry. "Pioneers Found Blue Mountains Main Obstacle on Oregon Trail." *Oregon Journal*. February 12, 1956.

Chandler, W.B. "I Was a Third Generation Pioneer." *Oregon Historical Quarterly*, Volume LXVI, Number 3, September 1965.

Clark, Ricky. "Mid-19th Century Album and Friendship Quilts 1860-1920." *Pieced by Mother*. Edited by Jeannette Lasansky. Oral Traditions Project, 1987.

Crawford, Helen. *Life of Mary Whitley Gilmour, 1931*.

Currier, Philip Joseph. *Currier Family Records of U.S.A. and Canada*, Vol. 2. Concord, New Hampshire: Capital Offset Company, 1984.

——. *Currier Family Records of U.S.A. and Canada*, Vol. 5. West Rutland, Vermont, 2002.

Curtis, Susan, "Blessed Be God for Flowers: Nineteenth-Century Quilt Designs." Patricia Cox Crews, editor. *Flowering of Quilts*. Lincoln, Nebraska: University of Nebraska Press, 2001.

"The Dibbles and the Dibble House 1856-1859." Author unknown. Gena Cline, Molalla, Oregon.

Garoutte, Sally. "Marseilles Quilts and their Woven Offspring." *Uncoverings: The Journal of the American Quilt Study Group*. Edited by Sally Garoutte, 1982.

Goddard and Robison Family Papers, Bonnie Furry, Medford, Oregon.

Grafe, Steven. "Walking in Strange Gardens: Early Floral Design in the Columbia River Plateau." *Painters, Patrons, and Identity: Esssay in Native American Art to Honor J.J. Brody*, edited by Joyce Szabo. Albuquerque, New Mexico: University of New Mexico Press, 2001.

Greer, George, "The James Greer Family." Polk County Pioneer Sketches. Dallas, Oregon: *Polk County Observer*, 1929.

Gunn, Virginia. "Romance and Reality: A Century in Quilt Scholarship 1890-1990." Paper presented at the Bibliography Conference, February 1992, Louisville, Kentucky.

Ham, Edward. "Journey into Southern Oregon: Diary of a Pennsylvania Dutchman." *Oregon Historical Quarterly*. Volume 60, Number 3, September 1959.

Hargreaves, Sheba. "The Letters of Rozelle Putnam." *Oregon Historical Quarterly*. Volume 29, Number 3, September 1928.

Harlow-Tandy Family Reunion Notes, Rosalie Willet, Thibodaux, Louisana.

Hazelton Family Papers, Lane County Historical Museum, Eugene, Oregon.

Helfrich, Devere. "Applegate Trail 1971." *Klamath Echoes*, Number 9.

Hyde, Anne. "The Significance of Perception and Interpretation in the History of the American West." Paper presented at the National Endowment for the Humanities Research Conference, July 1992, Utah State University.

Jones, Catherine Leonard. "Letter to Mrs. C.H. Dye, November 12, 1900." Patricia Erlandson, Medford, Oregon.

Keller, Rosemary Skinner. "Creating A Sphere for Women." *Women in New Worlds*, Hilah F. Thomas and Rosemary Skinner Keller, eds. Nashville: Abingdon, 1981.

Lieuallen, John Wesley, Letter to Josiah Lieuallen, 1864.

Lieuallen, Lena and Mabel Lieuallen Wagner. *Memories of Grandpa and Grandma Lieuallen*. Gilberta Lieuallen, Adams, Oregon, unpublished manuscript.

Lieuallen, Sally. "Diligent Search Gains Century Farm Award." *Pioneer Trails*. Pendleton, Oregon: Umatilla County Historical Society, June 1980, Volume 4, Number 3.

Madden, Mary. "Textile Diaries: Kansas Quilt Memories." *Kansas History*. Volume 13, Number 1.

Martin, Charles W., ed. "Report of Captain Medorem Crawford." *Overland Journal*, Summer and Fall, 1984, Volumes 3 and 4.

McCormick, Gail. *Everything's Fine-O in Mulino!* Mulino, Oregon: Self-published, Volume 2, Number 4.

McKenzie, Winifred. "Noah Franklin Lieuallen 1839-1876." Lieuallen Family Papers, Gilberta Lieuallen, Adams, Oregon.

Menefee, Leah Collins and Lowell Tiller. "Cutoff Fever." Oregon Historical Quarterly, Volume 78, Number 3, September 1977

Meyer, Suellen. "Pine Tree Quilts." *The Quilt Digest 4*. Edited by Michael Kile. San Francisco, California: Quilt Digest Press, 1986.

Meyers, E.L. *Barlow Toll Road 1846-1919: The Story of Two from Fort Deposit*. Portland, Oregon: Genealogical Forum, 1972.

Morris, Henry. "Eliam Morris Family History 1811-1958." *Champoeg Pioneer*, Volume 2, Number 30, July 1958.

"Mrs. Lucinda Spencer." *Transactions of the Fifteenth Annual Reunion of the Oregon Pioneer Association for 1887*. Portland, Oregon: Press of George H. Himes, 1887.

"1985 Aurora Colony Quilt Show." Aurora Colony Historical Society, Aurora, Oregon.

Olch, Peter D., M.D. "Trailing the Elephant's Tail." *Overland Journal*, Volume 6, Number 1, Spring 1988.

Osaki, Amy Boyce. "A 'Truly Feminine Employment' Sewing and the Early Nineteenth-Century Woman." *Winterthur Portfolio*, Volume 23, Number 4, 1988.

Palmer, Rosemary G. "The Sabbath According to Female Diarists on the Trail." *Overland Journal*, Volume 22, Number 4, Winter 2004/2005.

Perkins Family Papers, Yamhill County Historical Museum, Lafayette, Oregon.

Riggs, Lois. "The Zadoc S. Riggs Family." *Polk County Pioneer Sketches*. Dallas: Sarah Childress DAR Polk Chapter #6, 1927.

Roberts, Adda. *The David Roberts-Jane Anderson Family History*.

Root, Mabel Glover. *Family History of the Oregon Pioneer Families of Philip Glover and John H. Palmer*. Louise Godfrey, Portland, Oregon.

Royal, James H.B., "Journal of James H.B. Royal While Crossing the Plains in 1853." Eugene, Oregon: University of Oregon Archives.

Schminck Family Papers. Schminck Memorial Museum, Lakeview, Oregon.

Seely, A.C. Family Papers, Douglas County Museum of History and Natural History, Roseburg, Oregon.

"Settlement Records 1878." Aurora Colony Historical Society, Aurora, Oregon.

Skeeters, Grace Jane Simpson. "The Life of Mrs. Grace Jane Simpson Skeeters." Southern Oregon Historical Society Archives, Medford, Oregon.

Smith Family Papers, Yamhill County Historical Museum, Lafayette, Oregon.

Soukey, Bippi, "Ashland's Original Granddaughter." *Ashland Plaza*, May 1978.

Spraker, Hazel. *The Boone Family: A Genealogical History of the Descendants of George and Mary Boone who Came to America in 1717*. Baltimore, Maryland: Genealogical Publishing Company, 1922.

Starr-Riggs Family Papers #2637, Oregon Historical Society, Portland, Oregon.

Starr Family Donation Accession Files 1967 and 1976, Oregon Historical Society Research Library, Portland, Oregon.

Stauffer Family Papers, Vera Yoder, Woodburn, Oregon.

"Teasels: Woolen Industry." Scrapbook 38, Oregon Historical Society Research Library, Portland, Oregon.

Wagner, Mabel Lieuallen. *Water from the Spring*. Gilberta Lieuallen, Athena, Oregon, unpublished manuscript.

Ware, Joseph. "The Emigrant's Guide to California." *The Emigrant's Guide to New Mexico, California, and Oregon Giving the Different Overland and Sea Routes Compiled from Reliable Authorities*. J. Disturnell, 1849.

Will, Clark. "Colony Mothers Help Write Colony History." Aurora Colony Historical Society, Aurora, Oregon.

——. "Eighteen-sixty-three Water Trip for the Knight's and Genger's Families." Aurora Colony Historical Society, Aurora, Oregon.

William Whitley House Historic Site. Kentucky Department of Parks, 1992.

Woodroofe, Helen Barrett. "Quilt Recalls a Strong, Good Woman." *The Callaway Journal*, Volume 8, 1983.

Wright Family History, Bertha Nolan, Milwaukie, Oregon.

Census Records

U.S.Census 1850 Missouri, Cass County, Sixteenth District, 95.

U.S. Census 1860 Missouri, Mercer County, Morgan Township, 141.

U.S. Census 1860 Oregon, Jackson, Ashland, 95.

U.S. Census 1860, Oregon, Multnomah County, Portland, 25.

U.S. Census 1860 Oregon, Polk, Monmouth, B.

U.S. Census, 1860, Oregon, Washington County, Forest Grove, 1226.

U.S. Census, 1870, Iowa, Keokuk County, 353.

U.S. Census 1870 Missouri, DeKalb County, Polk Township, 503.

U.S. Census 1870, Oregon, Clackamas County, Canimah.

U.S.Census 1870 Oregon, Douglas County, Calapooia Precinct, 104.

U.S. Census 1870, Oregon, Jackson County, 40.

U.S. Census 1870, Oregon, Lane County, Pleasant Hill Township, 508.

U.S. Census 1870, Oregon, Lane County, Springfield township, 52.

U.S. Census 1870 Oregon, Marion County, Aurora, 74.

U.S.Census 1870 Oregon, Marion County, Aurora Precinct, 150.

U.S. Census, 1870 Oregon, Wasco, east of Deschutes River, 59.

U.S.Census, 1870 Oregon, Washington County, 483.

U.S. Census 1870, Oregon, Washington County, Forest Grove.

U.S. Census 1870 Oregon Yamhill County, Sheridan Precinct, 544.

U.S. Census 1880 Nebraska, Richardson County, Falls City, 427.

U.S. Census 1880, Oregon, Jackson, Eden Precinct, 133.

U.S.Census 1880, Oregon, Lane County, Springfield Precinct.

U.S. Census 1880, Oregon, Marion County, 30.

U.S. Census 1880 Oregon, Umatilla County, Greasewood, 104.

U.S. Census 1880 Oregon, Umatilla County, Weston Precinct.

U.S. Census 1900 Oregon Lake County, Crooked Creek Precinct, 188.

U.S.Census 1900, Oregon, Lane, South Eugene Precinct 2, 121.

U.S. Census 1900 Oregon, Umatilla County, Weston Precinct.

U.S. Census 1910 Oregon Lake County, Crooked Creek Precinct, 18.

Acknowledgments

The Oregon Trail Quilt Project began as a search for a quilt exhibition during the celebration of the 150th Anniversary of the first wagon train over the Oregon Trail in 1843. The results of that project were an in-state traveling exhibition; a series of lectures across the country; and this publication. Over the last twelve years, the professional and personal rewards have been many and varied. The book won the 1994 Benjamin Franklin Award for Outstanding Publication in the category of history/politics from the Publishers Marketing Association. The book and lectures won an Award of Merit from the American Association of State and Local History. I have had the opportunity to travel across the country lecturing from the Smithsonian Museum of American History to the church basements of rural Oregon.

I am pleased to have Peter and Nancy Schiffer of Schiffer Publishing Ltd. recognize the ongoing value and importance of this book as an educational tool. Their acceptance of my request for reprinting the book is greatly appreciated. I especially credit Trish Herr and Sue Reich for recommending my scholarship to this new publisher.

This book and my second book have been used for educational programs at all age levels, and in public presentations including religious sermons and television documentaries.

Initially, the project could not have been undertaken without the interest and support of institutions, quilt documentation projects, and individuals throughout the country, particularly the Northwest. Contact information for the institutions is listed in Appendix C. The support stemmed from the growing recognition of quilts as cultural artifacts of women's history. Many responded to my first survey inquiry while others gladly opened their storage and records for follow-up research. They have greeted the reissue announcement with enthusiasm. I extend my continuing appreciation to all that have helped.

For the actual beginning, I acknowledge Jim Renner, Interpretive Director of the Oregon Trail Coordinating Council and the initial person assigned the task to develop the celebration. Through his awareness of my proposal, I came in contact with Daniel Robertson, Director of the Douglas County Museum of History and Natural History to co-direct the survey and research phases in preparation for the museum-sponsored traveling exhibit. This partnership enabled funding from the Oregon Council for the Humanities and the Friends of the Douglas County Museum of History and Natural History to support the work.

Responses to my survey of over one hundred institutions and quilt projects shaped my travel itinerary and led me to the quilts. These also provided much of the information described in Appendix C about documenting and donating quilts.

Later, a fellowship from the Oregon Council for the Humanities to attend the National Endowment for the Humanities Research Conference, "A New Significance: Re-Envisioning the History of the American West," helped to shape my findings and focus my conclusions.

On the national level, the institutions that provided access to their resources through use of their libraries directly or by computer linkup were the Library of Congress, the National Museum of American History of the Smithsonian, the Daughters of the American Revolution Museum, all in Washington, D.C.; the New England Historical and Genealogical Society in Boston; and the Family History Centers and International Genealogical Index of the Church of Jesus Christ of Latter-day Saints, based in Salt Lake City. These resources as well as Ancestry.com provided valuable family genealogy and history to validate and enrich my research.

Following this initial quilt research, many individuals answered questions, provided key leads, and assisted with the project.

Some of the owners of previous Oregon Trail quilts remained the same while others are now in the possession of other descendents who are continuing the tradition of preserving these treasures. The owners now include Vera Yoder, Patricia Leicher, Louise Godfrey, Wanita Propst Haugen, Donald and Gilberta Lieuallen, Michael Woodroofe, and Joanne Nelson.

Eight additional quilts have been added to this new edition. The owners who generously shared their quilts and their stories are Shannon Applegate, Susan Queen, Champ and Maria Vaughan, Cydney Bush, Charlotte Enfield and Nancy Walker Morgan. Appreciation is expressed to the Martingale and Company of Woodinville, Washington for the use of the transparencies for the Coyle and the Morgan quilts. Two of the quilts are from museum collections: American Folk Art Museum in New York City and the Museum of the Oregon Territory in Oregon City. They generously shared the quilts while family members shared information: Laura Jean Jory, John Coyle Beckman, Laura Jean Hevel, and Janice Zuger.

In addition, with the magic of the Internet and the new information that has surfaced, each of the stories of the quiltmakers from the first edition was greatly enriched. Contacts with the following family members and museum personnel who made contributions include: Barbara Bowerman, Kevin Mittge, Rosalie Willet, Robin Helman, Joan Staley, Shirley and Don Knepp, Monica Lawson, Patrick Harris, David Porter, Susan Seyl, Lucy Berkley, Marlene Wallin, Evan Schneider, Shawna Gandy, Merrialyce Blanchard, Janey Fire, Jan Wright, Bob Hart, Cheryl Roffe, Sandy McGuire, Judy Chambers, and Stella Shannon. Some of the staffs are small and depend on support from volunteers. Among the volunteers who assisted in this project are Susan Doyle, Lila Hill, Peg McCormick, Bob Higgins, Gaye Ingram, Anita Linscheid, and Isabelle Williams.

This edition is enhanced by the inclusion of maps and William Henry Jackson watercolors. Robert Hamm generously loaned the historic map of Oregon and Upper California. Rose Ann Tompkins used her knowledge of the western trails and talents in map design to create a map of overland routes used by these westering families. Finally, the William Henry Jackson collection of watercolors is part of the extended collection of the Scotts Bluff National Monument in Gering, Nebraska. For these Robert Manasek lent his research assistance and Roger Blair shared his transparencies.

Photography credit is given to Bill Bachhuber, George Champlin, Charlotte Pendleton, Matt Strieby, David Anderson, and Mark Gulezian.

Technical support came from Brad and Debbie Brotherton. Initially, it was the guidance and support of Bob Burco who edited early versions of the book and brought it to fruition. Now, it is the wisdom and editorial expertise of Robert P. Newman that has helped me achieve the goal of keeping the books in print.

Finally, I acknowledge the personal support from my family and friends across the country as I created a meaningful contribution to women's history and the history of the western migration over the Oregon Trail. I owe you all my grateful thanks.

Index